11|17

STANDING MY GROUND

D1434050

www.transworldireland.ie

www.**transworldbooks**.co.uk

STANDING MY GROUND

THE AUTOBIOGRAPHY

Brendan Cummins
with
Jackie Cahill

TRANSWORLD IRELAND

TRANSWORLD IRELAND PUBLISHERS
28 Lower Leeson Street, Dublin 2, Ireland
www.transworldireland.ie

Transworld Ireland is part of the Penguin Random House group of companies
whose addresses can be found at global.penguinrandomhouse.com

First published in the UK and Ireland in 2015
by Transworld Ireland
an imprint of Transworld Publishers

A CIP catalogue record for this book
is available from the British Library.

ISBN 9781848272217

Typeset in 12.5/15.5pt Ehrhardt by Falcon Oast Graphic Art Ltd.
Printed and bound by Clays Ltd, Bungay, Suffolk.

Penguin Random House is committed to a sustainable
future for our business, our readers and our planet. This book
is made from Forest Stewardship Council® certified paper.

1 3 5 7 9 10 8 6 4 2

For Pam, Paul and Sarah – the greatest
backroom team of them all

Contents

Foreword

I first met Brendan Cummins in the winter of 1996, when I was called into the Tipperary senior hurling squad. He was just twenty-one years of age but what immediately struck me was how he absolutely lived and breathed Tipperary hurling. I had the honour of playing alongside him before becoming his manager in later years.

Brendan's leadership qualities set him apart and marked him for success at the top level. Never interested in taking the populist view, he would always give it to you openly and honestly. During my time as manager, I quickly realized that skirting around issues can lead to bigger problems. Brendan always cut to the chase, most notably after we lost in the first round of the Munster championship against Cork in 2010.

We met in the Horse and Jockey for a debrief a couple of nights after the game and Brendan laid it on hot and heavy. We were either going to fold or regroup in search of the big prize. We chose the latter, but, after some initial dancing around the real issues among the group, Brendan's input completely changed the tone of the meeting.

Failure wasn't an option for Brendan. For a guy who wasn't covering 10km in a game, his fitness levels were phenomenal. I knew what he put himself through in order to be ready. It started with that run up the mountain at home every November and his work would remain hugely consistent right through to the end of the following year's campaign.

Some intercounty players think about the game for fifteen or twenty hours a week but I always felt that Brendan used every waking hour to make sure that he was mentally and physically in prime condition for matchday. He knew exactly what he had to do and he nailed it every time. Mental strength, self-belief and his ability to be in peak condition when the stakes were highest were his winning traits.

His absolute drive for improvement amazed me and while his shot-stopping was always beyond question, his ability to go from long to precision puckouts was honed and reached a peak when we won the All-Ireland in 2010. Brendan had to adapt, and he knew that too. He was completely open to change, provided it was in the right direction and made him a better player.

One of my abiding memories of that 2010 campaign came from asking the group to write a personal message to each of their teammates. There is nothing more powerful than positive, heart-felt feedback from your peers. The comments I received for Brendan from his teammates blew me away. 'Leader.' 'So reliable and a great friend.' 'Daddy of the team.' 'Rock solid.'

Off the pitch, we got to know each other well. As player and manager, you've got to be conscious of that relationship and manage it, but Brendan and I spent a lot of time together as friends. In 2011, we travelled to San Francisco on a GAA All Stars tour. We visited Alcatraz, the Golden Gate Bridge, and sat on a bench chatting about hurling and life – fabulous moments. I always feel comfortable in his company. My wife Mags and Brendan's wife Pamela forged a really good relationship too over the years. What you saw with Brendan on the field was what you saw off it. Just as you could rely on him in the heat of battle, you could call upon him in the morning if anybody was ever in trouble.

Picking him up after 2007 was difficult, I must admit. We played a game early in 2008 and Brendan was back in goal. He was hesitant. I urged him to be himself. 'Hey, pal, what's the story?' Slowly but surely, Brendan's confidence levels returned; they had taken a battering. Watching him put that point over the bar in the 2010 All-Ireland final was an incredible moment. He sent a message to the rest of the group, to management and to the Kilkenny players: on this day, we would not bend or break.

It was Brendan's redemption. I had been confident that he would bounce back. It's the trampoline effect. The further you go down, the more room there is to bounce straight back up again.

As Brendan himself has said, the knowledge that there were some exciting young players coming through helped to keep him going. I had some of them as minor manager when we won the All-Ireland in 2006 and Declan Ryan managed the 2007 winners. These graduates came into the senior set-up without a care in the world and with that winning mentality, but they would have learned so much from Brendan too, in terms of the extremely high standards he set and the demands he placed on himself and on those around him.

He's been asked many times about saves he's made; a few stand out for me. The save he made from Niall Gilligan at the end of the 2008 Munster final is mentioned in the book and there was also that fabulous save from Henry Shefflin in 2009. I remember another against Cork in the 2009 Munster championship when he literally put his head in the way of oncoming danger. A goal for Cork then and we were headed for the back door again. Those are the saves that stand out for me.

On a personal level, it's a tremendous honour to have been asked to pen this foreword. Brendan Cummins as the Tipperary player is a closed chapter now, but as a potential future manager he has a massive role to play. This will be the second part of his journey and I'm certain that Brendan will remain involved at the top level. Given what he has achieved and the drive he possesses, he will fulfil further ambitions on the touchline. Of that, I have no doubt. If he has the same influence on his players as a manager or coach as he had on the Tipperary group as a player from 2008 to 2010, he's going to make one hell of a contribution.

Liam Sheedy.

1

Generations

You will know me as Brendan but I could have been John. My grandfather was Johnny, known as 'Mr Football' in the South Tipperary village of Ardfinnan, situated 9 kilometres from the town of Cahir. My dad's name is John, and when I was born in Clonmel on 11 May 1975, the feeling was that I'd be called John too. My parents called me Brendan instead. They didn't want me to be known as 'little' John.

Grandad Johnny was a legend in the local area. He came from Grange, a village 6 kilometres from Ardfinnan. On the nights before big club games, Johnny cycled around Ardfinnan on his High Nelly, checking in at the local pubs to see if any of the players were out drinking. On the sidelines, he wore a long trench-coat, like the famous Liverpool manager Bill Shankly.

Johnny played on the first Ardfinnan team to win a major championship, in 1934, when the club's juniors won the county title. Ardfinnan went on to win county senior crowns in 1935 and 1939 and, in later years, Johnny would play a vital role in the continuing development of football at the club, along with James Teehan and 'Butcher' O'Brien. The hard work of these men paid off in a thirteen-year spell from 1962 to 1974, when Ardfinnan won five county senior football championships. Thirty-one years would pass before Ardfinnan won their next one.

In the 1960s and 1970s, Michael 'Babs' Keating was the star player for Ardfinnan and Ballybacon-Grange, the sister hurling club. Johnny revered Babs, whose exploits for club and county were noted far and wide. My dad played hurling and football with him. The hurlers played a running game in those days and the idea was to make progress up to the opposition's 45-metre line before passing the ball to Babs, who did the rest. He was the man who catapulted our clubs towards the top in Tipperary.

Whenever I talk to Dad, or any of his friends who played with Babs, they speak about him as though he was some kind of Olympic record holder. He really was that good. But Babs recognized that he needed good men around him to supply him with the ball so that he could work his magic.

Dad and the other lads didn't mind that Babs was the man making the headlines because he was helping them to win medals. I think what happened at that time rubbed off on me when I played football for Tipperary. We had a star man in my era, Declan Browne from Moyle Rovers, and I usually found myself kicking the ball in to Declan. His teammates were the supply line to Declan and, at our peak, we went close to winning the Munster senior title in 2002.

Home for Johnny Cummins and his wife Moll was Gortnalour in Ardfinnan. It was also the house I grew up in. My love of football stemmed from knowledge of Johnny's history and the fact that my dad was an exceptional player too in his time, representing the club with distinction and also lining out for Tipperary county teams.

Dad was just fifteen when Johnny died of cancer and he became the breadwinner in the family. He left school to work as a carpenter with Hally's, a local construction company, and provided for Moll and my aunt Marie, who was working in a local shop. Marie was just eighteen when her father passed away. For the family, these were challenging times, but they did the best they could. Moll gave Dad enough spending money for him to get by and that responsibility which had been thrust upon his shoulders helped to shape a man with a strong work ethic and good morals. It must have been a difficult transition for Dad, who went from a secondary school classroom with peers of his own age to a building site full of adults.

Hally's was one of two major centres of employment in Ardfinnan, along with the Woollen Mill, situated beside the bridge on the River Suir. The Mill opened in 1869 and closed in 1973. During World War Two army uniforms were produced there and, at its peak, the Mill employed two hundred people. Moll worked there as a weaver from the age of fourteen. She was forty-eight when her husband died.

Before my grandfather died, he asked to visit three places special to him – Grange, the bridge in Ardfinnan and Factory Hill, which is visible as you head to Cahir from Ardfinnan. From barely halfway up the hill, you can see the parish of Newcastle. The bridge was dear to Johnny's heart because when local club teams won county championships, the returning heroes came back home across the bridge and were greeted by a bonfire on the green. A friend of the family's, Alfie McDermott, took Johnny to those three spots for a last look around.

Dad told me that he ran up the back garden when he heard the news that Johnny, who was just fifty, had passed on. He was confused as people called to the house to pay their respects. You can imagine how he felt, not quite knowing what the future held in store. Johnny's funeral was one of the biggest the local area had ever seen. When Johnny was around, club games almost became adventures for people who wouldn't often stray outside their home

patch. He regularly organized buses to ferry players and supporters to and from matches against other clubs. The GAA was
the glue that held people together, and life revolved around the
green, the parish hall and the church. That sense of place and
community was instilled in hurlers and footballers when they
went into battle. They realized that what they achieved on the
field of play really meant something to the people they represented. Men like Johnny, James and the 'Butcher' O'Brien made
sure of that.

My father and mother, Anne, met on the green in Ardfinnan.
Mam is from the far side of the village, on the border with Cahir,
and Dad hails from the other end of the village, bordering
Ballybacon. If you can imagine it, the centre of the village is
almost like a gorge because of the many surrounding hills. They
were introduced at the travelling carnival that came around once
a year. Run by a man named Davy Whelan from Mitchelstown,
the carnival stopped for a fortnight on the green during the
summer. I'm told that it first made an appearance in the early
1960s, serving as a fundraiser to help renovate the church in
Ardfinnan. Pongo bingo, bumpers and swinging boats were huge
attractions. Davy also had a stall packed with delph and he sold
raffle tickets for the chance to win plates, cups and saucers. The
sound of music pulsed through the long evenings as local folk
enjoyed marquee dancing and live bands. The carnival ran for at
least ten years in Ardfinnan, until enough money was collected to
cover the cost of the renovation. While the new church was under
construction, Mass was held in the local hall. Dad was one of the
many people who helped with the building work.

I was sad to see the carnival leave because I can still remember
some great seven-a-side football matches played in the evenings,
before the bands struck up. There was a real primal feel to the
pitch on the green, with timber goals and a log for a crossbar.

Flies hovered over the grass, visible in the rays of the sun, and the only real concern for us as kids was when the ball drifted into the river. There would always be a mad rush to see if it could be scooped out before it went out of reach and drifted away towards Clonmel. Thankfully, we always managed to cobble together a few bob to buy a new one.

One of my fondest memories is of scoring a penalty to win a juvenile game for Ardfinnan. I can only have been eight or nine years of age at the time. I stuck it in the left-hand corner of a big red net. Although I was still just a young boy, it was an incredible rush. It was a goal that made local people smile.

When the young kids had finished their games, it was time for the matches between the senior teams. I saw how competitively adult players slogged it out. My dad played, and Liam Myles travelled down from Dublin to take part. Seamus Butler and Paddy Noonan are other local men I can recall playing for Ardfinnan.

People would come from far and wide to watch these games, even from Ballymacarbry and The Nire in Waterford. I could always sense that something bad had happened when Ardfinnan lost because the club prided itself on its seven-a-side team. Clonmel Commercials were one of the big local rivals at the time. I can recall a box of plaques destined for the winners being carried through a losing Ardfinnan dressing room on one occasion. Those mementos were so close that our men could almost touch them.

It would always take a while for life to return to normal after the excitement of the carnival. Our house in Gortnalour, or the 'top of the Rock' as it's known, was a bungalow with three bed-rooms, a sitting room, a kitchen and a bathroom. My bedroom was tight enough, 10 feet wide by 8 feet long, with just enough room in there for my bed. My Aunt Marie left home some years before I was born, when she got married, but Moll lived with us when I was a very young boy. Moll, who I was very close to, moved out to live with Marie when I was seven years old.

Thankfully, I've been blessed with a good memory and can remember my first day at primary school. My next-door neighbour, Alison Browne, started on the same day. I can remember the sensation of entering a new environment and how big the classroom was. I was given building blocks to play with but Alison was inconsolable beside me, in floods of tears. Ms Curran was my first teacher in junior infants and I struck up a rapport with her from the start. Ms Walsh was another teacher of mine, and Ms Ryan was with us when a local hero paid a visit in 1984. Gerry Ryan was a member of the Tipperary minor football team that won the Munster title and he came to visit with the cup. He walked in with a big smile and made a huge impression. The memory of that occasion and how it impacted on me is no doubt linked to my strong connection with Ardfinnan National School. When I played with Tipperary, I visited the school with my first All-Star award in 2000. There were many more visits after that with Munster and All-Ireland cups. Mairead Condon is the administrative principal and Liam O'Sullivan the deputy principal at the school now and both are enthusiastic GAA people.

At school, I was an average student. I was happier when I was out and about kicking a ball or pucking around. I did just about enough to get by. My report card frequently read 'must try harder' but the teachers were never too hard on us. They noticed some academic potential in me but with big classes of up to thirty there was no learning support or any room for individual attention. The teachers didn't have time to get around to everyone. You either kept up or got left behind.

Sport was my thing and, as kids, we played a lot of soccer. It was jumpers for goalposts stuff. We played in the Castleview estate, a two-minute walk from the village, hell for leather until sunset. On the way home from there, five or six of us would play another game under the streetlights. Sean Maher, Cathal Hennessy, Davy Ryan and Paddy Ryan were some of the boys I used to knock around with. Derek O'Mahoney and Liam Barrett, two of the three lads who stood with me on my wedding day (my good friend Mike English was the other groomsman), joined in those games too, although I didn't get to know them properly until we were older. Liam lived in Castleview and Derek was from the other side of the village.

At home, the contest was always against myself. I would imagine that my left- and right-hand sides were the opposing teams. I'd hit the ball up in the air and catch it again before it hit the ground. In the bedroom, it was right hand versus left up against the wall with a crumpled piece of paper. Because I had so many friends to pal around with, not having brothers or sisters was never something I gave much thought to. Besides, Dad and I were more like brothers than father and son.

Gaelic Football was the game I was first exposed to and my early education was served with Dad. He was manager of the adult team in Ballyporeen, a village less than 13 miles from Ardfinnan. I went to the training sessions with him, kicking the ball back to the players from behind the goals. On Saturday mornings in Ardfinnan, we played football on the green. It was the dominant game in our locality, but I loved hurling too.

We had a pitch in Ballybacon, on a hill, with improvised goals made from trees. We hurled with Ballybacon-Grange juvenile teams, and there were a number of men instrumental in driving underage development. Dad was one, along with John English and Eamon O'Gorman. The late Fr Pat Moran, who passed away in July 2014, was another major influence. Fr Pat had been involved with Ballybacon-Grange since he was a young boy and served as president of the club for many years.

When I was five, Fr Pat began work on rejuvenating the club and took charge of the intermediate team. He was innovative in so many ways – he could well have been the first hurling trainer to use a video recorder to show players where they were doing well or badly. The club won a South Tipperary final under Fr Pat and he became more and more involved with the juveniles as the years passed. He showed us drills and brought great structure to training sessions for young players. Fr Pat had his number ones and number twos. Each player was assigned the number one or number two and he'd call out the numbers to ensure uniformity in drills. Number one would run out and roll-lift the sliotar, before it was number two's turn. The same principle applied for the jab-lift, and so on. While this might sound like incredibly simple stuff, it was an easy way to communicate with young kids who might otherwise have struggled to understand what he wanted them to do.

Jody Spooner played his part too, over the course of one key weekend. Jody was from Roscrea and won an All-Ireland 7s title with his club in 1979. He was also a Munster senior club medallist in 1970 when the men from North Tipperary went on to win an All-Ireland title. Jody coached us for a weekend and I got a real sense of enjoyment from his work. His approach ensured that there were more touches of the ball, for instance. Normally at underage training you might not have too much involvement in the game. All too often in juvenile matches the star player on one team might run the length of the pitch and then stick the ball in the net. Play would resume, only for the star player on the opposing team to do the very same thing. For most of the players on the pitch it was like watching a game of tennis.

Babs was living in Dublin at the time but put in an occasional appearance at the local field to help out with coaching. He was trying to change the way I held the hurley when I was eight or nine. I held it with my left hand on top, right hand under – the golfer's grip; Babs wanted me to hold it right hand on top and strike off my right-hand side, with my left hand on the bottom. Like any coach, Babs was trying to do the right thing for a young kid. But he knew too that I was enjoying myself and that there's little point in trying to make drastic changes when that's the case with a young lad.

When Babs was a star of Tipperary teams the big intercounty games were obvious attractions for village people. I dreaded the prospect of travelling to matches in Dublin because it could take you four hours to get home but I loved the Croke Park experience and the atmosphere the place generated. I sat on Dad's lap in the Upper Hogan Stand of Croke Park in 1982 when Offaly beat Kerry in the All-Ireland football final. Kerry were going for the five-in-a-row and I cried when they were beaten. I was a massive Kerry fan, and I was back at Croke Park in 1986 when they won the All-Ireland final against Tyrone. I managed to get on to the pitch after the game and met the Tyrone midfielder Plunkett Donaghy. He had blond hair and I idolized him. He was so strong and tall. I remember thinking that he was a monster of a man.

Manchester United were my soccer heroes, from the time I could walk. Dad supported United too and our very own Theatre of Dreams was the back garden at home. I dug it up with the studs of my boots because whenever I watched the English soccer matches on TV, the pitches were always mucky and cut up. That was the scene I wanted to create. Dad even installed a floodlight connected to a length of timber maybe 20 feet long so that we could play into the night. The first time we played under the light, I can remember kicking a new blue and white football and the sound it made off my boot was lovely. When I dived to save Dad's shots I could see my reflection in the shadows sweeping across the garden. For me at that age, it was just like Old Trafford.

We loved cricket too. I first watched it when we had BBC TV installed at home for the FA Cup matches. If there was no soccer on, I switched on cricket. There were times when the aerial perched on the flat roof would lose the signal and I'd climb up the ladder to adjust it, with Dad shouting from the front door to let me know when we were up and running again. Our Theatre of Dreams in the back garden became Lord's, The Oval or the Melbourne Cricket Ground. Dad had some 2 × 1 timber and used it to cut stumps and bails for a homemade wicket. I grasped the game quickly, and to this day I'll sit down and watch an entire Ashes series. When England's Andrew Flintoff was in his prime during the famous 2005 matches against Australia, I didn't have Channel 4 on TV so I sat outside on the grass at home and listened to the closing stages on the car radio.

The concept of winning and losing struck me from a young age. It was part of daily life in our house because of Dad's involvement in the GAA. Mam also displayed an interest in what we were doing and claimed that she once scored a goal on the local green to win a ladies match. But I never felt that I had anything to prove because I was the son of John Cummins. He was a nurturing figure in my development and encouraged me to carve my own niche, if that's what I wanted to do. He was never the type to stand behind the goals at matches, shouting and roaring. Experience of coaching young players, including the Tipperary minor footballers, had taught him that there are few things worse than the sight of a parent cosying up beside team selectors in an attempt to influence their thinking. I would have to stand on my own two feet, and that suited me just fine.

2

Connie

I was nine or ten years of age when a group of us travelled from Ardfinnan National School to Thurles for a primary schools football trial. I don't remember anything about the game itself but I do remember a man calling out the list of players who were deemed good enough from what he had seen. The numbers were quickly whittled down but the man was short one at the very end, with just a few of us left in with a chance. My friend Lee Crowe was standing beside him, and as Lee was the first kid he noticed, this man beckoned to him and Lee duly joined in with the others. I was crushed. For the first time, I felt a burning anger strong enough to leave an imprint on my soul.

Rejection comes in many forms. How you deal with it is the key to determining whether it's a destructive or a constructive force. I have always tried to turn a negative into a positive. If something went wrong, there had to be a way of fixing it, I reasoned. The underlying consequences of rejection are more complex. Hurt, temper and residual pain must be explored, processed and dealt with if you are going to move forward with a sense of resolution and purpose. One of my favourite sayings to people is that if they are going to come to me with a problem, they must also bring a potential solution.

The best lads from our school had travelled to Thurles that day. Davy Ryan was picked, Sean Maher too, Cathal Hennessy and Lee, but not me. When I got home, I lashed my football off the shed wall at the back of the house in a temper. The searing frustration felt like it was burning a hole in me, and it had to be released. What had happened was nobody's fault but my own. I hadn't been considered good enough to make the cut but I still wanted to play. Hell, I *needed* to play. I knew that something had to change so I worked out what I would do differently if a similar situation ever arose again. The next time a selector called out his list, I made sure that I was standing beside him, looking into his face as if to say, 'I defy you not to pick me.'

As a boy, I would cry when things didn't work out as I'd planned, like in school when I was caught doing something by the teacher and was asked to explain myself in front of the class. Those weren't tears born out of anger. It was more to do with temper and frustration aimed at myself because I'd found myself in a difficult situation. I became aware of an inner monologue, a voice inside my head calling me names. 'Look at the situation you find your-self in now, you fool' was a regular insult from my mind.

I can recall a day in primary school when I was on lookout as a few of the other boys were throwing wet toilet paper, sticking it to the ceiling. We got caught, and more tears of temper followed. Over time, I learned to channel that frustration in other ways.

Even when things went well, I'd sometimes get upset. When I was eight years of age, I scored a goal in a South Tipperary U12 hurling semi-final against Carrick Swan. The game was played in Marlfield, a village not far outside Clonmel. I scored it in the first half. It flew in. At half-time I was crying because my dad, who was involved with the team, said something to me. He wasn't giving out or anything like that. 'I'm only advising you,' he would always say. Ray Duggan was our other corner-forward and he was blubbering as well. Ray's dad, Jim, had him in tears too after offering some pearls of wisdom!

There were some great lessons along the way. One time I played in an U12 South football final against Commercials and decided that I would go for a cycle earlier in the day. It definitely took something out of me because by the end of the match I could barely walk. Commercials had players who were much bigger than many of us. I was marking Niall Dempsey, who was a big lad. Niall and I used to mark each other in plenty of those underage games. He was the star man for Commercials and I'd try to take him on at midfield. On the night of the U12 final, I blew a gasket and Dad wondered what had happened to me. I told him that I had been out for a cycle that morning. 'What did you do that for?' I argued that I was still young and wanted to enjoy life, that playing matches wasn't the be-all and end-all.

There was another day when I was in goal at a hurling match in Clonmel, with Eamon O'Gorman standing behind me. A shot came in and Eamon shouted at me to leave it off, as he felt it was going wide. But the ball ended up in the back of my net. Dad told me later that I had to learn always to make my own decisions in goal.

I wanted to be a goalkeeper because of Connie Naughton. He played junior soccer with Cahir Park, on the same team as my dad, and he was class. Connie was too small to make it at League of Ireland level but he had everything else in his goalkeeping artillery. I loved how he looked in his black and white jersey with the pads on the elbows. Black togs, black and white socks, white gloves, blond hair. That was Connie. He'd come and collect a cross with a roar of 'Keeeeppppeeerrrr!' I stood behind the goals when Cahir Park trained and played matches, just to watch

Connie. He inspired me, and I remain in contact with the man to this day.

One of my regrets is that I never got to play in a competitive eleven-a-side match at any level. I've always wondered what I would have been like as a soccer goalkeeper, wearing the kind of gear that Connie did and coming from my line to collect crosses from the skies like him. I did make up the numbers in training games with Cahir Park from time to time but I wasn't very good. Because I was a hurling goalkeeper, I had a tendency to drift off my line, and in soccer that meant I was invariably chipped. I never had the time to devote to soccer because of my GAA commitments but it's a sport I've always loved. In every big match I played from 1993, I wore a Manchester United shirt under my playing gear.

United's Danish goalkeeper Peter Schmeichel was a hero of mine. He had an unbelievable presence in goal. I wanted to emulate him in my own sport. I had a blue United T-shirt that I'd wear too, along with a Moyle Rovers jersey with the number 20 on the back that I'd found discarded in one of the dressing rooms in Ardfinnan. I usually felt very cold before matches. It's how my body reacted to nerves, and I countered the cold by layering up. It's why I wore tracksuit bottoms in my early years playing with Tipp. On my torso, the United T-shirt went on first, followed by the Moyle Rovers jersey, the red United top and my own goalkeeper shirt – four layers that eventually became two. With wear and tear, the United T-shirt developed big holes, and I lost the Moyle Rovers jersey somewhere along the line. But the red United shirt remained with me until the day I retired in 2013. I liked United, and the shirt was comfortable and helped me to relax.

In March 1995, I travelled to Old Trafford with Willie Barrett and his son Liam to watch United play Arsenal. They won 3-0. Mark Hughes, Lee Sharpe and Andrei Kanchelskis scored the goals. I walked into the Theatre of Dreams and the sight of the green carpet inspired me. It was floodlit, magical. It took me back to those nights at home in my own back garden. Why couldn't Croke Park, Páirc Uí Chaoimh or Semple Stadium be my Theatre of Dreams?

It was after I moved on to secondary school at St Joseph's in Cahir that I linked up with a Tipperary hurling squad for the first time. It took time for my body to develop and jerseys were usually too big for me. There's a picture from the annual Tony Forristal tournament for U14 county teams in 1988 and I'm in the back row. It really looks like I'm an U12 player but I made that squad out of sheer bloodymindedness. A man called Jim Lynch from Cahir was a selector and he warned my dad that Tipperary would carry only one goalkeeper on the panel. Shay Killeen from Knockshegowna was first choice and Jim would always say to me before training, 'Young fella, don't make a mistake today. I want to get you on this panel.' I didn't make a mistake, and rarely did, so they had no choice but to keep me involved.

It was the second year in a row that Tipperary won the competition and we had a fantastic team. Shay was in goal and there were other brilliant players like Frank McGrath from Nenagh, our captain who was named player of the tournament, a young chap by the name of Tommy Dunne from Toomevara, who would go on to achieve great things, and Brian Flannery, who won a Munster senior hurling medal in the colours of Waterford in 2002. That was my first experience of success as a Tipperary player and it whetted my appetite for more.

As in primary school, my studies didn't progress in tandem with my sporting career. At St Joseph's, my report card was direct and to the point. The gist of it was that I needed to concentrate more and to cop on to what was happening in the classroom. Sport at St Joseph's wasn't particularly well organized but the principal,

Gerry Grufferty, did helpfully accommodate us. If we put the team together, Gerry would look after the rest.

I was now developing far more of an interest in the Tipperary senior hurling team, and I was at Croke Park in 1989 when they won the All-Ireland final against Antrim. I stood on the Canal End terrace watching John Troy play in goal for Offaly in the minor final. I was taken by the size of his hurley. I noticed that he was using an outfield hurley and I decided that this was the new course of action for me. I had played an U14 game for Tipperary against Wexford and let in a soft goal because my hurley was too big and heavy. I'd even struggled to puck the ball out because of the weight of it. I changed to a smaller stick after watching John play for Offaly.

As I progressed through secondary school, my Intermediate Cert results were nothing to write home about. I put in a much bigger effort for the Leaving Cert. I needed grinds twice a week from Patsy O'Halloran, a man in Clogheen. I didn't particularly like those but the grinds were a necessary evil because I was falling behind in maths, one of my weakest subjects. I didn't know a huge amount about numbers but I did know that I wanted to study Industrial Computing at Waterford Regional Technical College. I didn't really have much of a clue about Industrial Computing but the fact that it involved computers was good enough for me.

When the Leaving Cert results were being handed out, I was met at the door of St Joseph's by Mr Grufferty.

'You didn't do too bad, Cummins,' he said.

He handed me the envelope, and on the drive home, Dad stopped the car so that we could share the moment. I tore open the envelope, and not only had I passed, I'd done quite well. Dad started crying and I wondered why. Was it because he was happy or could he simply not believe how good my results were? He was proud, I knew that, and thankfully I had achieved enough points for Industrial Computing at Waterford RTC.

I wish that I could say I was the model third-level student with a voracious appetite for work. Not a bit of it. Industrial Computing was, in a word, carnage. I was fine when it came to the technical part of computing but I was out of my depth with the maths, just like in secondary school. By some miracle, I passed the course. Gaelic Games helped to keep me sane. For the most part, I still look back on my time in Waterford with real fondness. In 1996, we won a Division 2 Higher Education League title, which enabled Waterford RTC to compete in the prestigious Fitzgibbon Cup.

Hurling was a major sport there but the problem for me in my first year was the fact that Alan Hickey from Cork stood between me and the goalkeeping position. I was seventeen and realized that Alan was first choice, leaving me with a decision to make ahead of my debut year in the Fitzgibbon Cup, in 1993: I could either settle for second best or try to force my way on to the team in another position. Corner-forward was a position I fancied, but to achieve that I needed to turn up every single night for training, to make it impossible for them to drop me, just like the Tony Forristal team. I didn't miss a session. Dad would come down to collect me and drive me home because I didn't stay in Waterford when I studied there. I'd be up at 6.45 the next morning to catch the 7.30 bus back down to Waterford. That's how it was, and that's how it had to be. When I trained, I tried to win as many runs as I could, to do as much as possible to stay on the shoulder of that selector so that whenever he looked round he would see me. I was determined to ensure that I would not be ignored.

My efforts were rewarded when I was handed the number 15 shirt for our Fitzgibbon Cup semi-final against University College Cork. I'd played well in a previous match and scored a few points, which helped my cause, but UCC represented a massive step up in class. I lasted the first half, during which time I managed to hit one of my teammates, Tipperary's Brian O'Meara, on top of the head with my hurley. Brian was fortunate that I didn't crack his skull open. I was taken off at half-time.

Management had probably seen enough of my forward 'skills' to realize that they would be better served by having me between the posts, and I was goalkeeper in 1994 and 1996. We had some terrific players, lads that were household names in their respective counties: Ollie Moran from Limerick, Waterford's Tom Feeney, Peter Barry and PJ Delaney from Kilkenny, and our own Tommy Dunne and Brian O'Meara. Sod's Law dictated that I would finish my third-level career without a Fitzgibbon Cup medal. Waterford IT won the competition in 1995 but I was ineligible to play because I had to take a year out to gain a Diploma in Quality Assurance as part of my studies. At times like that, you wonder if you're ever destined to be successful, to win big things. The Fitzgibbon Cup had been won the year before I arrived in Waterford and in the season I took out. Still, the competition provided me with some invaluable experience. It was raw, primal hurling played at the time of year when pitches are soft, and the hits went in hard and often. So many great players have cut their teeth in the Fitzgibbon Cup, with good performances in the springtime often indicating to intercounty managers that players could get down and dirty as well as producing the summer flash.

But by now I was well on my way to carving my own niche. After leaving college, it was time to step out into the big, bad world and stand on my own two feet. Little did I know how much of a roller coaster ride adult life would turn out to be.

3

Making the Grade

There were flaws in my game that needed to be addressed before I could make the step up to minor level with Tipperary. I failed to make the grade in 1992 because I couldn't strike the ball as well off my left-hand side as my right. So almost every night, I went to the local ball alley to practise on my weak left side. Dad would soak a sliotar in a bucket of water the night before to make it heavier and more difficult to strike. It took months, but eventually I could hit the ball as far off my left-hand side as my right. A weakness in my game was never acceptable to me, and this aspect that I had neglected between the ages of twelve and fifteen had left me playing catch-up with the other boys. Still, I had a brief glimpse of the minor panel in 1992, as my experience of that grade began with more of a whimper than a bang.

I was called into the panel for a game against Limerick in Mitchelstown. Kevin O'Sullivan from Cashel had been picked to play in goal ahead of Shay Killeen but there was panic in the team hotel before the game as it appeared that Shay was not going to show up. As it transpired, Shay was held up but team management feared that he had decided not to travel in protest. The phone rang at home asking me to hightail it to Mitchelstown as quickly as possible. That wasn't a problem as I lived just 18 miles away. My dad and John English drove me over, but I didn't realize at the time that I was being brought in as an emergency in case Shay was a no-show. Before we reached Mitchelstown, however, I was made aware that Shay had made it on time and that my services would not be required.

I was a victim of circumstance, but after being asked to travel at the eleventh hour, I was still anxious to feel part of the night. I approached the dressing-room door and Pat Fox was standing there, blocking my path. Pat was a senior star for Tipperary at the time, holder of two All-Ireland medals, and it was a common practice to have an influential figure present on matchdays, to help relax the younger players.

'Where are you going?' he said.

He didn't know who I was, but Jim Lynch, a former selector with the Tony Forristal U14 team, was part of the minor set-up and spotted me outside.

Jim pulled me into the dressing room but I felt really awkward in there. It was no more than fifteen minutes before throw-in and I was a complete stranger to these players, who were togged out and ready to go, the familiar waft of Deep Heat filling the air. If you're not involved in a game and you walk into a dressing room more or less as a complete outsider, it's not a good place to be. A dressing room is a sacred place before throw-in and I felt like a gooseberry in there. I sat in the dugout for the match but left immediately afterwards. Fr Tom Fogarty was the team manager and he tried to make the best of a bad situation, asking me to join the team for a post-match meal, but I politely declined. In fairness to Jim Lynch, he called to my house the next day for a chat. He thanked me for coming over, explained the misunderstanding and informed me that I wouldn't be joining the panel for the rest of the season. I think Jim felt as embarrassed as I did.

My chance came in 1993, and this time I was to become a fully paid-up member of the Tipperary minor hurling panel.

This was more like it as we progressed to a Munster final with Cork at the Gaelic Grounds in Limerick. Fr Tom was still the manager and we had a really good team: Colm O'Flaherty was full-back, Andy Moloney at midfield, Johnny Enright on the frees. We played before the senior game between Tipperary and Clare and I made a really bad error for Cork's goal. Cork were awarded a free 10 yards in from the touchline, 65 metres from goal, and it dropped short into the square. I shouted 'my ball' but the sliotar slipped into the net off my outstretched hand. Disaster.

There was silence among the Tipperary supporters standing on the terrace behind me, until a voice piped up: 'You fucking eejit.' I remember thinking that he was dead right, but now I was faced with a fight-or-flight moment at a very crucial stage in my developing career. My first Munster final in front of a large attendance and I had messed up, big time. So I picked the ball out of the net, reset and got on with the game, really angry with myself. Nothing else mattered but making up for that mistake.

It was a horrible feeling, bending my back to fish that ball out of the net, but I had a chance to make some amends when a line ball was cut in during the second half. I was far more decisive this time, coming out to catch the ball between two players as it fizzed across the face of goal. Panic over. What had I been worried about? I played extremely well for the remainder of the game. Perhaps that mistake had to happen for me to throw off the shackles and express myself. We won by three points and I was a Munster minor medallist for the one and only time in my career.

Tellingly, the mistake is what I remember from that game. I can still feel the sensation of the ball rolling between forefinger and thumb, believing for a millisecond that it was in my grasp before it leaves the edge of my hand and drops over my left shoulder. I cursed myself and wondered if there was some way I could have that moment back, for just a second, but I couldn't. I had been playing so well and this error came from nowhere.

We lost the All-Ireland semi-final to Galway and that one really stung. I'd seen Michael Ferncombe play in goal for the Tipp minors at Croke Park in 1991, making saves at the famous Hill 16 end of the ground, and I wanted some of that. As it turned out, I would have to wait until 1997 to play there for the first time.

There was still plenty of life left in my underage career with Tipperary after the minor grade. I played for three years at U21 level, and another chastening experience came my way during that time. A Brian Corcoran-inspired Cork team beat us in 1993, and a year later I found myself on the outside looking in. I suspect that my commitments to football had a part to play in that as I had played on the Tipperary team that won the McGrath Cup in 1994. Some football and U21 hurling training sessions clashed and I had to try to combine the two as best I could.

I'll never forget when team management dropped the bomb-shell in the function room of the Park Avenue in Thurles. Chairs had been laid out and I was sitting five rows from the front, fully expecting to get the nod. Kevin O'Sullivan was picked, and that old, familiar temper rose in me. One of the selectors had told me earlier in the year that it would be OK to excuse myself from some of the hurling sessions because of my commitments to the footballers. I was told that I would still be picked on the U21 hurling team, but that didn't prove to be the case. The U21 grade is crucial for any player looking to make the jump from promising underage player to potential senior.

We were beaten by Waterford away from home in 1994 and we assembled in a local hotel in the city for a meal after the game.

The selectors were naturally subdued, as were the players, and, after we had eaten, I took the chance to give them a piece of my mind in private. 'I'm disappointed for the team but I'm not disappointed for ye.' Should I have said that? I'm still not sure to this day, but that anger was boiling inside me and I felt at the time that I had to let it out. It was probably the wrong thing to say because it's one of the few times in my life that I've addressed a management team before I was first spoken to.

The 1995 season brought with it a hint of fresh promise for our U21 team. Michael Doyle was manager and Tommy Dunne ran the show on the pitch like a man possessed. We beat Clare in the Munster final to win the provincial title for the first time in five years. I remember that game because of the controversy that surrounded it as Ger Loughnane, Clare's senior manager at the time, pulled his senior panellists, including Ollie Baker and Frank Lohan, out of the U21 final. I recall that there was some doubt about whether the match would go ahead at all but it did, eventually, when Clare hopped off the team bus togged off and ready to play. The game ended with dusk descending, and you know it's a dark evening when you can see the lights from the press box glowing in the Old Stand at Semple Stadium.

We beat Antrim in the All-Ireland semi-final in Navan and I remember being particularly nervous ahead of that one. The commonly held belief was that we would win comfortably, and that assumption swept through the camp. I had never played against an Antrim team before and this was a step into the unknown, but we got the job done comfortably to set up a final meeting with Kilkenny in Thurles.

My old football favourites Kerry were involved in the U21 football final that preceded our game and they got the job done against Mayo, with future senior stars Diarmuid Murphy, the goalkeeper, Darragh Ó Sé, Johnny Crowley, Liam Hassett and Dara Ó

Cinnéide playing their part. It was a glorious September day but I knew that the sun would prove a tricky opponent as it dipped to the right over the New Stand as the evening drew in. During the second half an advertising hoarding on the right-hand side of the pitch on the 45-metre line bounced an occasional flash of reflected sunlight, but I would have more problems to contend with than that.

While I made a very good save to deny Kilkenny's Denis Byrne, the goal the 'Cats' scored was a scrappy one to concede. A scruffy effort bobbled into the net over my right shoulder and for a moment it felt like this was the 1993 Munster minor final all over again, an avoidable goal in a very big game. This was the first time I had ever seen the words 'All-Ireland final' stitched into the commemorative jerseys that you wear on the biggest occasions. Before many spectators had even settled into their seats I was picking the ball out of my own net. But we recovered well to score a 1–14 to 1–10 victory, with Philip O'Dwyer coming off the bench to score the clinching goal. The win sparked a massive celebration in Dundrum later that night as our team captain, Brian Horgan, hailed from the local Knockavilla-Kickhams club.

The celebrations were another eye-opener for me as I was a teetotaller at the time. I didn't drink until I was twenty-three. I never really knew what drink was and it didn't click with me that if you got drunk, you could have good craic. I was in Galway on a night out when I had my first drink. Liam Barrett was with me and I ordered two pints of Bulmers cider. I handed one to Liam.

'Who's the other one for?' he asked.

'I'm drinking that.'

'Aw Jaysus!'

I drank that first one but returned to 7Up for the rest of the night. I now know that if I'm out in company and I feel uncomfortable not drinking, at least I can order something. But I never needed Dutch courage or to be rat-faced drunk to hold conversations with boys or girls. My dad never drank and my mother seldom did. Drink culture simply wasn't part of my experience growing up. My memory is not of my dad heading out to the pub but of my dad playing football and hurling with me in the back garden. I never knew it to be any other way. So I never felt like I was missing out.

That night in Dundrum, some of the lads were falling around the place, high on a cocktail of natural elation from winning the match and the alcohol that rewarded it. This was alien to me and I didn't want to stay out all night. We'd won, it was my first All-Ireland medal and that was great, but I wanted much more than that. There have been hundreds of promising players who won minor and U21 titles but never went on to fulfil their potential on the biggest stage of all. I wasn't prepared to fall into that bracket. As far as I was concerned, this was only the start.

I didn't want to be just another guy who played in goal for Tipperary. I wanted to be remembered, and the only way I could do that was to do things on the field that others could only dream about. I was trying things, like diving to catch the ball with my hand rather than using the hurley. The Clare senior goalkeeper, Davy Fitzgerald, left a lasting impression on me in the summer of 1995. We trained with the U21s after Clare played Limerick in the Munster senior final, and as I approached Semple Stadium, Davy was surrounded by a group of jubilant Clare supporters after they had made history by winning the competition for the first time since 1932. The people there thought he was the bee's knees and Davy was smiling from ear to ear. I looked at him and thought: 'I want some of that.' That's where I saw myself, playing in Munster finals and winning them. I had played in the same championship as Davy earlier in the summer but he was light years ahead of me in terms of what he had now achieved.

I always studied other goalkeepers, and the impression I got was that Davy was like a coiled spring before games, ready to release when he crossed the chalk. He sent out his own unique message that he was going to fight with everybody on the terrace if he had to. Not everybody liked him but he was fine with that. In fact, it was fuel to his fire. Wexford's Damien Fitzhenry was the standard-bearer in my eyes but I wanted Davy's energy. I aspired to be a composite of the best of Fitzhenry and Fitzgerald. Inside I'd be Davy but the external me would be cast along the lines of Fitzhenry, cool, calm, composed, master of all that he surveyed.

The common thread running through all three of us remained constant throughout our careers: it was taken as an insult if an opponent scored a goal against us, an affront. That's the way it has to be if you want to succeed as a goalkeeper at the top level.

4

Stepping Up

'Well done today, that's you they're talking about on the radio, and it's well deserved.'

Words etched on my consciousness ever since Ken Hogan uttered them on the way back from Cappoquin, County Waterford, in November 1993.

'If Carlsberg did intercounty debuts . . .' You could have run an advertising campaign on the back of what happened against Waterford in that National League fixture, which was the first time I had pulled on the Tipperary senior shirt.

Babs was our manager and he rang my father a few days before the game to pass on the message that I would be playing on Sunday. I had played minor and U21 for the county earlier in the year but I hadn't even trained with the seniors yet. What's more, the Tipperary senior hurling team was a world that existed outside the circles I had operated in until that point. I hadn't seen them playing a match since the 1989 All-Ireland final at Croke Park. I wasn't there in 1991 when they beat Kilkenny to win the Liam MacCarthy Cup.

We met in Cahir in the morning and the other lads from the South, Brian O'Meara and John Leahy from Mullinahone, were brilliant to me, taking me under their wing right from the start. I thought I was the bomb, dressed in my shiny blue tracksuit, and here I was getting ready to play alongside superstars of the game. I didn't recognize some of the faces, mind you. Noel Sheehy, the full-back, walked in and I thought he was Paul Delaney.

The game itself was Roy of the Rovers stuff. Waterford forward Paul Flynn hit a shot from 8 or 9 yards out and, after the ball struck me on the arm, it hit the post, fell at my feet and I was able to pick it up and clear it comfortably. I felt at home pretty much straight away and what helped was the fact that Páraic Fanning, a mentor of mine in college, was playing at full-forward for Waterford. I felt that I knew him better than any of my own team-mates. To top it all off, we won, and Babs delivered the post-match team talk as he towelled himself off after a shower. He spoke about how the day went and how he was pleased with the result. It was Tipperary's third League outing of the season and it had brought a third victory.

On the bus journey home, the radio hummed with news of how Tipperary had unearthed a promising new goalkeeper. In the build-up to the game, much of the talk centred on how Ken Hogan, the regular first choice, had been dropped. This media-driven hype was new to me, and thrown into the mix was the Babs ingredient. Favouritism was the obvious inference as Babs and I hailed from the same club, but this was a run-of-the-mill League game and I guess the newspapers needed some angle to spice things up a little. Ken's reaction was incredible. He could have been forgiven for feeling aggrieved but his first instinct was to congratulate me on my performance. Look at it from his point of view: here was this cocky young upstart, just eighteen years of age, parachuted in from practically nowhere to take his place, and from the manager's club. Instead, he pointed out that the radio commentator was talking about me, and I was left feeling incredibly humbled.

I was still involved in the new year, a sub against Galway in 1994 when we played them in Nenagh. I got back in for the Cork game and kept a clean sheet even though we lost by two points in Thurles, but problems surfaced in early March when Down travelled to play us. I was now beginning to realize that people were talking about me, but any young player who thinks he's having it easy is in for a rude awakening at some point.

Before the Down game, Babs told us that he was rating every player out of ten. This didn't go down too well with one of our star players, Nicky English, who gathered us in the shower area to deliver a rather blunt message: 'Listen, don't mind what he's after saying about player ratings, we'll be rated as a team, not as individuals.' It was an early insight into Nicky's mindset, but as an individual I was well below par, leaking three goals in a performance that put the kibosh on my debut season. That was it for me for the rest of the year, and I couldn't really complain. After all, I had been plucked from virtual obscurity and my main goals were senior football with Tipperary and the U21 hurlers. Jody Grace and Ken battled it out for the goalkeeping position with the senior hurlers, and when Tipp won the National League in May 1994, I was pucking around in my back garden, listening to the game on the radio of Dad's maroon Mazda.

Even though I hadn't finished the campaign, that victory meant that I had secured my first medal as a senior hurler with Tipperary. The problem was that I didn't feel I had deserved it, having only featured in two of our eleven matches. On the night of the medals presentation in Thurles, I sat outside the Park Avenue Hotel in the car, afraid to go in. All dressed up and nowhere to go. Pat Fox and Nicky English were in there, for Christ's sake, and the team had won a National Hurling League title while I was playing for the footballers. It didn't feel right. There was a certain sense of belonging, but it wasn't strong enough for me to collect the medal, which was later delivered to me in the post.

Just weeks after winning the League, Tipp were knocked out of the championship by Clare at the first hurdle, a defeat that signalled the end of Babs's reign after eight seasons. The appointment of Fr Tom Fogarty as his successor was encouraging news for me. I had played well in 1993 when Fr Tom was manager of the minor team, and while Jody Grace had played in the Clare game, I felt that I had a significant advantage on him because Fr Tom knew what I was capable of. Ken retired after the 1994 season but, in truth, an error against Galway in the 1993 All-Ireland semi-final had signalled the end of his successful intercounty career. The pathway was now clear and my persistence was rewarded with a senior championship debut against Waterford in May 1995, when Jody was ruled out through injury. Taking over from Jody was real pressure but the help and advice he sent my way eased that. Even though Ken had stepped away, he was brilliant too, having had the experience of playing in Munster and All-Ireland finals.

Advice is one thing but it still won't fully prepare a player for the sheer magnitude of a senior championship debut. And on that Sunday afternoon at Páirc Uí Chaoimh, I was a crumbling, nervous wreck during the pre-match parade. It hit me all at once that this was serious, this was Munster championship and this was knockout. Tipperary had won the All-Ireland final in 1991 and here I was, getting ready to play alongside some of the most iconic names in the county's history: Noel Sheehy at full-back, Declan Ryan, John Leahy, Michael Cleary, Nicky English and Pat Fox. The voice returned: 'Uh oh, shit. I'm out of my depth here.' The more I tried to reassure myself that everything would be OK, that I had the ability to survive in this magnificent cauldron, the worse I felt. Thankfully, the lads out on the field were in Playstation mode and we posted a massive tally of 4–23.

I was standing as a virtual spectator for most of the game, watching Fox, who came on as sub, Ryan, Cleary, Leahy and English strutting their stuff as arrows slung mercilessly above and below the Waterford crossbar. I had very little to do but Waterford's only goal shot in under my legs with my eyes looking elsewhere. On one occasion I ventured towards the touchline and fell. I was like Bambi on ice, or more Coco the Clown with my tracksuit bottoms on. All I was missing was a red nose to complete the look. I was a wreck, but my teammates bailed me out with their scoring power. In essence, I was a minor player togged out in senior attire, and I feared for my place after that.

The voice in my head savaged me later: 'You had the chance, you have the ability and everything going for you, but you blew it. You took it for granted because you went in there feeling that it was just another game, but it wasn't.' What had happened – and I didn't realize it at the time because I simply didn't understand it – was that my mental preparation was inadequate. Physical skill alone is only half the battle on championship Sunday. Mental attitude, strength and experience are just as important for generating a good performance but I didn't have those key attributes yet.

Luckily, I had the chance to redeem myself with the senior footballers, who trained a couple of nights later. We were brought to Thurles in a taxi and Pete Savage, a football stalwart from Ardfinnan, was with me in the car. That's the way it worked at the time. Taxis were cheaper than hiring a bus, and Pete didn't drive.

'Tipp have a great team and they could win the All-Ireland,' the taxi driver mused, referring to the performance of the hurlers. 'But only if they get rid of the goalie.'

I squirmed in my seat.

Pete, smiling, warmed to the theme. 'Ah, he wasn't that bad, was he?'

'Oh, he'll never make it, that fella.'

When we finally arrived in Thurles, after what seemed like an eternity, I had been well and truly shelled.

'Listen,' Pete said as we left the taxi, 'that goalkeeper you were talking about, well he's here now so you can tell him what you really think of him!'

It was the taxi driver's turn to squirm, and after he mumbled what I can only assume was an apology, he sped off.

He had made his point, a valid one, but the goalkeeper that had played at Páirc Uí Chaoimh wasn't me. I had got it so badly wrong that I began to train without tracksuit bottoms, just regular togs. If I wanted to be a senior hurler, I had to look like one, not this child with the tracksuit bottoms and the socks pulled halfway up his shins. Look the part and then you might feel the part. I looked at myself on the highlights from that game and cringed.

Fr Tom, as usual, was a port in the storm. 'Put that behind you, you'll be playing the next day,' he told me.

Those words were like music to my ears. I don't know if he meant them at the time or not but I can only presume that he did. Jody Grace broke his thumb two weeks before the Limerick game and an SOS went out to my old nemesis, Kevin O'Sullivan. He was back as if he'd never been away, and Kevin was a real threat. This time, the voice consoled me: 'The good thing is that Kevin is concentrating on soccer and he can't really focus too much on the hurling. And Fr Tom told you that you'd be playing the next day so don't worry about it.'

I did play against Limerick, and I played well, even though we lost by a point. It was a strange thing, playing without tracksuit bottoms for the first time, but I felt that I'd made a statement. Jody's injuries hadn't helped his cause but I'd managed to see off the challenge of Kevin, which at the time was considerable.

In seventy minutes of hurling, the boy had become a man.

5

Fuelling the Fire

'Lads, what ye did to Brendan in there was a disgrace.' Michael Ryan is angry. I've just been filleted at a team meeting after the 1996 Munster hurling final. I'm the fall guy after Limerick came from ten points down to draw at the Gaelic Grounds.

I'd already had a taste of the verbals against Waterford in the quarter-final, when some of their players targeted me after the pre-match parade. We played them at Walsh Park and Waterford were seeking revenge after we beat them in 1995. I was the only weak link in their eyes, having let in a poor goal on my debut. 'You'll let in another soft one today.'

I could deal with that, but having my own dressing room turn on me was a new challenge. In the Munster final, we played with a gale at our backs. Liam Cahill stuck a goal in the bottom corner, Michael Cleary picked off a line ball and sent it fizzing back over the crossbar – we were on fire. Ten points ahead at half-time, we looked home and hosed, but Limerick came roaring back to level. Nicky English and Pat Fox were sprung from the bench and we pushed two clear again before Limerick rallied once more, Frankie Carroll popping the equalizer over the bar in stoppage time. Every time I pucked the ball out, it seemed to rain back over my head. Limerick scored nineteen points and salvaged a replay.

I was playing in my first Munster senior final and still, at twenty-one, a relative greenhorn. When the game was analysed a couple of nights later, some of the more senior players were looking for a victim, and found one. The consensus was that my puckouts were the problem and the clear message was that I was the reason we had blown such a big lead. But Michael Ryan wasn't happy and lashed back in my defence. 'It wasn't all Brendan's fault,' he stressed.

Fr Tom was also present but decided to let it slide. I'm sure that he would have called a halt if the criticism had become over-personal but, in his own way, he was backing me to work my way out of this one. He knew that this would really sting but it was also a test of my resolve and would make me stronger. He managed it well, and sometimes you have to let players vent, even if there's collateral damage along the way. I was it.

In the car on the way home, I cried. I had to let it out, but at home I never mentioned a word about what had happened. I processed the events, internalized them, and vowed to make amends.

We stayed in Cork the night before the replay and I roomed with Conal Bonnar. I tried to kill time downstairs in the hotel as I felt dreadfully anxious. When I returned to my room, my pillows were gone, so rather than disturb Conal, I rolled my coat into a ball and used that. Instead of acknowledging the fundamental fact that I was on the same team as this guy, I was overawed. Conal had taken a couple of extra pillows yet I didn't have the courage to ask for them back.

I was still working through that public dressing down and it was my first real experience of the heat championship hurling can generate if the result doesn't go your way. It wasn't right but I was in a dressing room that was packed with older and far more experienced players. Maybe I was the problem on the day but I wasn't the only problem, as Michael had pointed out.

We should have finished them at the first time of asking but a couple of key moments kept Limerick alive. Joe Quaid, their goalkeeper, pulled off one of the greatest saves I have ever seen, from Aidan Ryan, and Nicky was denied a blatant free when Mike Nash tugged his jersey. I was angry, but I didn't play particularly well in the replay. Limerick scored four goals against us at Páirc Uí Chaoimh, Owen O'Neill kicking two of them. The current Limerick manager, TJ Ryan, scored another, after I had almost cut the legs from under our corner-back George Frend as a high ball led to chaos in our goalmouth. Carroll scored the other Limerick goal and our season was over.

Fr Tom fell on his sword, part of the natural attrition. It was also the last time that Nicky and Pat wore the Tipperary senior shirt, and one of my most prized possessions is the jersey I wore in that game. I later had it signed by all of the players.

Len Gaynor, a man who won three All-Ireland senior medals as a player, was unveiled as our new manager. He was also the man who lit the touchpaper for Clare's hurling revolution, handing over the reins to Ger Loughnane after managing the Banner County in 1993 and 1994. Len was joined by Michael Doyle, our U21 All-Ireland winning manager in 1995, and Murt Duggan from Ballingarry. There had been speculation about an approach for Babs Keating but Len had an impressive track record, having led his club Kilruane MacDonagh's to an All-Ireland title in 1986. He had also coached a number of other clubs in Tipperary and his most recent achievement before taking the county job was to mastermind Newport's first North Tipperary senior hurling success in fifty-one years. Len had also been a Tipperary selector in the mid-1980s.

Len was old school but an incredibly passionate man. He brought real freshness to the set-up and had total commitment from the players right from the start. One of our panel members, Liam Jones from Newport, trained with us on the morning of his wedding day. But there was an early setback in 1997 when Brian O'Meara, one of our key players, broke his kneecap in a League match against Limerick. In an era when players were encouraged to 'run it off', Brian was placed in the corner-forward position but gestured to Dr Peter Murchin – the surgeon who dealt with the players, and who would go on to have a more hands-on role with the team in later years – that he couldn't walk. Peter examined Brian and informed a member of the management team that his kneecap was severely damaged. The selector asked Peter if he had applied painkilling spray to the injury. 'I don't think you heard me,' Peter replied. 'His kneecap is split in half.'

The men in charge of our team had spilled blood for the cause and demanded the same from us. Len was a powerful orator, the type of man who could deliver a sermon from a mountain and captivate the audience below, who would be hanging on his every word. But we were hurling in an environment that contained the Clare team he had helped to create. I can only compare them to a bunch of animals left out of a cage, and they were revolutionizing the game of hurling with unparallelled fitness levels. More than that, they went for your throat right from the start, bringing huge aggression to the table. It took us a while to adapt, but Len was desperately close to winning Munster and All-Ireland titles in 1997. In both games against Clare, John Leahy had late chances. A goal in the Munster final would have drawn us level, and in the All-Ireland final, if John had found the back of the net we would have won the game. The problem was that it was almost impossible to devise a gameplan to confront Clare. They had brilliant hurlers, and that should never be forgotten, but we could not match that raw, naked aggression.

Our championship campaign began with victory over Limerick at Semple Stadium, with almost fifty thousand present. I was incredibly excited after that game because after losing to them in 1995 and 1996 we had finally managed to get one over on them. What was even better was the knowledge that a potential path to Croke Park had now opened up – a venue I had never played in before. 'Yeesss!' I roared as I collected my hurleys from the back of the net. 'We beat the bastards!' When I turned round, Limerick's Gary Kirby was there, to offer congratulations.

'Ah, there's no need for that, Brendan,' he said, half smiling.

'Jesus, I'm sorry, Gary.'

Clare and Tipperary didn't particularly like each other and one of the more uncomfortable moments of the year occurred when I was summoned to the radio gantry at Páirc Uí Chaoimh, after we lost the Munster final. I was face to face with Clare's Brian Lohan, fielding questions from the interviewer, and it felt really weird. A gripping rivalry between the counties was quickly developing and it was particularly fierce in the linked towns of Killaloe and Ballina, separated by an arched bridge, with Killaloe on the Clare side and Ballina on the Tipperary side. On that bridge, Clare supporters perched a door – a reference to the fact that we were now faced with the 'back door' route to revive our season.

Losing the Munster final wasn't the end of the world, however, as one more fence would take us to an All-Ireland semi-final. We jumped it comfortably, against Down in Clones, and were pitted against Wexford, the reigning All-Ireland champions. This was my first taste of Croke Park and it was the first time all year that we really clicked into gear, winning by 2–16 to 0–15. Leahy, O'Meara, Tommy Dunne and Cleary were flying, firing the type of long-range points that were still rising as they cleared the crossbar. With a few minutes remaining, the game was effectively won and our supporters were ready to invade the pitch in celebration. I looked to my right and my friend Derek O'Mahoney was there. 'Come on, we're going to do this!' he roared.

At full-time, I commiserated with a number of the Wexford players including Martin Storey, who was pulling on a cigarette. And this was the first time that I experienced the sensation as a senior player of supporters running towards me. We had lost Munster finals in 1996 and earlier in the year and the images you carry with you from those losses are watching opposition players being carried shoulder-high from the pitch, legs flailing, hurleys in the air. Now it was our turn, and as our fans streamed out of Croke Park, the battle-cry went up: 'We want Clare, we want Clare!'

They had beaten Kilkenny by four points seven days earlier and the scene was set for the first all-Munster All-Ireland final. I looked ahead to the game with a huge sense of anticipation, but not anger. I never bought into the simmering rivalry between the counties until the pot bubbled over in later years, when Nicky English was in charge. It got more personal then, because it was Loughnane against Nicky, and I wanted Nicky to win. In 1997, I was driven by the sheer excitement of playing in my first All-Ireland senior final.

Superstition kicked in as I had worn a white jersey in the Munster final and felt good in it. Because of the colour clash between Clare's saffron and blue and the yellow Tipperary goal-keeper shirt, white would be the order of the day again. I was seated beside our full-back Noel Sheehy on the bus journey to Croke Park and Noel was very much in the zone. Through gritted teeth he tapped the seat in front of him, repeating his personal mantra: 'I feel the need, the need for speed.' He was so bloody determined, angry, even. I loved playing behind Noel. It was like playing at home with Phil Walsh at club level. Phil would turn round every now and then and ask, 'Are you OK, young fella?' Noel would glance back at me through the helmet, teeth grinding, and I knew that he was looking after me.

Noel was like that fictional Dutch character, the young boy who saved his country by putting his finger in a leaking dyke. He was determined that nothing would pass and he would stand there and repel the opposition no matter how bad the danger was. We might stumble but Noel insisted that we would never fall. He had ability but he was also a player who got every last drop out of himself. If Noel was a doused sponge before throw-in, he was bone dry at the end. He played in that 1997 final with his right hamstring practically torn, yet he did fine.

Walking around in the pre-match parade took me back to All-Ireland football final day in 1982, when I sat on my father's knee in the Upper Hogan Stand as Offaly beat Kerry in that famous game. As the game reached a conclusion, the flashing letters and numbers from the electronic scoreboard in the Nally Stand seemed to light up the stadium, just like the Subbuteo table football set at home when I was a child. It wasn't enough to have a green piece of cloth and the basic accessories for my flick football set, with Dad providing the opposition on Christmas morning. No, I had to have the scoreboard and the floodlights too – anything to make it seem more real.

Jamesie O'Connor's winning point over the Hill 16 crossbar was the decisive score but we had a late chance to win it. I held my breath looking through the crowd of players on the pitch as John Leahy wound up for one last effort. I didn't know what had happened until the ball squirted out to the side. Davy Fitzgerald saved John's shot and Clare were champions.

I got lost after the final whistle, not knowing the way back to our dressing rooms. Everybody else seemed to be gravitating towards the Canal End and I met Ger Loughnane in a dark tunnel. I was anxious when I saw him because this was Loughnane, a mythical figure in many ways, the saviour of Clare. Here we were, just the two of us, in a tunnel after Clare had beaten Tipperary in an All-Ireland final. 'What's going to happen now?' I wondered. 'He hates Tipp.' He was extremely gracious in victory and we shook hands. 'Hard luck, you'll have plenty more days.' His kind words were in stark contrast to the image Clare wanted to portray, that the whole world was against them.

Clare needed that, and they made sure that nobody was going to laugh at them any more. Loughnane's fire-and-brimstone approach enabled his players to make the sacrifices that they did and to extract maximum reward from the ability they possessed. Clare won All-Irelands with just a couple of recognized scoring forwards. The rest worked like dogs to make sure that the ball made its way to them and they had a half-back line capable of scoring long-range points. Their superb centre-back, Seanie McMahon, would launch one of his long-range frees and I'd lose it in the clouds. Seconds later, it'd be dropping over the bar from 100 yards. They had incredible leaders all over the pitch, from Davy Fitzgerald in goal to the Lohan brothers, Brian and Frank, Liam Doyle and Anthony Daly. That Clare defence was like the Iron Curtain. They were bloody good hurlers and formidable people, with the same determined look as Noel Sheehy in their eyes.

We needed some of that, and you would think that losing Munster and All-Ireland finals in such heartbreaking fashion in 1997 would fuel our fire for the following season. But there are times when a manager can lose the dressing room for no other reason than it simply drifts away from him, and that's what happened to Len. The excitement of playing in an All-Ireland senior final kept me going through the winter and I wanted more of that. Tommy Dunne was another player just waiting to explode, but 1998 was one of those years that passed us by, as can often be the case in Tipperary. It wasn't for the want of trying on Len's part. For example, he brought in a rugby league coach from England for one of our training sessions. At the time I felt it was strange, but Len didn't want to be seen as the old stook averse to change or new ideas. It was a great idea to get this coach in, with a new perspective on strength and conditioning and game-playing, and when he left, we held on to a few of his drills. Every manager takes a punt on something, but the relationship between the players and Len drifted. When we were knocked out of the Munster championship by Waterford in 1998, we were like players clinging to a lifebuoy who simply let go.

Complacency wasn't an issue, but the team was a year older. Noel Sheehy had also retired after 1997. We didn't have much young blood coming through but 1998 wasn't any different to other years when we underachieved. We had gone soft, and there was no sign of anybody trying to arrest the malaise. The players must take responsibility for that. The leaders that would emerge over the next few years were not yet in a position to exert any real influence. Once again, the clarion call went out from the Tipperary county board for a new captain to steer the stricken vessel. God heard the rallying cry.

6

The Rock

I thought I was dead when I left the recovery room because the Holy Bible states that no man can see the face of God and live. But there he was, Nicky English, the man who was God in the eyes of Tipperary supporters.

'Are you all right?'

'I'll be fine, I'll be back.'

'I know you will.'

It was February 1999, and I had just undergone surgery at Our Lady's Hospital in Cashel – a procedure that would save my career. I was injured playing on our local field, for Ardfinnan against Clonmel Commercials in a club football game. I had gathered possession and, attacking the village end goals of the pitch, I hopped the ball to go around the giant Commercials midfielder Eamonn Hanrahan, nicknamed 'Tiny'. He was 6 feet 7 inches tall. I had a way of rolling my hand over the ball and when I swivelled my hips, that was enough to send an opponent the wrong way and I could get past him. Eamonn stuck out his knee to stop me, a natural reaction from a player on the back foot, but the quadricep muscle in my left leg connected with his left knee and I was left in a crumpled heap on the ground.

It wasn't too bad for the next twenty-four hours but by the Monday night my leg had swollen and I had to wear tracksuit bottoms to work the next morning. Wearing a pair of jeans or normal work pants was too painful, and I visited Cashel hospital on Wednesday, where a doctor stuck a needle in my leg, thinking that he could draw out the contusion. A dead leg is quite a common injury but also a quite serious one, with many underlying factors at play. My quad had taken a traumatic blow from Eamonn's knee and the impact had caused the muscle to crack against underlying bone, resulting in internal bleeding. If a player decides that he can try to 'run off' this injury, the bleeding can increase, meaning that the muscle recovery will be much slower and the risk of more permanent damage rises. I had not tried to run mine off, I'd come straight off the pitch.

At 5.30 a.m. on Thursday morning, I was roaring like a bull in bed at home due to the pain. At this stage I could wear nothing but my underwear on the lower half of my body because my quad had swollen to such an extent that it was almost double the size of the other one, and purple in colour. My mother rang for an ambulance, and if somebody had told me there and then that they could ease the pain by cutting my leg off, I think I would have accepted that. Morning had broken when the ambulance arrived and I was taken to the hospital in Cashel, where I met Dr Murchin.

I remember telling somebody in the hospital that I needed morphine and when I glanced down at my foot, I noticed that the veins in it had collapsed. There was now no blood flowing below the knee. One doctor tried the previous trick of sticking a needle in my leg to draw some fluid out, but the result was the same as the first attempt a couple of days earlier. Nothing.

Then Dr Murchin arrived. He took one look at my leg and insisted that it was a case for the operating theatre, and fast. The bleeding was deep enough in the muscle to form a pocket of blood known as a haematoma. In many cases the human body reabsorbs and processes this blood over time, but if the haematoma does not work itself out, surgery is required to remove it. This was the situation I now found myself in, and I was scared. I paid a visit to the toilet before the operation and almost soiled myself with fear. Picture the scene: I was sitting on a toilet encased by grey marble walls, my leg outstretched in front of me, the veins in my foot collapsed.

I was anaesthetized for surgery but I came to during the procedure and insisted that I wanted to look down and see what they were doing. I pulled the towel to one side and was greeted by the sight of my leg with no skin on it but still as big as it had been before. It was like a brief out-of-body experience, and I soon fell back to sleep again.

My next memory is of the recovery ward, when I placed my hand under the bedcovers to feel my leg. My hand got covered in blood and the bottom half of my body felt wet, as if I was after wetting myself, which I thought I had. The problem was much more serious than that as an artery had burst and my leg was pumping blood on to the bed. During the operation, my leg swelled to such an extent that it was impossible to sew the skin back together when the procedure was completed. The wound was left exposed, with the skin peeled back on either side. Dr Murchin had cut a 12-inch hole in my leg, allowing blood and tissue to flow from the injury on to the operating table, thereby alleviating the pressure that had built up and caused the swelling. The area was then cleaned out, and Dr Murchin decided that the wound would be stitched once the swelling had gone down even more. The problem was that the associated damage below my knee came rushing to the upper part of my leg, causing the femoral artery in my quad to burst. A second trip to the operating theatre was needed. Dr Murchin was on his way back home when he took the emergency call to return to the hospital. Thirty surgical clips later, the problem was solved and the road to recovery could begin.

Nicky was outside when I was wheeled out. The doors opened on to the main corridor, and as I was being ferried back to my room I glanced to my left and there he was. Nicky was Tipperary's new senior hurling team manager and his visit provided with me a real sense of comfort. He was the one man I needed there, to tell me that everything would be OK, because I feared that I would never play again.

On a daily basis during the early phase of recovery the dressing on the wound was changed and I asked Dr Murchin if I could watch what he was doing. I really shouldn't have as the light that shone from above highlighted the gravity of my injury. There was no skin on my left quad muscle and all I could see was pus, red and green in colour. The skin looked like it was dead, rolled back on either side, but four or five days after surgery, the wound was finally sewn. Dr Murchin started at one end of it, a nurse at the other, and they met in the middle.

As I lay on the table before the procedure, I looked out through the window and was greeted by a spectacular sight, the Rock of Cashel. Coincidentally, the Tipperary county board decided after the 1999 championship that the team crest would be redesigned, and the original was replaced by an image of the Rock of Cashel, with two crossed hurleys and a football underneath. To many people it's just a crest, a symbol, but to me it represents much more than that. Any time I pulled a shirt over my head with that new Tipperary crest sewn into it, I thought about the day I lay on that table in Cashel hospital, with two people stitching a gaping wound in my leg. In my mind, they had done much more than a job with needle and thread: they had effectively knitted my career back together.

The Tipperary crest stood as a shining beacon of hope for me, and a constant reminder of what I had almost lost.

7

Nicky

The biggest compliment I can pay to Nicky English and Liam Sheedy, who both guided us to All-Ireland senior titles, is that they were almost a mirror image of each other as managers. Their styles differed in subtle ways but the pursuit of excellence and high standards was very much the same. Nicky had my back from the moment I met him for the first time after his appointment in 1998, at the Anner Hotel in Thurles. That vision of him at my side in hospital a few months later is forever etched in my mind.

He also helped to provide focus in my professional life. I was operating in a comfort zone, and Nicky knew it. He asked me if I was happy in my previous job. I told him straight out that I had gone soft. He asked me what I would like to do, and if I would consider a job in Allied Irish Bank, for whom he worked. I didn't need to be asked twice and a meeting was arranged with Pat Murphy, who worked for Ark Life at the time, AIB's insurance wing. 'Talk to this fella,' Nicky said, 'he'll know from speaking to you whether you'll be able to do the job or not.' Pat was impressed enough by what I had to say to offer me a role.

Before joining AIB, I had been working as a sales

representative with McMahon's, a timber company covering Limerick, North Cork and South Tipperary. It was a super education because when I first started in the job I was armed with little more than a printout of potential customers and left to my own devices. I would either sink or swim, but I did well and built up a solid customer base. Eventually I sank into a comfort zone. I was whizzing around in a green two-litre Ford Mondeo with a spoiler on the back. People were ringing my dad advising him that he should tell me to slow down before I went in over a ditch. AIB was the fresh challenge I needed, and after a four-week course to gain product knowledge, I officially joined and have been working with them from that day to this.

Ever since, it's been a cycle of meeting customers, advising on life cover and dealing in pensions and savings. It's a very dynamic job but working across different branches through the years has suited me. I enjoy working with and motivating people. The team-building aspect of the job has helped me in my hurling career too. Every day throws up a new challenge.

With Nicky in charge, I also hoped that my hurling career would really take off. His philosophy was built on commitment and communication – commitment to the group and communication in terms of building characters. Nicky didn't just make me a better player, he made me a better person, just like Liam Sheedy would in later years. There was always a sense that you had let Nicky down if you lost a game, and when the phone lit up with an incoming call from him, the reaction was almost psychosomatic in nature, a pang of anxiety and a small bead of sweat on the brow. The phone might ring three times before I would answer with a tentative 'Hello?' The worry was always that I might have done something wrong. It was as though Nicky was my hurling conscience. If he told me I had done something wrong, then it meant that I had and there was no comeback.

He was never angry, more disappointed, and that made me feel even worse because we realized how much Nicky was investing in the project to transform us from perennial underachievers into winners. We worked in a safe environment where constructive criticism was key. You were criticized as a player but respected as a human being. On that basis, Nicky and Liam could say whatever they wanted to a player, safe in the knowledge that he would take it in the right spirit. That's why they achieved success because Tipperary in any given year have the raw materials to win an All-Ireland title but the most crucial ingredient, that X factor, is provided by the manager. That's the key, and it's no coincidence that it took Nicky three years to get us there. Liam the same. It's no surprise either that Tommy Dunne was Nicky's captain, his leader on the pitch, and Eoin Kelly was Liam's. They were the go-to men. Whenever I looked out at Tommy or Eoin on the pitch, I knew they meant business. By Jesus, I was desperate to do my job because I would have followed those guys to the ends of the earth.

Having Nicky as manager was the first time in my intercounty career that I'd had a former teammate in charge. It was an unusual feeling because I'd been there in 1996 when Limerick beat us in the Munster hurling final replay and Nicky retired in the aftermath of that defeat. I had never really operated in Nicky's social circles but I was always in awe of him. He was a hero of mine and every other Tipp youngster who grew up harbouring dreams of playing senior hurling for the county.

Nicky had Ken Hogan on board with him, a man I'd huge respect for since 1993, and Jack Bergin, another former Tipperary player who I didn't really know. It had become apparent from early in the summer of 1998 that Nicky, despite his lack of intercounty managerial experience, was the man that county board officials wanted to take over from Len Gaynor.

Our first team meeting with Nicky was really impressive. He was very big on one-to-one communication with players and he asked me to write down a few ideas to sum up my commitment to the cause. I wrote that I always hated it when players broke into a round of applause to welcome home the back markers at the end of punishing training runs. Surely the lads who finished first or who were leading the way should be applauded? Those were the standards I lived by and I made a written promise to Nicky that I would be one of the first in the training runs. It was my way of indicating to him that I wanted to emerge as a potential leader. Actions would speak louder than words and I wouldn't applaud any guy who trailed in last, particularly as I might have lapped him on one of those lung-bursting runs. Nicky told me that we needed everyone to raise their standards if we were going to win anything and I signed the bottom of my declaration, confident that we would move forward in the right direction.

Some of those early training sessions with Nicky were killers. He brought us up the Devil's Bit, a wild mountain near Templemore that is almost 480 metres above sea level at its highest point. The valley in which the town of Roscrea stands separates the south-western part of the Slieve Bloom mountain range from the Devil's Bit. It's raw and rugged and the sheep we passed along the way on those bitterly cold mornings must have wondered what in God's name we were doing up there. It seemed that not even their woolly coats could protect them from the chill. From the outside looking in, I believe that Nicky had identified softness in Tipperary players in 1997 and 1998, and he wanted to separate the men from the boys. The training was boot-camp in nature, and when I made it back from injury in 1999 we were training on Saturday mornings before Sunday League matches. We never really played any League game that season on full throttle but still managed to win the competition. Nicky knew damn well that because of the training we had been subjected to over the winter months, the dogs of war that he needed for championship battle would emerge, and they did.

Philly Maher and Eamonn Corcoran were ferocious competitors. John Carroll was another, and even though he finished up a few pounds heavier at the tail end of his career, he was still a great man to train. Eddie Enright was another solid guy and Tommy Dunne was a machine, pure and simple. One of the lads would bear the brunt of Tommy's wrath if he didn't hit the line to complete a sprint at training, pulling up a couple of yards short to ease off. That was anathema to Tommy, who set high standards and demanded them of others. 'Go to the fucking line the next time, come on now, boys.' Tommy was the benchmark for me and I knew him well, having played on underage teams alongside him from U14 right through to senior. Nicky's mantra was that we would go to the ball, take a chance and make things happen. But I had to get fit to do that, having suffered that career-threatening injury.

After I had gazed out at the Rock of Cashel and he began to stitch my leg, Dr Murchin had told me that I would be back in five weeks. I returned in April 1999, when we beat Waterford by three points in Thurles, welcomed back by a Paul Flynn dipper of a free from 35 metres out that spun over my head and pinged off the crossbar. It was great to be back. The injury had been a setback, but the only question in my mind was how long it would take for my hurling career to resume. There was a danger that it could have been the end, and it would have been but for Dr Murchin. I credited him in a newspaper article that carried the clever headline 'Thanks Very Murch'. I have been left with a 12-inch scar and there is no feeling on the outside of my left upper leg to this day, but my career was safe and that was the only thing that mattered to me. Those low moments when disinfectant strips were placed in the wound to aid the healing process were consigned to the memory bank when I got back on the training field and, more importantly, on to the pitch.

We won the League against Galway in Ennis on 16 May, three weeks before our Munster championship opener with Clare. It was Tipp's first League title in five years and my first on the field of play. I remember the day even more because Manchester United won the Premier League, with goals from Andy Cole and David Beckham wrapping up the first part of an historic treble. We were chasing a treble of our own on the back of League success, with the Munster and All-Ireland championships up for grabs.

Clare were sure to provide us with fierce opposition on 6 June and they didn't particularly like Nicky. Petrol was poured on the Clare–Tipp rivalry when he was appointed because their players and supporters reckoned that Nicky had been laughing at them when Tipp won the 1993 Munster final by eighteen points in Limerick. TV cameras captured what became known as 'Nicky's smile' as Tipp put Clare to the sword but I don't believe that he was being intentionally derogatory in any way.

A couple of weeks before we played Clare in the championship, a guy rang and asked if it would be OK for him to film me from behind the goals throughout the entire game. I agreed, and I'd love to know where that footage is now because it was one of my best ever games for Tipp. Before the match, Nicky presented us with a piece of writing from the former US President Theodore Roosevelt, which really summed up the journey we were on. I've kept it to this day as a reference point because it encapsulates the life of an intercounty hurler. Roosevelt urged the reader to ignore critics; credit belongs to the man who is at the coalface trying to achieve his goals. If failure comes at the end of the process, that must be accepted too, but it's better to have tried and failed than not to have tried at all.

Those words set me up perfectly for the visit to Páirc Uí Chaoimh, which was my favourite playing surface. I could always feel the studs of my boots sinking into the carpet there – a beautiful sensation – and on that pitch the ball always hopped true. We played well too, unlucky to be caught by Davy Fitzgerald's penalty at the end to draw the game. When Clare's Conor Clancy gained possession some distance from goal, he ran, and ran, and ran. In my eyes he over-carried the ball and should have been penalized, but it was our full-back Fergal Heney who was penalized, for a foul, and Dickie Murphy awarded a penalty. I had an injured Liam Sheedy on one side of me and Mick Ryan on the other as Fitzgerald's penalty hit me on the foot on its way into the net. It was a real sickener because we emptied the tank that day and still came up short. Davy had pulled off a brilliant save from Paul Shelly at the other end of the pitch and that was probably the turning point.

All was not lost as we had a replay to look forward to six days later. We spoke during the week about how Clare appeared to be tiring and Eddie Tucker did particularly well on Seanie McMahon when he came in. Declan Ryan was left out from the start for the replay, the only change in personnel, but the plan was that he would come in with fifteen or twenty minutes left to finish the job, with Eddie Tucker starting. Leaving Declan out was a big call and he was summoned from the bench far earlier than expected.

The idea was that my puckouts would come thick and fast and wear Clare out. When they were tired, it would be Declan's time, like Moses parting the Red Sea. That was fine in theory but there was still life in Clare and they scored freely. Naively, I kept pucking the ball out like I'd been told to until I was urged to stop. It was a massive learning experience for me, but the only way a player can learn and improve is to go through something like that. It was one of many mistakes we made in the early part of Nicky's tenure and it was no surprise that it took him three years to bring us to the top. He persisted with a number of players and you have to accept that guys will make mistakes along the way. Some fall by the way-side, that's just how it is, but the core group needs to make mistakes together in order to learn.

That's how it was for us as Nicky attempted to bring us to the summit. We made mistakes, and never more so than on that Saturday in Cork when Clare beat us by ten points. We had thought that Clare would tire, but what we didn't realize was that a couple of their players had vaulted out over the barrier in front of the covered stand as they roared from the tunnel. They were like men possessed, and they ate us alive. It was a case of All-Ireland contenders against pretenders, and the manner of our defeat provided clear evidence that, while we had come a long way in a short space of time, we still had a long road ahead of us.

8

Gladiators

'There's plenty of flak coming your way tonight, and rightly so.'

Nicky's cards are on the table and he knows what's coming at training in Thurles, just a couple of days after we've lost the 2000 National Hurling League final to Galway in Limerick.

'The puckouts weren't good but you're to take it, and I'll sort out the rest.'

With that, Nicky handed me a CD and an A4 sheet of paper containing all of the times I could have gone short with my puckouts or tried something different. The idea was that I would cross-reference the CD with his notes, and improve from there.

Forearmed is forewarned and I was ready for the team debriefing which had been called to review our defeat. Declan Ryan wasn't happy, and while I apologized for the puckouts, a fire now raged inside me. 'Fuck ye, I'll show ye.' Declan's criticism would fuel my fire for the remainder of the season, but when I studied the footage of my display later that night I saw that Nicky was right. I could have mixed them up a bit more. Nicky being Nicky, he was ready with his own response to the critics. 'Right, now ye have had yer say. From now on Brendan will hit the ball where ye want it, but it's up to ye to win it.'

That was that, no more was said about it, but I had a right bee in my bonnet. I wasn't the reason why we had lost that League final but suddenly I had something to prove. As the goalkeeper, I was a legitimate but easy target. Ken Hogan had warned me once that 'if the team loses the match, it's always going to be your fault'. I say that now to some of the goalkeepers I coach. They'll tell me how they're being blamed but my response is always the same: 'I'm sorry, but that's the way it works.' There are six defenders, two midfielders and six forwards on a hurling team but only one goalkeeper. No forward is going to come into the dressing room after a game and thank the goalkeeper for the great puckouts he sent his way during the game, but that he's sorry he didn't catch them, because what he's really saying there is that he should be dropped the next day. I resolved that I wouldn't find myself in that position again, but our forwards started to win puckouts and we beat Waterford and then Clare to ignite our championship season.

The night before the Munster semi-final against Clare in Cork, we went to the cinema and watched the film *Gladiator*. In it, Russell Crowe's character Maximus Decimus Meridius utters the immortal line 'At my signal, unleash hell', before the Armies of the North went into battle. Against Clare, we unleashed hell and gave it to them, big time. It was as if a torrent of fury and frustration came raging to the surface, and we blew them away, just like they had done to us almost twelve months before. In his post-match interview, Nicky even referenced the date of that 1999 replay, 12 June. He hadn't forgotten, neither had we. Our body language was different. This time it was Tipperary players vaulting that barrier after emerging from the tunnel. Tommy Dunne sparked it, and where he led, the rest followed.

That performance closed the door on the hurt we'd carried for almost a year, but our training was more refined in 2000. Those punishing runs up the Devil's Bit faded into the background, to be replaced by speed, agility and quickness (SAQ), work championed by our physical trainer, Jim Kilty. The tackle bags were still there and we were careering into them now, with almost reckless abandon. Nicky would order forty press-ups and then see how our touch was with fatigued arms.

We were moving forward but this time it was Cork, All-Ireland champions at the time, who provided the shock treatment. Tommy Dunne scored two brilliant goals but we still lost the Munster final by two points, as Cork racked up 0–23.

The All-Ireland quarter-final draw pitted us with Galway at Croke Park. After taking a blow to the head in the first half, I was in trouble. Lying on the turf, I could feel the warm sensation of blood dripping down my face from a head wound. Our team doctor, Gerry O'Sullivan, rushed to my aid and Nicky was just a couple of paces behind him. The TV cameras flashed to Eoin Kelly sitting in the stand. Still eligible for the minor grade, Eoin was a precocious eighteen-year-old attacking talent who had been named on the bench. Nicky had gambled again by naming Eoin, who had played in goal at underage level, as my back-up for the day. That was a logical move as Nicky had an extra outfield player on the bench and it's rarely necessary to replace a starting goalkeeper. Gerry bandaged my head and that got me through to half-time.

'Gerry, is he right?'

'Yeah, I'm just giving him an injection.'

'Don't mind that, stitch him.'

At half-time, Nicky ordered Gerry to perform emergency remedial action, and he stitched me up without local anaesthetic. Not a pleasant thing but essential patchwork at half-time in a game of such magnitude.

The full-time whistle brought an end to our season and I was angry. This was Nicky's second year in charge and we seemed no closer to winning an All-Ireland title. We had beaten Clare, the benchmark team, but lost to Cork and now Galway had taken us out. Were we really moving forward at all?

That was the question I asked myself during the winter months as we prepared to do it all over again the following year. Nicky was never under any pressure to vacate his position; the only pressure present was self-created, and he was a man hellbent on taking us to the summit. When my initial anger subsided, I realized that we had made further progress. While that was motivation in itself to stick with the Nicky project, a newspaper article published in 2001 provided more. Along with Tommy Dunne, I was named in the wrong kind of team, 'the best 15 players never to have won an All-Ireland title'. I should have been flattered, but this was a selection of championship hard-luck stories.

We won the League again in 2001, beating Clare at the Gaelic Grounds just four weeks before our championship meeting. In the dressing room, Nicky fished a black rubbish bag from his pocket, packed the League trophy into it, tied the bag in a knot and flung it lasso-style on to the rack above where we were sitting.

'That's what that's worth now if you don't put Munster and All-Ireland titles with it – absolutely nothing.'

The intensity of our training increased as we prepared to meet Clare in that Páirc Uí Chaoimh cauldron once again. They were now men on a mission after we beat them in the 2000 championship and again in the League final. The flames of rivalry rose high. We didn't particularly like each other. They liked to mouth off at us during the pre-match parade, but that was Clare's thing. They got off on raw, primal aggression, and Nicky understood that. We were now almost three years into his project, hitting tackle bags even harder and at a stage where we had been stripped down at the Devil's Bit in Templemore, and built back up again.

Now we were hurling, attacking the ball, and we had an Eoin Kelly in 2001 that was lighting the place up. When special players like that come along, sometimes just once in a lifetime, you have to win. Nicky and Fox were the two players that lit up the generation when Tipp won All-Ireland titles in 1989 and 1991, now we had Eoin and Tommy.

The Clare game was passionate, angry hurling. Huge skill levels on show but played with a temper. At the throw-in, hurls flew like helicopter blades on a roasting hot afternoon, the kind where you struggle to catch your breath. Eoin took a ferocious dunt from Ollie Baker in the first half and was turned upside down but he bounced up immediately and fired the ball towards the Clare goal. Thinking about that moment now is enough to give me goosebumps. It was tight and tense but one of the most enjoyable afternoons I ever experienced in a Tipperary shirt. With seconds left on the watch we were a point up and, standing over a free deep in our own half, I looked up and saw Declan Ryan pointing to the corner flag. That's where the ball went, and as it drifted out of play, Declan caused a kerfuffle big enough to encourage Dickie Murphy to blow his full-time whistle.

Bar the two All-Ireland final wins, that was probably the most excited I've ever been after a game.

In the Munster final against Limerick, Brian O'Meara came up trumps and we hung on in that one too, by our fingernails. Nicky was down at my end of the field for the last three or four minutes. He was always down around the 20-metre line when the final whistle blew, drawn to that area of the field as we repelled the opposition. I met him on the pitch after the final whistle and to have that sensation of making Nicky happy was just brilliant. In my seventh full season as a Tipperary senior hurler, I'd finally won a Munster medal.

Again, Nicky stressed that the job wasn't done. We had League and Munster titles in the cabinet but the big one was still there for the taking. Our All-Ireland semi-final opponents were Wexford, and to prepare for the game we went on a team-bonding weekend to Wicklow. Nicky let us take the shackles off as we ate pizza and drank wine. I was rooming with Lar Corbett on this weekend and my brief was to talk to him about the importance of discipline, keeping the head and maintaining composure. I laugh at the irony of it now because Larry had a club match back home on the Sunday and he was on the dry. He didn't go out at all but I arrived back to our room in a heap. I was sick on the way back to our accommodation. If Larry learned anything that night, it was that when a fella that normally doesn't drink decides that he will, the end result is never good.

I was suffering the next day when we went paintballing. I stayed in the 'dead zone' for the majority of it, sweating and covered in flies. I was a sorry sight. Declan Ryan ran out of ammunition and the sight of him dressed in what I can only describe as a BMX helmet and a pair of overalls was enough to make me grin for the first time all day. Our sub goalkeeper at the time was Darragh Rabbitte, a great character, and Declan asked him for a few extra bullets. 'No problem,' said Darragh as he fumbled for spare ammo. With that, Declan loaded up and shot Darragh from two feet! That weekend was reflective of the great atmosphere we had engendered in the camp. It was serious when it had to be but we had incredible fun along the way too.

All the while, we never lost sight of the prize that was potentially just 140 minutes from our grasp. But before then, Wexford would provide me with one of the most uncomfortable afternoons of my entire career. With just minutes left in our All-Ireland semi-final, all I wanted to do was get the hell out of Croke Park.

9

The Promised Land

The 'yips' are described as the loss of fine motor skills without apparent explanation, in any one of a number of sports. They're most commonly associated with golfers, who suffer involuntary wrist spasms when they're trying to putt. The hurling 'yips' paid me a visit in the second half of that 2001 All-Ireland semi-final against Wexford, and if someone had provided me with the chance to run out of Croke Park when the heat came on, I would have taken it.

We were in a good position, leading by five points, but Wexford had rocked us with a couple of goals from Larry O'Gorman and Rory McCarthy and were in the ascendancy. I ventured out to our full-back, Philly Maher, seeking reassurance from him while also trying to settle his frayed nerves.

'We'll get through this,' I said to Philly, 'there's only a few minutes left.'

'Yeah, we will,' he replied.

Earlier in the half, one of the umpires behind my goal had remarked on how well we were moving. Now, with just a few minutes remaining, he's telling me that we'd better hope the referee blows this one up soon.

I was in a strange space. Larry O'Gorman's first goal flew over the top of my hurley and, while I saw it all the way, I couldn't do anything about it. In my mind, the ball was travelling at real speed, but when I'm in the zone it's as if the world around me is moving in slow motion. Anxiety had released high levels of lactic acid into my blood and my forearms were immobilized. It was a desperate feeling, a complete lack of control over my own body. The more I told myself to snap out of it, the worse it got, and I had reached a stage where my mind was telling me to get out of Croke Park because I simply couldn't function. With four minutes remaining, another high ball in around our goalmouth dropped to O'Gorman, who pulled on it. Thunk! A familiar sound, sliotar striking the wooden skirting in the corner of my net. Wexford scored two further points to tie the game but we had played our get-out-of-jail card and escaped with a replay.

There comes a time with every player when he's had enough and he just shuts down. You look at him and he's visibly mal-functioning and there's nothing he can do to stop it. That was my time, and it very nearly cost us. I never saw it coming because I'd been man of the match in the League final and good too in the Munster championship. Then we had a six-week lay-off before the Wexford game and I felt I had done everything right to cope with the gap. We were well ahead but then Wexford came back and I collapsed to a point where my mental faculties were shutting down with every passing moment. It was a sickening feeling. It wasn't the time to endure a power struggle in my own head, hanging on in the last few minutes of an All-Ireland semi-final against a team coming at us in waves. I worked my way through it in the days that followed, refusing a newspaper interview request ahead of the replay. Normally I would oblige journalists but I wondered if I'd been speaking to too many people during the year. It was time to get selfish because I needed to perform.

The replay was overshadowed by the red cards issued to Wexford's Liam Dunne and our own Brian O'Meara. We won comfortably and all through the game I was fuelled by the self-directed anger I had carried from the drawn game. I was desperate to atone for a poor performance, and an eleven-point victory and 'clean sheet' eased my guilty conscience. We were so disappointed for Brian, though, as he would miss the All-Ireland final through suspension. That entire process galled me because Liam Dunne spoke passionately in Brian's defence at the disciplinary meeting, urging Croke Park's men in suits not to deny him the chance of playing in the biggest game of his life. Liam said that he had niggled Brian and Brian niggled him back, the type of stuff that you'll see every Sunday, but the GAA bigwigs coldly said 'no' and Brian's suspension was confirmed.

I remember thinking how wrong it was that Brian had to sit through all of that, at the end of a table, as complete strangers pontificated and played judge and jury. Had Brian done enough to warrant not playing? No, and while these administrators would have said to themselves that they did a great job sticking by the rules, they stopped a man from playing in an All-Ireland final. They weren't the ones giving up four or five nights of their week to go training in wind and rain only for a referee to make a harsh decision. Look at what's been happening in more recent times, with yellow and red cards rescinded on a regular basis. It's good that younger people are becoming administrators because they seem to be more in touch with what's happening on the ground. They seem more inclined to give due weight to a sense of natural fairness and the spirit of the game rather than always adhering to the strict letter of the law. In cases like this, people in positions of power in Croke Park would do well to remember that without players, we wouldn't have such a great game.

Brian took his medicine with typical grace, even though he was approached about taking out an injunction. He did think about it but such was Brian's selflessness to the cause that he felt it might have put Nicky in a tricky situation, with media talk before the team announcement centring on whether or not Brian would be named. He said in an interview later that the All-Ireland final was probably the hardest hurling match he was ever involved in, even though he wasn't there at the coalface.

I knew his absence would make our task even more difficult but I felt that we had enough experienced heads to get the job done. Still, an All-Ireland final can do strange things to even the most composed characters.

I had suffered the sporting equivalent of a mental breakdown in the Wexford match but that experience stood to me when our corner-back Tom Costello went through a similar experience in the final. I could see that he was mentally slipping early in the game and, during a break in play, I jogged out to meet him.

'Are you all right?'

'I'm all right, I'm all right.'

'You're not, you're gone. Relax now, just follow your man around for the next few minutes, let that be your focus.'

I knew by Tom's body shape that he was in trouble. His head was down, looking at the grass; he was playing his man from behind rather than getting out in front and dictating the match-up.

'You're not on your own here,' I said to Tom. 'Get in front, get in front.'

'Yeah, OK.'

My puckouts were going to Eoin and Tommy the way we had planned but at half-time John Leahy had a go at me over them, even though he wasn't playing because of injury. Tommy picked up the baton and demanded more puckouts in his vicinity. Tommy knew that he was flying, and when you're going that well you want the ball all of the time. Early in the second half, I let Tommy have one, drilling the ball low to him at ankle height. With one delightful touch, Tommy gathered possession, instigated an attack and turned to me with a thumbs-up. He was in the zone, like the famous American footballer Tom Brady making plays. Tommy was the difference between Galway and us that day, setting the tone with a glorious early point from the sideline. If he had been playing for Galway, they'd have won the game.

Seconds before referee Pat O'Connor blew the final whistle, I had the ball in my hand preparing to take the final puckout of the game. Those were precious seconds that I allowed to linger, a magical feeling knowing that the job was done. I remember Philly Maher's smiling face and Nicky racing to embrace us before we fell in an ecstatic heap on the ground. In the dressing room later, we closed the doors and formed a tight circle. Tommy placed the cup in the middle of the floor and we linked arms.

'We've done it,' Tommy said, smiling. 'This is what it's all about, boys!'

We'd formed plenty of circles during the three years that Nicky was with us but there was always something missing. Now we had it, and it was vitally important for each and every one of us to look one another in the eye and offer that knowing glance, to feel that you played your part in giving the man beside you the happiness he now radiated from every pore.

I fished my mobile phone from my gear bag and thumbed through the texts that were flying in at a rate of knots. One from earlier in the day still shone brightest of all for me. That morning, Darragh Rabbitte had sent a message to each member of the panel. 'Tipperary, champions 2001' flashed on the screen. Darragh just knew. We all did.

10

The Big Ball

'**B**rendan, you're either in or you're out.'

Tipperary's greatest ever footballer gave it to me straight after a National Football League match against Laois in February 2002. We'd drawn with them in Portarlington and they were formidable at the time, just eighteen months away from winning their first Leinster senior title since 1946. Fergal Byron in goal, Tom Kelly and Joe Higgins at the back, Pauric Clancy middle of the park and talented players such as Brian 'Beano' McDonald and Chris Conway up front. We still managed to take a point from the game. There was a real sense in our camp that we were going places. Declan Browne was a massive leader, the only football All-Star in Tipperary's history. What's more, he won the individual accolade twice, in 1998 and 2003.

'Look, Brendan. We need to kick on here but it's not acceptable that you just turn up when it suits you,' Declan said. 'That's the way it's been for a while now.'

He was dead right. I was picking and choosing games with the footballers and playing in them without doing a massive amount of training. At the time, I was fully focused on hurling, but on a free weekend I played football because I loved the game. It had now reached a stage where the footballers were ready to go to another level. Declan's tongue-lashing had the desired effect. I reached some common ground with Nicky and devoted more time to football.

My first League game for the senior footballers was back in 1993, a week before my hurling debut. I played minor and U21 football earlier in the year, featuring in the Munster minor final against Cork. We lost by eight points but Ollie Cahill scored one of the finest goals I've ever seen at Semple Stadium. Ollie went on to become a fine soccer player, joining Northampton Town in England a year later, before returning home to win every domestic honour with various clubs. My performance was far less memorable. I had one kick at goal but it went wide on the left from 35 yards out.

There was no success at U21 level but I made my senior championship debut in 1994 against Clare in Limerick. It was remarked upon at the time that I played senior football for Tipperary before lining out for my club. Dad reckoned that senior club football was too physical for a teenager. Muiris O'Sullivan was the ref, I recall, and even though he was a great friend of Dad's and I'd met him many times, there was no room for sentiment when he booked me. I hit one of the Clare players a belt of a shoulder under the stand on the 45-metre line, one of those times when I pleaded to the ref that I got there as fast as I could!

We played in the Munster final in 1994 and were well beaten by Cork at Páirc Uí Chaoimh. It was my debut Munster senior final in either code. On the evening before the game I went to the pitch in Ardfinnan with Eamon Ryan, our sub goalkeeper at the time, to practise my free-taking. I ripped the inside of my boot while kicking the ball and Eamon had to loan me a pair for the game. At the Silver Springs Hotel in Cork, where we convened before the match, I found myself chatting to a couple of people about what it would be like to mark Brian Corcoran, the Cork dual star. It was hardly ideal preparation, going into a big match without my regular football boots and shooting the breeze with complete strangers. At the bus station on the Monday morning, I read reports that Tipp might have been closer had Brendan Cummins been more accurate on the frees. It was a fair assessment.

1997 was one of my best football years in terms of form but I was in and out again because of hurling commitments. I came on against Limerick for the second half of the Munster preliminary round replay and scored eight points. Our football team manager at the time, Paddy Morrissey, had called me up for the game during the week when injuries hit the camp and my name wasn't even listed on the official match programme. I did well against Waterford in the quarter-final but I was back on the bench for our semi-final defeat against Kerry. In an era when we played the Kingdom five times between 1995 and 1999, that game in 1997 was the one that got away. We had them on the rack in Tralee, Declan Browne was on fire and we were dominant. I came on as a sub in the second half. In the end we lost by five points, but we gave them a real fright. A year later, we welcomed Kerry to Thurles for a Munster final and lost by four, with James Williams scoring a late goal. We needed another point quickly to pressure Kerry but they responded at the other end of the field with a score and managed to close the game out.

In 2002, I played in my third Munster senior football final, and Tipperary almost ended a famine dating back to 1935. That match against Cork, played at Semple Stadium, was the undoubted high-light of my football career at intercounty level. I had played a senior hurling qualifier against Offaly the previous night, but while I felt tired at the end of the football game, that was more to do with the effort we had put in on the day. Declan Browne was flying and scored 0–8, five from play. We had a serious chance of winning. In fact I was sure we would win, but in the end we needed a late equalizer from Niall Kelly to salvage a draw. We couldn't raise our game again for the replay and Cork won by nineteen points. It was mission impossible. The game was over after the pre-match parade. We were flat, and our psychology played a part in that. If you're the underdog, and a chance like we had in Thurles presents itself, you have to take it. After the first game it appeared to any neutral observer that we were on a par with Cork but we had been driven by the fear of being annihilated. That brought a real edge to our play, but it was lacking in the replay, and Cork took us apart.

I shouldn't have played in the second game, having suffered a torn stomach muscle in the drawn match. I was receiving a pain-killing injection at half-time when our manager Tom McGlinchey told me that I wouldn't be going back out anyway. It was the right call. I was too slow going down for the pick-up in the first half because of the injury and paid the price as a Cork player drove me out over the sideline with a well-timed shoulder. It was my last ever football match for Tipp because even though I was due to play in the qualifiers against Mayo in July, the injury still wasn't right, certainly not for an outfield role. Instead, my next outing was when I played in goal for the hurlers in the All-Ireland quarter-final against Antrim.

All told, my senior intercounty football championship career spanned nine seasons and sixteen games. I played in three Munster finals, four if you include the Cork replay in 2002, but finished without that elusive Munster medal. It's a regret, of course it is – it would have been lovely to win one. Then again, I played for almost twenty years with the hurlers and finished with just two All-Ireland medals – another haul that could have been so much better. The bigger regret from my football career is that I never really fulfilled my potential. That was due to a combination of factors. I scored freely in club matches but never really stepped up to the mark in a Tipperary shirt. I didn't give the big ball as much attention as I could have either. There has always been a sense in the county that hurling is king.

I must admit that my preparation for hurling games was more meticulous than it was for football. Hurling was the game I was devoting far more time to at intercounty level; football was more 'off the cuff' for me. I played the game with more freedom and enjoyment, which allowed me to express myself better. Curiously, I always found that when I really committed to football for a period of time, I never got the best out of myself. It was as if I was trying too hard, trying to make things happen, rather than playing off instinct.

There was a time when we played Clare and I swapped jerseys with an opponent. A bill arrived for my jersey soon after and the cost of it was deducted from my expenses. I also remember a day when we played a National Football League game in Thurles and throw–in was delayed because the man with the keys to Semple Stadium couldn't be found. It really was as if football was an afterthought.

Hurling remains the dominant sport in the county, but football has improved dramatically. The football board, a separate entity, receives good support from the county board and the Friends of Tipperary Football raise money to support the various teams. When Barry O'Brien was appointed county board chairman in December 2008, he told delegates that Tipp should be winning an All–Ireland senior title by 2020. It was a bold claim to make, but Barry appointed Kerry man John Evans as the county senior team manager and he made terrific progress, while also putting some really good underage structures in place. The combination club team in North Tipperary, Thomas MacDonagh's, won the county senior football title in 2011. A player hailing from the traditional hurling stronghold that is North Tipperary, but who loves football too, now has an outlet. In recent years we've seen Tipperary underage teams beating Cork and Kerry and there is now a real production line providing talent to the senior set-up.

The question is, can we make a major breakthrough at senior level? I don't like saying this, but my hunch is that it won't happen in the short term. We looked like putting up a good show against Kerry as recently as 2015, but even with a depleted team and a host of big names on the bench they still won by six points. We'll continue to struggle because I look at players like James O'Donoghue, Kieran Donaghy and Colm Cooper in Kerry and wonder how we could ever produce that class of player. I think back to Cork in 2002 and their brilliant forward Colin Corkery who scored 0–18 over the two games. There's always a player with the X factor, like Declan when he was in his prime for us, but the big teams always have at least three or four players at that level. Look at Dublin with Paul Flynn, Bernard Brogan, Diarmuid Connolly and Kevin McManamon, to name but four.

So, to win an All-Ireland senior football title remains an unlikely dream for Tipperary. A Munster championship, however, is not beyond the bounds of possibility. But that will also prove difficult. Support is an issue too. Our footballers regularly play in front of paltry crowds, with no more than a couple of hundred attending League matches. It was encouraging to see over eleven thousand in Thurles for the recent Kerry game. We need more of that. I have talked to one or two of the footballers and they insist that a lack of support is not a problem and that they're self-motivated guys, which is great to see. I just hope they stay on course and remain disciplined. They may have to take one or two beatings along the way before a breakthrough comes, like the Clare hurlers in 1993 and 1994. The big test will come during the winter months when they're face down in the mud again, asking themselves why they're putting in the effort. Those might not be the nights when Munster and All-Ireland titles are won, but if your attitude in pre-season training is not up to scratch, there are little grounds for hope.

11

Club

Not long after winning the 2001 Munster senior hurling final, a letter arrived at home. It was on Ardfinnan GAA headed paper. My first thought was that the club had written to pass on congratulations. I couldn't have been more wrong.

The envelope contained confirmation that I had been suspended for missing a club championship football match against Moyle Rovers. The game was fixed for a Saturday, and following a sales conference with work in Dublin, I stayed in the capital on the Friday night. I got held up in traffic on the way down and rang one of the club officials to tell him that I wasn't going to make the match on time. It wasn't a knockout championship game and I didn't think any more of it.

The club held a specially convened meeting where the decision was made to send me a letter confirming that I was suspended from playing activity with immediate effect. The news had a devastating impact on my family as three generations had represented the Ardfinnan club with pride and distinction.

Why hadn't somebody spoken to me about this letter before it was delivered? It's a question I still can't answer to this day. It was all very confusing and the other club players were caught up in a situation that was not of their making. I spent some time wondering what exactly I had done wrong. OK, I had missed a football championship match, but the response was excessive. I sent a return letter to the club, apologizing for missing the game and pointing out that nothing like this had ever happened before. In it, I stated that I found the club's actions strange and unusual, and explained how I had been held up in traffic and had contacted a club official to let him know. I also expressed my extreme disappointment with the club's subsequent decision to suspend me.

There were attempts to resolve the issue in the intervening years, instigated by people I would have had great respect for, like Stan Barlow and Stephen O'Brien, when he was appointed chairman. But I didn't play for the club again until 2005. The stumbling block was that I wanted an apology in writing and if I didn't get it, I wasn't going back. Those were dark days, and while the players, many of them good friends of mine, would have asked me to come to training, I needed that letter confirming that my suspension was lifted. My beloved grandmother Moll was caught in the crossfire and it cut her to the bone. 'If he's that good, why did his own football club suspend him?' was one question directed at her.

I hoped that it would be resolved in 2003, when Ardfinnan reached the county final. There were rumours that I might return after Kilkenny beat Tipp in the All-Ireland hurling semi-final. I trained by myself but no moves were made at official level to solve the impasse. I sat at home while my wife Pamela went to the match. She told me how it went when she came home. Cahir won by three points to claim their first ever county senior football title.

In early 2005, club stalwarts Peter Lambert and Willie Barrett called to the house one evening and handed me a letter. 'Let that be the end of it,' they said. 'We're sorry that this thing got so out of control. We want you to be a servant of Ardfinnan football.' I agreed to return, and kicked a big score against Galtee Rovers from Bansha in one of my first games back. We progressed to the latter stages of the county championship and I scored 1–2 in the semi-final replay victory over Clonmel Commercials. The goal was a penalty and I never struck a ball as well. It was a foot off the ground all the way before nestling in the bottom left-hand corner. I'd never had a great record from penalties since that evening on the local green when I was a young boy.

Johnny English scored our other goal against Commercials but both of us would miss the final because of an AIB work holiday to Australia and New Zealand that was planned well in advance. Ardfinnan hadn't won a county senior football final since 1974 but the famine ended against Loughmore, when the team ground out a 1–5 to 1–4 victory. When Johnny and I got home, we played against Nemo Rangers in the Munster club championship, a game the powerful Cork champions won by ten points. Still, I was glad to be back involved.

It was a massive learning experience in so many ways and proved the old adage that when your back is against the wall, you discover who your true friends are. My true friends stuck by me when doing so was almost viewed as treason. I committed a minor crime, in sporting terms, but served a long and lonely sentence. The experience left a scar, but it was still not strong enough to sour my love affair with Ardfinnan.

It's a club that's dear to my heart, and during my career I was also fortunate to play alongside my father on the same team. I was going along to watch a game but with the team short of numbers, I played at corner-forward. He had my back on the pitch too in a junior match against one of our local rivals. I had played well in the first half and as we trotted off at half-time, I heard a shout. 'Duck!' I ducked as a fist came flying over my head. Dad had saved me from a right clatter from an opponent who wasn't too pleased that I was doing well.

Playing against Commercials in a South junior final was another highlight. I was marking Brendan Walsh, a super player who represented Tipperary at underage level. My dad marked one of the Commercials lads that he would have slugged it out with for years. Here we were, two generations fighting it out for our club. I was trying to win my battle against Brendan, with Dad laying down his own marker.

I still line out at club level when I can, opting to play outfield these days for the Ballybacon-Grange hurlers. You might have seen the AIB advertisement on television where I talk about the game we lost against Upperchurch in Tipperary town. That was the 1998 county intermediate hurling final when we were pipped by a point. Victory would have seen our club achieve senior status, as the intermediate winners gain promotion to the elite ranks of club hurling in the county. I thought I was destined never to play senior club hurling so I explored the option of linking up with neighbouring clubs to make a strong combination team. It was a suggestion that met with a lukewarm response from other clubs but I was advised to float the idea of an amalgamation at county board level. I had seen how it worked in other counties. In Cork, for example, Joe Deane hurled at junior level with Killeagh but was exposed to the senior grade with divisional team Imokilly. The county board refused my request but the South Board, which controls the affairs of the South Tipperary division, agreed that we could play senior hurling on an experimental basis. It wasn't the South senior championship but an exercise worth trying nonetheless. Ballybacon-Grange joined up with Newcastle, and I remember we played Eoin Kelly's Mullinahone in a match in Clonmel. Even though we lost, it was still a good night in many ways as we could finally claim that we had played senior club hurling.

At intermediate level I have won nine South titles but the county crown continues to elude me. Success in the South Tipperary Intermediate Championship in 2007 stands out for me because that competition was my only opportunity to show what I could do that year. After losing my place with Tipperary, playing well with my club provided me with a sense of comfort that all of the training I was putting in was worthwhile.

Tweaks in the senior hurling championship, allowing for more clubs to compete, enabled Ballybacon-Grange to play at that grade for a few years but we were relegated back to intermediate in controversial fashion in 2012. We had originally beaten Cashel in a senior relegation play-off but, following a series of protests, a replay was ordered and we lost. The saga dragged on for six months before our fate was confirmed. I argued vehemently that we should not have played Cashel again, as was decreed following a series of boardroom battles at county and Munster levels, but we did and we lost. It was difficult sitting back and watching all of this unfold but I have discovered on a few separate occasions that the spirit of fair play is sometimes lost in rulebooks.

12

Transition

The 2002 Munster final defeat to Waterford marked the beginning of the end for Nicky English as manager of the Tipperary senior hurling team. Eddie Enright and Paul Ormond had recovered from injury but were left on the bench. Nicky dropped John O'Brien and Eugene O'Neill from the starting line-up, with Lar Corbett and Benny Dunne, making his full championship debut, drafted in to start. With Eddie and Paul injured before the championship, Noel Morris and Donnacha Fahey came in and played well. Nicky was reluctant to tinker with a winning team but he was also cognisant of the pitfalls of the past. One of those was the habit of playing the same team over and over again. Nicky didn't want things to become stale. We carried a degree of over-confidence into the Waterford game but we also met an extremely good team with players like John Mullane, Ken McGrath and Tony Browne. Men on a mission.

We had beaten our arch-rivals, Clare, and Limerick to reach the final and these were clear signs that we were ready to kick on after winning the All-Ireland in 2001. Before the Limerick game, I was very ill, suffering with dizzy spells, a high temperature and vomiting. My condition worsened as the week wore on, reaching a peak on the Friday before the match. The rumour circulated that I wouldn't be playing and our team doctor, Gerry O'Sullivan, visited my house to give me an injection on the Saturday night, to allow me to sleep. God knows how I played because I was in a daze. I came out to a ball and while I could have cleared it off my left-hand side, I went to sweep it away off my right. I threw the ball up but fell on my arse, having suffered another dizzy spell. At half-time in the dressing room, I slept for five or six minutes. Gerry drove me home that evening and I avoided the post-match meal.

The good thing was that we were avoiding the potential land-mines in Munster. The expectation in Tipperary after an All-Ireland success is that we will fall flat on our faces when the time comes to defend hard-earned silverware, but we had passed two stern examinations against Clare and Limerick. I suspect that Nicky felt he simply had to freshen things up, that the players on the starting fifteen were beginning to feel a little bit too cosy. We had bounced into another provincial final without doing a whole lot, from the outside looking in. From the inside looking out, we felt in control of what we were doing, but Waterford hit us with a tornado at Páirc Uí Chaoimh to win their first senior Munster final in thirty-nine years.

The back door provided a potential path to redemption. After beating Offaly comfortably, we drove into an Antrim roadblock. We were two points down at half-time and Nicky took a step back. 'Ye created the problem, ye fix it.' We won by ten points but we were struggling, stale again. Getting that fright should have been the kick in the arse that we required, and meeting Kilkenny in an All-Ireland semi-final was surely the spark that would get us going. We'd heard the slagging from 2001 that we'd won a 'soft' All-Ireland, avoiding Cork and Kilkenny along the way.

We did give it everything when we played Kilkenny in 2002 but everything wasn't good enough. Even though we played to our maximum, the extra edge that had been there in 2001 was missing. We hurled with a more cultured and relaxed approach but lacked frenzy. Remember that I had seen that team in the paper with my name listed among the best players never to have won an All-Ireland medal. That was a statement and a half to hang my hat on and drove me absolutely berserk in pursuit of the Holy Grail. The motivation is always there to win it again, not to waste the opportunity, but that desire needs to be infused in everybody. Numbers 20 to 30 on a panel are the guys that win you All-Irelands, with the pressure they're applying to the starting fifteen and the recognized five subs expected to come in. With that team selection against Waterford, Nicky would have tried to recreate that competition for places again, but the real deep want was gone.

Nicky, to his eternal credit, had given us another year when he could just as easily have stepped aside after the magic of 2001. We let him down, and little did we know that five barren years would follow, years in which we would struggle to be competitive. Nicky's departure was expected and, while work commitments were a huge factor in his decision to step aside, he had given the Tipperary job everything he had. I was upset when he left, even more so because he was gone on a low point. He was another manager we had let down. On the other side of the fence, Kilkenny had Brian Cody, and while nobody knew at the time how great a dynasty he would create, continuity would prove crucial in their success. We had three amazing years with Nicky and one bad season, 2002. That was due to softness on our part, but Nicky could look us in the eye and say that he had no more to give. His tank was empty. I heard on the news that he was stepping aside.

Into his shoes stepped Michael Doyle, manager of the successful U21s in 1995 and a selector with Len Gaynor. Michael would quickly become a victim of circumstance because Nicky had extracted every last ounce from us in 2002, and we were now a busted flush. In 2003, we did contest a freakishly classic League final against Kilkenny but losing an eight-point lead hinted at systemic failures that would manifest themselves later in the year. Clare beat us well in the Munster championship and, while we recovered to beat Laois, Galway and Offaly, we were hooked up to hurling's version of a life support machine. In the All-Ireland semi-final, Kilkenny were ready to rip the plug clean out of its socket.

13

Moll

This is the Alamo. Kilkenny's Eddie Brennan fires in a shot but I manage to keep it out. Tommy Walsh is on to the loose ball in a flash and drives a shot towards goal. I save that one too but Tommy won't be denied, and at the second attempt he breaks through for a goal. It's the end of a passage of play that has been rerun many times on TV. I always stop the tape before Tommy scores.

At half-time in the 2003 All-Ireland semi-final we were two points up, but at the finish we were a beaten docket. Kilkenny tore us apart in the second half. We scored four points, they added 3–9. It was a rout. I remember making those saves and I remember being angry. In my mind, not only were Kilkenny trying to inflict as much damage as they could, they were also trying to end my career. If they scored seven goals that day, it could be my last ever game for Tipp. After all, how could the manager of the team pick a goalkeeper who conceded that many? In the second half of that game, I was fighting for my future.

Pam asked me how I felt after the game. I was naturally disappointed that we had lost so heavily – twelve points separated the teams at full-time – but I was relieved that they had been restricted to three goals and I still had a career. It didn't matter that I won the man of the match award or that the commemorative crystal was delivered to me by RTÉ. What really mattered was that I was still alive as a Tipperary hurler because I had played poorly against Galway. Somehow we escaped against them, winning by a point in Salthill, and while we'd played very well against Offaly for an hour, they scored two goals and made life uncomfortable.

The writing was on the wall, and Kilkenny took full advantage. Brennan skipped by Tom Costello early in the second half and I made a good save to my left. Tom O'Donnell, a man from Golden, was looking after hurleys behind the goal. As I went to puck out the ball after the Brennan save, Tom remarked, 'This is going to be some half, Bren.'

Soon, all hell broke loose, and instinct took over. While people will remember the passage of play that finished with Tommy Walsh sticking the ball in our net, what I remember most is dropping the ball that led to it.

The knives were out for our manager Michael Doyle after the game. Michael had a two-year term and was anxious to continue. He would have felt that he was still feeling his way into the job and dealing with some of the baggage inherited from Nicky's time. The overwhelming view of the players, however, was that Michael was not the man to take us forward. A team meeting was arranged at Dundrum House Hotel and at least twenty players were present. There was a rambling discussion for a while that was going nowhere before I asked the question 'If Michael is in charge, do we think that we'll win an All-Ireland?' The response from the room, including me, was no. It was also agreed that Tommy Dunne and Brian O'Meara would meet with Michael to relay the news. That meeting took place in Clonmel, and while Tommy received huge criticism in local circles at the time, he was simply assuming a captain's responsibility and passing on the views of the players. Tommy and Brian had their say at the team meeting, the same as everybody else. This was democracy at work, and they were the guys sent to deliver the message.

Michael told them that he didn't want to go. Tommy and Brian explained that this was how the players felt. We didn't want any hard feelings because Michael is a nice guy but we had stalled under him. It wasn't entirely his fault either because it was a difficult task replacing Nicky. He had managed to extract every last drop from us, and when Michael came in, we were stuck in the mud. No matter how much he tried, he was fighting a losing battle.

The move to remove him as manager wasn't a personal slight on his character. It was, in sporting terms, a business decision made by people who wanted to move forward. We had drifted again, the same as we had during Len Gaynor's final year in 1998. Personally I felt sympathy for Michael because once again a manager had lost the team without even knowing it.

Michael had given fantastic service to Tipperary, scoring two goals in Killarney against Cork in the famous 1987 Munster final replay. He was the son of John, an eight-time All-Ireland senior medallist, and was manager in 1995 when we won the All-Ireland U21 title. He was with Len for two years as selector but then found himself in a no-win situation when he took over the senior team. Nicky left Tipperary in a much better state than he found it and Michael was under pressure to deliver results. It didn't work out, and it wasn't nice to have two Tipperary men, Tommy and Brian, telling another that he had lost the dressing room. The repercussions were far-reaching. Opinions within the county were polarized but Michael was hurt more than anybody else. At least we, as a group, had each other. We were all GAA people, but sometimes hard decisions have to be made. Michael resigned in

Above: At home in Gortnalour. My grandmother Moll is pictured here on the left, with Grandad Johnny on the right and my father John in the centre.

Below: Mr Football, Johnny Cummins (*back row, extreme right*), lived for championship days. One of his favourite players was Babs Keating (*front row, third from left*).

Above left: I wonder what Dad's thinking here. Maybe he's hoping I can grow faster so that he can play hurling and football with me.

Above right: In my house you supported Manchester United or you starved! I'm proudly wearing my Red Devils shirt here and birthday cake is the reward.

Left: Here I am on my confirmation day, with my proud parents on either side. Leather jackets were all the rage back then!

Below: And they said I'd never finish the course! Graduation day at Waterford Regional Technical College.

Above: On Tony Forristal duty with Tipperary U14s. I think the jersey might be a little too big for me (*back row, third from right*)! A young Tommy Dunne is pictured front left.

Below: Club success! Ballybacon-Grange, South U21A hurling champions, 1995 (I'm in the back row, fourth from right).

Above: On the move! I wondered what it would be like being marked by the great Brian Corcoran. Here I am, trying to get past him in the 1994 Munster senior football final against Cork.

Right: Up close and personal with Kerry legend Maurice Fitzgerald. Few players ever got this close to the great man.

Below: Opening of the new pitch in Ballybacon. We played Waterford in a senior hurling challenge to mark the occasion. I captained Tipperary on home soil, a wonderful honour.

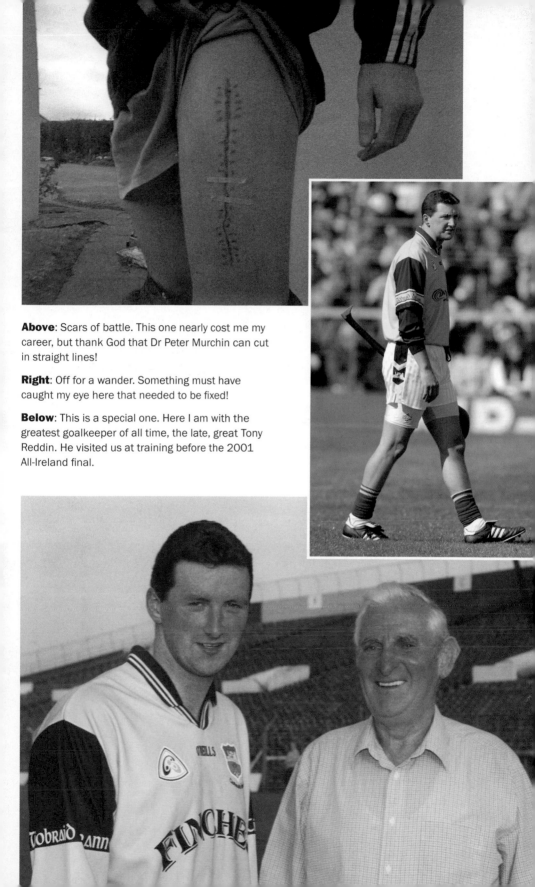

Above: Scars of battle. This one nearly cost me my career, but thank God that Dr Peter Murchin can cut in straight lines!

Right: Off for a wander. Something must have caught my eye here that needed to be fixed!

Below: This is a special one. Here I am with the greatest goalkeeper of all time, the late, great Tony Reddin. He visited us at training before the 2001 All-Ireland final.

Above: We've done it! I celebrate All-Ireland final glory in 2001 with 'God' himself, Nicky English.

Left: Declan Ryan won All-Ireland medals in three different decades. He was a big reason why we won in 2001.

Below: 'Spike' was never too far away. Here he is, on the left, as Dr Gerry O'Sullivan and I celebrate at the Hill 16 end of Croke Park after the 2001 final.

Left: 'Alone, all alone.' Back in Liberty Square in Thurles, sharing our victory with supporters as we join together in a rousing chorus of 'Slievenamon'.

Below: Home at last. I'm surrounded by a group of young supporters in the Glenview Lounge in Goatenbridge on a great night when Liam MacCarthy paid a visit.

Bottom: Long-standing Ballybacon-Grange club chairman Thomas O'Leary marks my 2001 All-Ireland success with a lovely presentation.

Above: A proud Gran. Moll loved to see silverware coming. In 2001, she got to grips with the All-Ireland, Munster and National League trophies.

Below: Beaming faces all around me. My parents are pictured here with my aunt Marie and uncle Billy. Moll is holding on tight to Liam MacCarthy!

late September and Tipperary had a third senior hurling team manager in as many seasons when Ken Hogan was unveiled as his successor.

In a nod to the recent All-Ireland-winning past, Jack Bergin was also back as a selector, with Colm Bonnar on board too. Bonnar had won All-Ireland medals with Ken in 1989 and 1991 and was involved in a backroom capacity with the Waterford team that had beaten us in the 2002 Munster final. The county board's thinking was that Ken and Jack had been involved with Nicky, and if the players didn't want Michael Doyle, they'd give us people who were familiar with success. The county board's sentiments were honourable. They were providing the kind of management team that the players wanted and the link to 2001 and All-Ireland glory was rekindled. The ball was now back in our court, but what did we do with it? We let it back under our legs.

Ken's association with Nicky should have added a layer of grit, but softness crept in. He brought back numbered training tops and a regimental uniform to training and matchday but he was swimming against the tide. We simply didn't have good enough players and we were working in an era when Cork had revolution-ized the game of hurling with their short-passing style of play, based heavily around possession of the ball. They beat us in the qualifiers in 2004, ending our season, and again in the 2005 Munster final, when we played well in the second half but had given ourselves too much to do by falling way behind.

The Tipperary hurling team was drifting along with no real direction and, what's more, we knew it. Ken tried to halt the decline by adding pieces to the jigsaw. I remember a team-building exercise where another player and I were asked to draw a shape on a whiteboard that had been revealed to the other members of the group. I was encouraged while fulfilling my task, but the other player was jeered when he tried it. Ken's idea was to illustrate how encouragement affected one player and how verbal abuse impacted on the other. It was a really clever exercise designed to promote positive communication. On the pitch, however, we were stuck in a rut.

We failed to make any real impact in the League and Waterford knocked us out of the 2004 Munster championship. We did manage to beat Limerick in the qualifiers, and while the gritty nature of this one-point victory suggested that we might be capable of regrouping, we were in fact building a championship challenge on sand.

The six-point defeat to Cork in Killarney ended our season, and that was a particularly low moment. We visited Fitzgerald Stadium a week before the game for a look at what were unfamiliar surroundings. It was almost impossible to visualize what matchday would look like – something I was always big on. The blood red of Cork jerseys in the stands and terraces provided an ominous backdrop on what was a gloomy afternoon. Cork scored 2–12 in the second half and we never looked like winning the game.

2005 was another largely forgettable season, although we did beat Limerick, after a replay, and then Clare to reach the Munster final. That Clare game is special to me because that one was for my grandmother Moll, who was sick in hospital at the time. She was a wonderful character and I loved her indomitable spirit. There's a picture of Moll and me when I accepted a player of the month award many years ago. She's looking at the trophy and I'm looking at her – a real moment in time. She took such pride in my achievements and I'd call to her every Friday at lunchtime. Her death had a profound effect on me because I thought Moll was indestructible. Her birthday was at Christmas time and we'd sit around the table to celebrate. 'This is the last one anyway!' she'd say with a smile. 'I'll say good luck to ye all now! I won't be here next year but ye can be here if ye want!'

Slot machines were her vice on visits to the beach in Tramore or Salthill in Galway. Those places were for over-eighteens only but I was eventually old enough to sit with her as she played. Dooly's arcade was her spot in Tramore. She'd start in there at midday and we had to pull her out of the place at lunchtime. After fish and chips, she went 'back to work', as we called it. The people that ran the place were amazing. It was a social outlet for the elderly people and there was a man called Wilf who would come round to the regular customers and give them a flowerpot full of coins to keep them going. If a player was making regular visits for change, the staff there recognized that they weren't going too well and helped them out.

Moll was on one of those visits to Tramore in April 2005 when she took a fall. I was working in Urlingford at the time when aunt Marie rang. 'Moll's not great,' she said. Moll was moved to Clonmel but insisted that she was fine. 'I'm a bit sore but I'll be OK,' she assured me. A couple of hours later, a priest was standing beside the bed giving her last rites. She was eighty-eight years of age but I couldn't accept this was the end for her. I rang Peter Murchin and he arrived to the hospital. I handed him her chart and asked what he thought.

'It's not great,' he said.

'Peter, what can we do?'

'I can help her to live for another four or five months but that's the best I can do. I can have a go.'

Peter worked his magic, and Moll made a remarkable recovery. Every night, one of us would have to stay close to her because she could jump out of the bed at any time. She was raving, talking to her husband, and back working in the Mill in Ardfinnan. We visited her one morning and, lo and behold, Moll was sitting up in the bed drinking tea and eating toast.

'What is after happening to you?' I asked her.

'I don't know, but I'm feeling better!'

She was brought to Clogheen, a ten-minute drive from Ardfinnan, to convalesce before returning home to Marie's house. We spent some wonderful time together in the summer of 2005. We chatted in Marie's back garden one day.

'Do you realize you were nearly dead?' I asked her. We had that kind of relationship, Moll and me.

'Do you know what? I didn't have a clue what was going on. Was I that close?'

I nodded.

'Brendan,' she said, 'the older you get, the more you realize that it's going to happen, and the more you accept it. I'm not afraid of it.'

We played Clare in the Munster semi-final on 5 June. I remember feeling really emotional during the national anthem before throw-in. It was a wet day and we won by six points. I met my cousin Anthony Power after the game, and he was crying. 'That was for Moll.'

A garda outrider took us from the Gaelic Grounds to the far side of Pallasgreen, just a few miles from the border with Tipperary, and I drove back to Clonmel with Dad. In her final few months, I spent as much time as I possibly could with Moll.

It was 24 August when she passed away. Early in the evening she was lying in her bed and I went in to say goodnight to her. I feared it would be the last time I would talk to her and I brought her a scratch card. She loved those and she did everything in her power to scratch it, with my hand helping her. I kissed her on the forehead before leaving. 'Good luck, Moll.' Something told me I would see her again before the night was out.

The phone rang at home in the middle of the night. It was Marie. 'Come up, Moll's after dying, she's gone.' This was a drive

I knew I would have to make eventually, and it was difficult. I ran upstairs when I reached Marie's house and there was Moll, eyes closed, exactly how I had left her just a few hours before.

I've thought about her every day since. I picture that twinkle in her eye. Whenever I went on holidays, I always brought her back a present. One Christmas I gave her a toy reindeer on a pole that sang 'Grandma got run over by a reindeer'. 'Look at what the other fella got me,' she said to the family, smiling. There was another time when I brought her home a toy soldier, a commando with a gun whose arms moved. We were coming home from Spain and Pam had him on the carry-on luggage in case he got broken. But the security staff at the airport were spooked and gave our little friend a thorough examination before he was passed for clearance. 'I nearly got jail over you trying to get this fella out of the country!' I told Moll. She got a real kick out of that. There's a teddy bear at home in my bedroom with the number 30 written on it. I have a photo of Moll and me on my thirtieth birthday, with the bear on top of her head and me behind her, laughing. I saw Moll as being Granny, but never an old granny because she was someone you could have a bit of craic and a laugh with. I knew how much I meant to her and she knew how much she meant to me. In each other's company, we both felt safe. It was just perfect.

She took a little part of me on her journey to the next world, the jersey I wore in the Clare game. That one meant so much to me. I had played well, kept a clean sheet and knew that would make her happy back in the hospital. My concentration levels were through the roof.

Our season should have opened up after beating Clare but Cork defeated us in that Munster final and Galway had our number at Croke Park in the All-Ireland quarter-final, winning by two points. We were up by six but still managed to let it slip. David

Forde scored a goal I could have done better with and Damien Hayes pushed Hugh Moloney to one side before crashing home another. It all seemed so inevitable.

With the greatest respect to the players we had, other teams had better. We were regressing again with no obvious talent coming through to provide fresh impetus. Nicky had tried new blood in 2002, and while that didn't work, at least he tried, because in Tipperary we tend to persist with players for too long. These are players that Kilkenny manager Brian Cody would look at for six months and then bin. A harsh filtering process should have taken place between 2003 and 2005 – three wasted years. Instead of sorting things out in three or four seasons, it could have been done in two. The process would have been painful, but it would have been the right way to go. We were living in the past, and you have to ask the question, why does that continue to happen in Tipperary?

After the loss to Galway, Ken called a meeting at Thurles Golf Club. I believe that he did so against the wishes of the county board. He told the players present that he wanted to continue. Ken insisted that he had more to offer and, when I was asked for my view, I agreed. County board officials thought otherwise and were already eyeing up his successor.

The next man through the revolving door was a charismatic figure, a man who led Tipperary out of a hole in the 1980s and moulded them into All-Ireland champions. When he was installed as Ken's replacement in October 2005, this man stated that nothing less than an All-Ireland title would suffice. He wasn't concerned about his legacy being tarnished in any way if his second coming didn't work out, insisting that 'it's better to have tried and failed than to not have tried at all'.

Babs Keating was back.

14

Babs

The return of Babs was greeted with huge fanfare. John Leahy and Tom Barry were on his ticket and John was a folk hero in Tipperary, winning All-Ireland medals in 1989 and 1991 when Babs was previously in charge. Tom was less high profile but with some pedigree nonetheless. He played with Thurles Sarsfields for over a decade until 1987 and also hurled with the Tipperary seniors in the early 1980s. He was a former Sarsfields manager and selector. The 'dream team' captured the imagination of the Tipperary hurling public in an instant. Supporters were talking about winning All-Irelands again.

Our 2006 League campaign began in low-key fashion with a draw against Limerick at the Gaelic Grounds. It was a decent result, considering that Limerick had more hurling under their belts than us and had won the pre-season Waterford Crystal Cup. It was a game we could take a lot of positives from because we scored 1–1 in stoppage time and Shane McGrath, a bright young star from Ballinahinch, made his debut.

We played Kilkenny in our first home outing and lost by nine points. I did well and didn't concede a goal in a man of the match performance. Babs was impressed and, when we travelled together to a Tipperary Supporters Club meeting in Clonmel, he spoke about my grandfather and how I was the best Tipperary goal-keeper since Tony Reddin, who retired in 1957. He had a way of making you feel good. Our first victory of the season was achieved against Antrim in Cushendall, a fortnight after the Kilkenny defeat. I was even made captain for that game.

The first problems surfaced after the Galway game, when Babs took us to task in the media. We lost by eight points in a tie that should have provided us with an opportunity to atone for the All-Ireland quarter-final defeat in 2005. It was a terrible performance, and there was an element of truth in what Babs said afterwards: 'We have serious thinking to do. We will do it but we are not getting the response from the players. We cannot get that drive with them. Our fellows were dead only to wash them.' In previous roles with the Laois and Offaly hurling teams, Babs had also run down his players in public. In 1998, he described the Offaly players as 'sheep in a heap' before an acrimonious split. By the end of that season, with Michael Bond in charge, Offaly had become All-Ireland champions.

Our preparation hadn't helped: a large number of children were allowed into the dressing room before the game to mingle with the players. I was particularly poor, letting in a couple of incredibly soft goals as Galway scored three. For one of them, I came to meet a ball on the half-volley as it hopped in front of me but it skidded into the net. With six minutes left, I came for a high ball but com-pletely misjudged it and turned our full-back Philly Maher upside down as Richie Murray exploited the open goal.

As the League campaign progressed, the team environment became increasingly dysfunctional but we still managed to make it through to a semi-final with Kilkenny. Our psychologist delivered the pre-match team talk. 'Come on, lads, let's go,' Babs said to John Leahy and Tom Barry. 'It's all yours now!' There we were, ten minutes before the off, standing in the middle of a dressing room with a sport psychologist who it seemed to me had never delivered a team talk in her life. She decided to put me standing in the middle of a circle, with the other lads gathered around me in a huddle. 'Close your eyes, boys, and visualize the first ten minutes of the match,' she said, thinking on her feet. 'Visualize going to the first ball, catching it, beating your opponent to the tackle, dispossessing your opponent.' Ten minutes into the game, Kilkenny were 2–3 to 0–0 in front. We didn't score for fifteen minutes. I'd been chipped by Martin Comerford, 5 yards off my line.

There was another bizarre episode at a training camp in Clonea, County Waterford. It was agreed that we would meet in the foyer of the hotel for a morning run at 6.30, before returning for breakfast. But when we gathered the next morning, there was no member of team management present to provide us with direction. We took it upon ourselves to get the run done. Over the course of that weekend, I trained the Tipperary hurling team for thirty-five minutes or so, with drills on the beach. Babs asked me to do it, saying that it would make a nice change for the lads.

It came to a head when we returned to training after the Kilkenny game. I stayed at one end of the field working on goal-keeping drills, with the rest of the group at the other end. I had asked permission from our trainer Brian Murray to do this, and he'd agreed. During the Kilkenny match, I should have cleared one ball off my left in the second half but I swept around to strike it off my right-hand side, at ankle height. Babs picked up on this and said that it was a big problem that I couldn't hit it off my left. He also accused me of placing our kitman, John 'Hotpoint' Hayes, in an unfair position because Hotpoint was helping me out with goalkeeping drills after training. My point was that there was no goalkeeping work during the session itself, but that wasn't a problem because I would stay behind and get it done later.

In my quest for improvement, I firmly believed that some extra work would get me back on the right road. I wanted to train harder and become better. I pounded a punch-bag, the idea being that I would fatigue myself and see how my touch was then. With the benefit of hindsight, perhaps I was wrong to train on my own and separate myself from the rest of the group. I could have handled my emotions better.

On a different occasion, Philly Maher was questioned about his weight, and was told that he was putting too much butter on his chips. John Leahy corrected Babs on this, stating that Philly was putting too much butter on his spuds, not his chips. In fact, our dietitian had told Philly that he was underweight and needed to eat more.

Out of sheer frustration, Philly rang Babs later in the year to inform him that he was leaving. Quoted in the press at the time, Babs said, 'Philip is getting married, building a house and he's under severe pressure.' Philly had done so much for Tipperary hurling, and while I'm not suggesting for a minute that every player should bow out shoulder high with trumpets blaring, the suggestion that his domestic situation had anything to do with it wasn't right.

I found myself in another strange predicament when I was played at wing-back in some of our training sessions. That particular arrangement came to a head one night when Babs walked across the middle of the pitch to sort out the starting positions for a game among ourselves.

'Brendan, go wing-back,' he ordered.

'Babs, I'm going in goal, I'm a goalie.'

I didn't consider that to be an unreasonable request. I can also recall the presence of TV cameras that night, to record footage of our session. How would it have looked if viewers had seen a goalkeeper playing outfield, with John Leahy standing between the sticks?

In the 2006 Munster championship, we beat Limerick and Waterford but lost to Cork in the final. In the fallout, our captain Ger 'Redser' O'Grady reportedly delivered a less than complimentary phone message to team management. On the Tuesday evening a few of the lads were socializing in Borrisoleigh. They were in the wrong place at the wrong time as Brian Murray was also the Borrisoleigh club trainer. He was conducting a session at the local field when a young boy arrived with his hurley that he'd just had signed by the lads in the pub. Word swept through the field, and Brian wasn't best pleased. We bore the brunt of his annoyance the next evening at Tipperary training, when he put us through the wringer with some extra running.

Ger's phone message was offside by a mile. Management dealt with the issues pretty well, and when we trained on Thursday, Conor O'Mahony, Shane McGrath, John Carroll and Micheál Webster were absent. Brian was training them separately in Templederry. Three of them – Conor, Shane and John – returned the following week and apologized to the squad but Redser and Micheál were cut loose. It was crazy living through that, and trying to win an All-Ireland at the same time. We had played quite well in the Munster final and the season was still very much alive.

Our progress to a provincial decider opened up a route to Croke Park and an All-Ireland quarter-final against Waterford. We travelled to Croke Park by coach and I recall one of our players, Darragh Egan, sitting on the floor. There was no seat available for him because Babs had invited a number of elderly people to travel with us. They had been staying at the same hotel as us and needed a lift to the match. There were a couple of lovely old ladies sitting down the back beside us. One of them asked me if I wanted to have a read through the newspaper. I politely declined as I was trying to get my head right for the game. We stopped at the Cusack Stand side of Croke Park to let them off and the Waterford team bus was nearby. I could see some of their players laughing as the elderly folk disembarked. Babs didn't see anything wrong with this. He was very open with people and, in his day, that's how it worked. You looked after everybody and you were nice to them. But there was a huge contrast with Liam Sheedy's time in later years when nobody outside the inner circle dared even look at the team bus, never mind travel on it.

Waterford knocked us out on a day when Dan Shanahan scored 1–5 for the winners. Babs's son was with us and decided to take part in my pre-match warm-up. Here he was, trying to fulfil what I can only assume was his childhood dream of scoring a goal at Croke Park. Our sub goalkeeper Damian Young looked on from the fringes in sheer disbelief. During the game, I was particularly happy with a save in that game from Ken McGrath, tipped over the bar from a penalty, but we were well beaten. The second coming of Babs wasn't working out.

I didn't know it then, but things were about to get worse. Much worse.

15

Warning Signs

Looking back, there were more signs of trouble. A few days before the 2007 Munster senior hurling semi-final against Limerick at the Gaelic Grounds, I met Babs on my way into the dressing room before training. He told me that Paul Curran had sustained a broken toe and Declan Fanning would be called in to replace him. We chatted about the positioning of our players when Limerick were awarded frees close to goal. I suspected that the Limerick forward Andrew O'Shaughnessy might take a chance and go low early on, but we would be ready for it.

Babs announced the team and in the huddle talked about how Hugh Moloney had told him that he didn't want to be considered for selection because of exam commitments. Babs said that it was great to see such honesty from a player, and reiterated this later in the week in an interview with the local radio station, Tipp FM. I'm not sure that Hugh had spoken to Babs at all in that time.

On the morning of the match, we met at Dundrum House Hotel for breakfast, before a team meeting. Our corner-forward, Willie Ryan, was informed that he would be taking frees. It was the first time that our regular free-taker, Eoin Kelly, heard about this. Willie was told to go for goal if we were awarded a 21-yard free in front of the posts, the opposite of what Eoin had been told a couple of weeks previously.

The bus for Limerick departed at eleven a.m. and we tucked into a pre-match meal at a hotel close to the Gaelic Grounds. I was sitting beside our team selector Tom Barry, who asked me about my memories of championship games from years gone by. I told John Leahy to let me know if there was anything wrong with my puckouts during the game. 'Don't wait until Wednesday night to tell me,' I said.

'Sure I'm always annoying you!' John responded, with a grin.

Babs wished me luck before we left the hotel. 'All the best today, young fella. We need a big one.'

'I'll give it a good lash, Babs,' I assured him.

The game itself was tough going. We struggled to win primary possession in the Limerick half and when one of my puckouts drifted out over the sideline, I heard a bark from the touchline. It was Babs. 'What the fuck are you at? Keep it in further!' At half-time we were level, and Darragh Egan, playing in our half-forward line, urged me to keep the puckouts coming long. I spoke to John Leahy and John Carroll and suggested a lower trajectory in front of Carroll. Leahy disagreed and insisted that I continue to hit them as high as possible, that Carroll would win them.

The Limerick captain, Damien Reale, had been sent off in the twenty-first minute and the gist of the half-time discussion was that it would be a disaster if we didn't win by seven or eight points, with Limerick down to fourteen men. For the second half, Paul Ormond was behind our goalmouth, providing water and spare hurleys to our players when required, and he had received a message from the sideline to keep the puckouts lower. The first couple went up John Carroll's wing and, while he got out in front of his man, he lost possession. Darragh was out of gas and lost the low ones that came his way.

Pat Tobin scored a late equalizing goal for Limerick, and near the end of the game I stood over a long-range free and thought about going for the posts. I decided not to as I didn't want to listen to any hassle if it went wide. I dropped it in around the Limerick goalmouth instead.

The game ended in a draw and Babs went nuts in the dressing room, describing how he had taken some criticism from supporters on his way down the tunnel. He couldn't understand why he was being blamed instead of the players who couldn't beat a Limerick team playing with just fourteen men for over two-thirds of the game. The players were silent, heads bowed. County board chairman John Costigan insisted that all was not lost and that the replay in Thurles six days later would be a different story. Tom Barry said that it was a good result, considering how Limerick had come at us towards the end of the game.

Before leaving the Gaelic Grounds, the players were left waiting on the bus for thirty minutes while the management team held a debrief. I went to the top of the bus and grabbed some water bottles from the cooler, to keep the players hydrated. Tom Barry asked the players if they wanted to avail themselves of ice-baths back in Thurles and we agreed that this was a good idea. When we arrived back to Dundrum House Hotel, we left wives and partners there before driving to Dr Morris Park, the training centre close to Semple Stadium, for ice-baths. This was now four hours after the final whistle, too long a wait for the recovery technique to have any real effect, but we followed instructions.

We returned to Dundrum House for a sandwich and a team meeting at ten o'clock. Babs kicked off by stating that we were never going to win any game because of my puckouts. He looked for feedback from the group, starting with John Carroll. He agreed with Babs, saying that he had to move back a few yards to get to the pitch of them. I responded by pointing out that I had discussed the puckout strategy with John Leahy, and had asked him to let me know if any tweaks were needed. At half-time I had also spoken to Leahy and the forwards. I added that enough people were at the game to tell me if the puckouts were wrong, and that past ten o'clock in Dundrum was too late for this kind of feedback. Ryan O'Dwyer, the current Dublin player, spoke in my defence, saying it wasn't entirely my fault and that the intended recipients should have done better under the dropping ball. The meeting concluded with discussion on other issues from the game and the players were told that they could enjoy a few drinks before bed.

I met Benny Dunne at the bar. 'I have enough of this,' I said. 'They covered their own arses in there while I was being slaughtered.' I was particularly unhappy with Carroll because of how he had behaved in the meeting. The plan was that the team would spend the night at the hotel but Pam and I left shortly afterwards. I explained to her that I couldn't stick around there much longer, in case I did or said something that I would later regret. Before leaving, I glanced through an upstairs window and noticed the three selectors – Babs, Leahy and Barry – talking outside the front door. Rather than passing them on my way out, I asked one of the staff to suggest an alternative exit from the hotel, and I left through the ballroom.

That night, I chatted with Pam's father for a few hours, trying to make sense of what had happened.

When we met on the following Wednesday night for training, a meeting was called beforehand to discuss puckouts for the replay. Tom Barry began by drawing large Xs on the flip chart, each one representing a forward player. John Leahy took control and asked each of the forwards what height they would like the ball delivered at. They responded by placing one hand in front of their faces – head high. We then decided on the hand signals we would use to indicate the direction of the puckouts – a good idea.

On the training pitch, we got to work. Goalkeeper Gerry Kennedy had been brought into the panel by Babs that year, and he and I practised with the forwards. I suggested to John that we should fill the spaces in front of the forwards with other players, to make it seem more like a match situation. He disagreed and asked me to hit the ball as I had been told to do. We did that for twenty minutes and all deliveries were pinpoint. It looked lovely, but there were no obstacles in the way and the forwards collected them with ease. At least we had a definite puckout strategy for the replay. It would soon be time to put it to the test.

16

The Axeman Cometh

'**B**rendan, we want a word.'

We've had our pre-match meal at the Horse and Jockey and Tom Barry calls me out. He's quiet as we walk to a separate room, where Babs and John Leahy are sitting. Here's how it went down.

Me: Well, lads. What's the craic?

Babs: Well, Brendan. The craic is that we are starting Gerry tonight.

Me: I don't believe this. (I put my head down on the table, feeling light-headed.) Am I allowed to ask why?

Tom: Well, we had identified with you earlier in the year that we wanted to see you bringing down more balls that were going over the bar, and you seem to refuse to do this. Also, there have been issues around the puckouts. We have always said that we want to see progression in training from every member of the panel. We are not seeing that progress in you.

Me: You are trying to end my career. This is the end of the road for me.

Tom: No. You still have a lot to offer this team.

Me: Obviously not, when you are dropping me. You are saying

I'm not up to it any more. Babs, why are you doing this to me? We are from the same club. What have I ever done to you?

Tom: Brendan, this is not about you or us. This is being done for the good of Tipperary hurling.

Leahy was sitting to my left, nodding as Tom spoke.

Me: I heard at the start of the year, Johnny, that you rang Gerry in Australia, telling him that if he came home, he would be in goal before the year was out. I thought that because I was playing so well that you couldn't drop me and I would get the year out of it. Obviously I was wrong about that.

Babs: I don't know where you heard that but it's all wrong. We made no decisions that early in the year.

Me: Anyway, it doesn't matter. Ye have made a decision and I have to respect it.

With that, I walked out the door, to murmurs of 'thanks, Brendan'.

When I got outside, I allowed myself to release the tears I had held back while I was in the room. I rang my dad. He didn't answer at first as he was driving to the game. I eventually got through to him and he was as shocked as I was to hear the news.

'Go nowhere,' he said. 'That's all he [Babs] wants, for you to run away and he can blame the whole lot on you.'

I spoke to Pam and her father, and they both said the same. I texted my friends Derek O'Mahoney and Liam Barrett, then returned to the room where the rest of the players were. I sat beside Eoin and relayed the news to him. He couldn't believe it, and soon word spread around the room. I ate a banana, an apple and an orange, trying not to scream.

Ryan O'Dwyer was the next man called out. He had a thumb injury and John Leahy took him to the car park outside and began hitting balls at him. Ryan caught them with his injured hand and hit them back. A member of our medical team examined Ryan and his opinion was that while he might have a small fracture, it was nothing too serious and the injury would not stop him from playing. Ryan had been picked to start in the team but was told he had failed the fitness test and was left out.

The three selectors returned to the room and said they had had a few tough decisions to make when picking the team they felt was best equipped to beat Limerick. The starting fifteen was greeted with silence, and my heart sank further as the names were read aloud. Babs said it was difficult to drop someone from his own club and the puckout signals discussed at training were reinforced with Gerry Kennedy, who would take my place. We were soon making our way to the team bus. I sat towards the back, with Paul Ormond and Micheál Webster asking what had happened in the meeting with the selectors.

Driving into Thurles was incredibly difficult. Looking up at the windows of the bus, children mentioned the names of the players they could see, including me, to their parents. That twisted like a knife in my gut. People gathered around the bus as it pulled in, saying hello to the players and wishing them the best of luck. John English, Eamon O'Gorman and Thomas O'Leary were there from the club. John had tears in his eyes, a man who had watched me develop as a player since I was six years old. He would have hurled with Babs.

'Is it true, Brendan?'

'Yeah, it's true.'

John's lips were trembling and I had to keep moving or I would have broken down too.

The dressing room was quiet. I sat two seats to the right of Gerry. We went out on the pitch for a few pucks to settle in. Jerry Ring, a well-known administrator and photographer in Tipperary, ambled across.

'It's the end of an era, anyway,' he said.

'Ah, yeah, Jerry.'

I didn't know what to say, but inside, I was boiling. This was not my obituary. It was a hole, and a pretty deep one, but it wasn't going to end here. Jerry meant no harm by what he said but his words cut me to the quick.

Back in the dressing room, I felt strange, with none of the butterflies I would usually experience before the off. Paul Curran told me that I would have to join a line outside the dressing room door, where the subs would pat the starting team on their backs as they made their way out.

'It's weird seeing you standing out here,' Paul said.

The public address system announced that the Limerick team was coming out: 'A chairde, Contae Luimní!' I looked to my left as the Limerick players raced down the corridor and turned to enter the light. That was strange as I'd never seen an opposition team emerge from their dressing room before: I was always holed up in our own dressing room, waiting for the knock on the door which was the cue to leave. Paul was told to give me Gerry's hurleys and gear to carry out on to the pitch. Paul brought them out instead. He probably realized that I was going through enough. As our players raced past I wanted to scream and run away, but I couldn't.

The really tough part came next as the subs followed the team out. When I emerged from the Old Stand tunnel, I was met by a flurry of flashing camera bulbs. Word had obviously spread that I wasn't starting. I left my spare hurleys in the dugout and when I turned to follow Gerry on to the pitch, I almost knocked down a couple of photographers who had moved across for a better angle. I had to help Gerry warm up because now he needed to be ready. I told him that I'd venture further out the field, between the 45- and 65-metre lines, and float a few shots in on top of him, to get his eye in and build his confidence.

The other players were hitting the ball across the pitch, and I was struck by a sliotar on the side of the head. Thunk! This was my *Fawlty Towers* moment, the scene where Basil Fawlty jumps out of his broken-down Austin 1100, shakes his fist in fury and shouts at the top of his voice! A cheer went up from some of the Limerick supporters who saw what had happened. They broke into a chant of 'Cummins isn't playing, Cummins isn't playing, la la la la, la la la la'. I smiled to myself. What else could I do?

When the warm-up ended, I gathered myself and wished Gerry the best of luck. Placing my hand on his shoulder, I said, 'You're the man. Fuck everyone else, you're the man now.'

As the pre-match parade made its way towards the subs bench, I realized that this wasn't a bad dream that I was going to wake up from any time soon. We were seated in the stand, not in the dugout. This was good because the photographers were a reasonable distance away. One of them trained his lens on me for the entire game – waiting for a response, presumably.

During the national anthem, I looked out over the top of the flagpole at the Town End of the stadium and closed my watering eyes. I thought of my late grandmother Moll in these moments and she was with me now, more than ever. 'I know you're looking down on me now, and I need your strength.' When I took my seat with the other subs, Paul Curran, Micheál Webster and Ryan O'Dwyer nearby, kids came over looking for autographs. They asked why I wasn't playing and this was embarrassing because I had no reasonable answer for them.

When the game got underway, we flew for the first half an hour, going nine points ahead. Gerry made a very good save from an Andrew O'Shaughnessy penalty. Babs turned to the crowd as one of our points went sailing over the bar, shouting, 'We have them now!' Micheál made as though he was going for a jog along the touchline to keep warm but Babs told him that there would be no warm-ups this evening. Perhaps he didn't want me to be seen parading up and down the line. I tried to keep sane by analysing the game as though I was in charge. At half-time we were ten points clear but I didn't join the team in the dressing room as the subs were told to stay where they were.

In the latter stages of the second half, and with Limerick roaring back, Eamonn Corcoran was taken off after receiving a particularly nasty belt of the ball between the legs. As he was being led down the tunnel, I went to check on him. Our masseur Mick Clohessy was looking after him. I decided to stay with Eamonn, allowing Mick to get back to the touchline. Eamonn and I chatted and he apologized for not coming to me before the game. He said that he wanted to focus and had planned to talk to me later. I texted Eamonn's wife Deirdre to let her know that he was OK.

Philly Butler, the groundsman at Semple Stadium, dipped his head in occasionally to let us know how the game was going. Limerick were clearly on the comeback trail. From ten points down, they were catching up. Pam was also texting me updates, and when O'Shaughnessy converted a late 65 in extra-time, a second replay lay in store.

The team trooped back into the dressing room and Babs hailed the players as heroes. John Costigan had his say too, praising management and insisting that the team needed to get behind them in order to be successful. I asked Hotpoint for the number 1 jersey, as I feared it might be my last for Tipperary: the team sheet released for the match programme earlier in the week had listed me as number 1, and Gerry wore 16. We arranged to meet at midday on Sunday for a recovery pool session at the Horse and Jockey, and I left Semple Stadium without showering.

I headed for the bus outside and met Pam, people murmuring as I passed. I decided to bypass the post-match meal at the Horse and Jockey. As we drove home, Pam and I broke down in the car.

It was at last possible to release the tension and emotion of the evening. I received a text message from the journalist Damian Lawlor, asking how I was. I rang him and he told me that he had heard in Nenagh on Friday night that I was going to be dropped. When we arrived back to Ardfinnan, we called to see my parents and Dad said that he had heard the rumour at a summer camp in Cahir on Saturday morning. It seemed at this stage that everyone had known that I was about to be dropped except me.

By now, it was becoming almost impossible to process the thoughts spinning through my brain. I needed to find a way to achieve some clarity in my thinking. I stayed up until past 2.30 a.m. that night before the idea struck me that I should record my thoughts and feelings about everything that was happening in a personal diary.

17

Holding On

The following morning was the hardest drive of my life, heading to the pool session knowing that it would be awkward. I arrived at 10.50 and the lads were hanging around, chatting about the game. I met Paul Kelly, who is always good for a laugh, and he didn't disappoint. None of them know what to say to me about the night before.

This is an excerpt from my diary, dated 17 June, the morning after the night before. I had texted Eamonn Corcoran before bedtime, to double-check what time the pool session was scheduled for. '11 o'clock' he messaged back. I was sure we had been told to meet at twelve.

Brian Murray was there to oversee the recovery work, which didn't start until 11.20. There was no sign of the selectors and Gerry was absent too, having rung to say that he was attending a christening. John Leahy appeared at 11.30, and when we were finished, I saluted him. He seemed taken aback.

Later that evening, disaster struck in a club football match for Ardfinnan against Aherlow. I was named at full-forward and started well, scoring a point before pulling my left hamstring. It was a bad tear and I had to be carried off, with ice applied to the injury immediately. The pain was excruciating but I had to make it appear that I wasn't too badly hurt, that coming off was just a precaution. I still held out hope that I would force my way back into the Tipperary team before the summer was out.

We were well beaten by Aherlow, and as the pain in my left leg increased, I knew that the damage was serious. On Monday I called to Brendan Browne, a local physical therapist, and asked for his thoughts on the injury. We were due back to training with Tipperary on Wednesday and I couldn't miss it. We decided that I would book into the cryotherapy clinic at White's Hotel in Wexford the next day, to help speed up the recovery.

Wouldn't you just know it, Eamonn Corcoran and Shane McGrath were there too when I arrived. They had been talking to Leahy, who did not know that I was going to be there. The lads promised not to tell anybody that they had seen me.

I returned home and met Brendan for more work. The leg was now starting to ease a little but the injury was turning black. Leahy rang me later that night, enquiring about my leg and wondering if there was anything he could do to help. South Tipperary is a small place, the news was bound to filter back. I denied that I was seriously injured, joking that the guy marking me was a right dirty bastard. If I admitted the hamstring injury, another goalkeeper might be drafted into the Tipperary panel, leaving me out in the cold completely. I was now in survival mode.

Me: What's the story, Johnny?

He asked if I was referring to myself.

Me: I felt the other night could have been handled a bit better. It seems that everybody around the county seemed to know. To be the last to know cut me to the bone.

John claimed that the decision hadn't been made until the selectors met at the Horse and Jockey.

Me: It was kind of unfair to Gerry as well, to be told that late, you know? I would have loved to sit down with Gerry, to talk to him and prepare him for what was coming.

I asked him what I needed to do to get back on the team, and what I needed to work on when we returned to training. John replied that it was a tough call and that they had a decision to make. The conversation terminated and I was none the wiser.

Training was scheduled for six p.m. on the Wednesday evening, earlier than usual. Maybe Babs didn't want any prying eyes. I met Mick Clohessy at his house at five. It was the first time he had seen my hamstring injury and he couldn't believe the mark on it. Mick's magic hands and Biofreeze pain-relieving gel would hopefully get me through. To hide the bruising I opted to wear knee-length togs, but when I pulled them on, I noticed that the blood mark had travelled down the back of my leg and into my calf muscle. Still, nobody would suspect anything if I wore track-suit bottoms, as I often did when I felt cold.

Hurling in pairs, I could almost feel the eyes of the selectors burning holes in me. They were seated in the stand, sheltered from the driving rain. I attacked the ball as best I could, to show them that I was prepared to work hard and show improvement.

We gathered together in the New Stand, the VIP section, to talk about the performance against Limerick. Babs said it was a great display from the team, battling through extra-time, but the best performance of the night was mine. Our eyes made contact and I didn't flinch as he praised me for the manner in which I had conducted myself. He once again insisted that it had been a tough decision for him to make, as we were from the same club and the only two men to bring All-Ireland senior medals to the parish. I continued to stare at him, roaring inside but holding my counsel as I rolled a sliotar in my hand.

Costigan's turn was next, and I gazed into vacant space as he spoke. It seemed that he was shouting my name every so often, trying to grab my attention, but I didn't look at him. He spoke about what a great servant to Tipperary hurling I had been, and how he had been there to watch my career from the very start as a minor. I tuned out. Babs spoke again and referenced the teams of the 1960s, and how they would never be able to hurl for ninety minutes like we had. It was his way of heaping praise on the current bunch, but it was lost on them.

We split into backs and forwards and Tom Barry took charge of a separate discussion based around defence. Tom wanted feedback from the group and would start with the substitutes. I said that we got carried away when we went ten points up, lost focus on what was happening between the white lines and struggled to put Limerick away. I held my composure, and as we made our way back up the pitch to rejoin the forwards, Tom said that he wanted to acknowledge how I had handled myself on Saturday night.

'Tom, I also want to acknowledge that it was the lowest thing that was ever said to me, that I had to be dropped for the good of Tipperary hurling.'

The session concluded with sprints and a warm-down, as a few of the usual diehards who rarely missed a training session filed in for what they thought would be a 7.30 p.m. start. The rest of the panel departed and I took Hotpoint down to the Town End goal for a twenty-five-minute goalkeeping session. I wanted to rid myself of the anger that had built up in me and also to show the people in the stands that I was still very much interested in hurling for Tipp.

When I had finished, we retired to the Horse and Jockey for a meal and team meeting. Babs summoned each one of the six backs to the top of the room and they were asked to mark with an X on a board where they should be standing when defending 65-metre and long-range frees. It was sad to see each of them heading up, pen hovering over the board before marking their spot. They filed quickly back to their seats and relaxed again once the spotlight was removed. The key to this strategy was to line the front of the goal, on the edge of our square, to ensure that nothing went through. This tactic would hopefully provide Gerry with adequate protection in the face of an aerial bombardment.

Arrangements for the following Sunday were also discussed. Eamonn suggested getting down to the Gaelic Grounds early for a few pucks, as this seemed to settle the players. Babs had a completely different idea, stating that it would be no problem to stop in Pallasgreen on the way and puck around there in our tracksuits, if the weather was good. This was not what Eamonn wanted at all, and the players thought the very same, but they were afraid to speak up and it was decided that we would meet fifteen minutes earlier on Sunday to allow for the stop in Pallasgreen.

For the first time, I prepared for a game I knew I wouldn't play in. When we finally arrived in Limerick on Sunday, a pre-match team talk was held and puckout signals were discussed again, with Gerry asked to stand up and explain them. Left hand in the air would signal a delivery down the left touchline, right hand for the opposite flank.

Limerick got the start they needed and with twenty minutes gone they were well in command and leading by six points. Eoin Kelly had resumed free-taking duties but he didn't appear entirely confident on them. I felt he was now looking over his shoulder too, as Willie Ryan warmed up on the touchline. Babs called Danny O'Hanlon from the bench to warm up and then told him to sit down again. He gave Danny his jacket to keep warm but when the rain came, he took it back and put it on himself. Danny, incidentally, had been standing on the terrace with his friends for the first Limerick game before being called into the squad. This time we came with a late revival, and a Seamus Butler point took the game into extra-time. We started well when Willie Ryan pounced for a goal but we could only manage another point and Limerick won by three. When the pressure came on, we buckled.

We were down but certainly not out, and I tried to rally our lads in the dressing room, urging them to keep the heads up as we had an All-Ireland qualifier against Offaly to prepare for six days later. I walked back to our team hotel and was greeted with a big cheer from Limerick and Tipperary supporters along the way. At a time when I needed it, this was a big lift, and the thought flashed through my mind that maybe, just maybe, the season might not be over yet. Training during the week would give me the chance to stake a claim for the start of a new championship.

18

Spike

Tom Barry was caught in a perfect storm. Fundamentally a very nice man, Tom's emotions were torn because he was the man who had explained to me why I was dropped from the team when two giants of Tipperary hurling, Babs and Leahy, had convinced him that this was the right thing to do.

On the Monday night after we lost to Limerick, the subs trained. Six of us were present – Paul Ormond, Liam Cahill, Alan Byrnes, Ryan O'Dwyer, Francis Devanney and myself. Brian Murray put us through our paces with the U21 team also present, looking at us and wondering what on earth was going on. Tom arrived twenty minutes into the session, and when it was finished, I asked Hotpoint to help me with some goalkeeping drills.

Tom stayed behind to watch and I knew that he was there. I urged Hotpoint to come closer and hit the ball at me harder. With Tom looking on, he would see what I could do and maybe he might be able to influence somebody. Any time the ball went wide or past me, Tom went behind the goals and threw it back. No words were spoken, but maybe this was his way of signalling that he was sorry.

My hopes of getting back in the team were dashed on Thursday evening. More players – Benny Dunne, Darragh Egan, John Carroll and Lar Corbett – were about to suffer a similar fate. We arrived in Thurles at 1.45 on Saturday ahead of a three p.m. start and Benny informed me that he was dropped. I couldn't believe this, and then he told me that Egan, Carroll and Corbett were axed too. The management team arrived at 2.15 and called the lads into the showers to deliver the news. The players who were coming into the team – Cahill, O'Dwyer, Devanney and Pa Bourke – had their tracksuits on when they were informed they were starting. Tom Barry announced the team and Cahill was sitting beside me when his name was called out. 'Jesus, I'm playing.' Liam was back, despite the fact that he was only recently recalled to the panel after a four-year absence. He had scored three goals and two points in a challenge match for a Tipp senior selection against the U21s, and Babs was suitably impressed. Liam, who had transferred clubs from Ballingarry to Thurles Sarsfields, was named at full-forward. Pa Bourke's inclusion wasn't lost on him either because Pa was replacing Lar, his Sarsfields clubmate, a neighbour, and a player he would have looked up to growing up.

At half-time, Babs made three substitutions. Lar, Benny and Carroll were all brought on, with Liam, Diarmaid Fitzgerald and Pa taken off. Diarmaid was injured, but with the scores level at half-time, Liam and Pa hadn't scored and were sacrificed. Offaly went five points up but folded and we managed to win by four, with Lar scoring a late goal. Babs congratulated the players but, speaking to reporters after the game, he said that the forwards were a problem. I changed and left Semple Stadium as quickly as possible.

At training on Wednesday evening, three days before our next outing against Dublin, Babs highlighted the error that allowed Offaly to score from a 20-metre free. He insisted that we should have had five players on the line instead of four but praised Gerry and the defenders for their performances. Babs told Tom Barry to take the backs to one side and sort out the issues he had raised. The team was announced for the Dublin game. I was not included.

Dublin went with a strategy of pumping long balls in on top of Gerry, attempting to expose him, but we won the game at Parnell Park by nine points. As I boarded the bus leaving the ground, our current county board secretary Tim Floyd and Babs were at the top of the steps. Tim said hello but Babs said nothing. When I was seated at the back of the bus, I thought of Pam and how I'd forgotten her, again. I was so mad after every game, I was all over the place. She boarded shortly afterwards and we travelled to the team hotel where the chat centred on what way the draw might go if we lost to Cork the following weekend.

In the week leading up to the Cork game, I tried to remain sane by training hard. One or two people had told me that there was a chance I might get back in the team. Babs spoke about how we could beat Waterford when we met them but was interrupted by Tom Barry, who reminded him that we would not be playing Waterford if we beat Cork. Babs continued to talk about Waterford in an All-Ireland quarter-final.

I had steeled myself for further disappointment when the team to play Cork was announced. We broke into backs and forwards at training and Tom Barry informed us that there would be one change in defence, with Alan Byrnes coming in. Shane McGrath and Eoin Kelly were told that they were being rested, to be ready for Croke Park and Waterford. As we warmed down with a jog after training, Eamonn Corcoran called the players into a huddle. He said that we could beat Cork, despite what management thought.

Preparations were dented, however, when Paul Ormond quit

the panel. Paul was disheartened as he had failed to break into the team for any of our games that summer. He didn't feature in any of the three matches with Limerick and was also ignored for the Offaly and Dublin qualifiers. He walked away on the Monday night before the Cork match, during the cool-down after training. 'I've enough of this,' Paul said to me before walking over to Babs to inform him that he was leaving.

It was a desperately sad sight watching Paul walk towards the changing rooms with his hurley and trademark yellow helmet. John Costigan ran after him but his efforts were in vain. Another guy I had the height of respect for had reached breaking point. I'll put it like this: if I was going to war in the morning and needed five men to come with me, I'd ring Philly Maher, Paul Curran, Eoin Kelly, Tommy Dunne and Paul Ormond. It's a shame that Paul and Philly were collateral damage when Babs was in charge. They deserved better than that.

Before the Cork game on the Saturday, we met in the Horse and Jockey. John Carroll was pulled aside and told that he wouldn't be starting. Darragh Hickey, who had joined the panel in the previous week, was in. Babs began by singling out Lar Corbett for special praise. Lar had stated in a newspaper article that all was well in the Tipp camp and that spirits were high. This, Babs felt, was an endorsement of his good work over the previous months. He spoke about the tradition between Tipp and Cork and, after John Leahy and Tom Barry added their tuppence worth, we headed for Thurles.

Cork appeared to be very cocky in the warm-up, strolling about as if the result was a foregone conclusion. They went five points clear in the first fifteen minutes, but a goal by Willie Ryan hauled us back into contention. He netted again in the second half and, against expectations, we hung on to win. The full-time whistle was greeted with a huge outpouring of joy from the stands as many people had drifted in during the second half when word began to spread that Tipp were putting up a real fight. It was Tipp's first senior championship victory over Cork since 1991.

There was huge excitement in the dressing room and John Costigan paid a glowing tribute to the management team. It went down like a lead balloon as the players knew that it was they who had pulled this one out of the bag. I congratulated all concerned and headed for the bus as quickly as I could. The crowd outside the dressing room was the biggest I had ever seen. As I walked out, I had to hold back the tears. A few people congratulated me but I had done nothing and I felt embarrassed. On the bus, the players were laughing because they had won despite the management's belief that we would be hammered.

When we reached the Horse and Jockey, Babs thanked the players for sticking with him and for this great victory. He also mentioned the wives and girlfriends for their dedication to the cause and how they were welcome to join us for the meal. I felt sick. I skipped the meal and went to visit Pam's parents for a chat before heading for home. Despite Babs making wholesale changes to the team, we had somehow managed to reach an All-Ireland quarter-final in which there was every chance that Tipp could beat Wexford at Croke Park.

Babs didn't travel to Dublin with the team the night before the Wexford match. He was involved in a golf classic that he ended up winning, and then stayed on that evening for the presentation. He showed up for breakfast the next morning. Paul Curran was fit to play despite picking up a serious facial injury in the Dublin game. Paul was praised for the speedy nature of his recovery but he wouldn't see any game time despite working hard to get back.

The trip to Croke Park was strange. When you have no hope of playing on such a big day, all sorts of thoughts run through your head. It really hit me when we reached the dressing room. I decided to get out of the way and disappeared into the shower area. Eoin Kelly was already there. We started tipping a ball to each other and I asked him if he was playing. He said 'no' three times, as if he couldn't believe it himself.

We started well in the game, but as the first half progressed it was clear that Wexford were finding a rhythm. Eoin was brought on after twenty-six minutes for Darragh Egan but he made little impact before half-time. In the dressing room, Babs let the players have it, telling them they were a disgrace and that if they were beaten today it would be their fault. We were three points up at the time and still ahead with ten minutes left before all hell broke loose. Damien Fitzhenry struck the fatal blow, goaling from a 20-metre free after referee James McGrath moved the ball closer to goal. Eamonn Corcoran had run over the ball and McGrath took issue with this, insisting that he had interfered with Barry Lambert. Eamonn was furious, explaining that he was just following his man, but Fitzhenry made hay and fired his shot over Gerry's head and into the net. We lost, and we were out of the championship.

After the full-time whistle, I met Damien in the middle of the pitch. We swapped jerseys and shook hands. He had been really supportive of me, keeping in touch with phone calls and text messages throughout the summer.

Babs resigned a week after the Wexford defeat.

The year was over, and now Pam and I could finally devote full attention to her pregnancy. Given the paranoia that prevailed in my life, Pam had worn baggy clothes to hide the fact that she was expecting. We didn't want to give management the chance to justify their decision to drop me on the basis that Pam was pregnant and I might need more time at home.

Despite what was happening in my hurling career, Pam and I

were enjoying our first year of marriage. We had met in 1999 and tied the knot in December 2006. After joining AIB, it took me a few years to get the money together to begin work on my house in Ardfinnan, on a site I sourced. The project began at the start of 2003 and was completed by the end of the year. Pam moved in before we were married, and we had both expressed a desire to have children.

But only family and a few close friends knew about the pregnancy. Not even one of Tipperary's most dedicated administrators, Michael 'Spike' Nolan, knew. Spike passed away in May 2008, and one of our last visits to see him was early in the New Year, not long after our son Paul was born.

'How have ye been doing?' Spike asked.

'Ah, we have a young fella at home keeping us on our toes now,' I replied.

'What?'

It dawned on us there and then: we'd never told Spike that Pam was pregnant. When we explained why we'd had to keep it under wraps, he nodded with an air of understanding.

'Ah lovely, a little boy, and a January birthday!' he remarked with a smile.

Spike was really angry about what had happened during the summer. In his role as county board treasurer, he was aware of how dysfunctional things had become but he felt powerless to halt the malaise. Spike was a great friend and a fantastic character to have around the Tipperary camp. Attention to detail was his hallmark. He'd lodge the money for the county board with all the notes facing in the same direction when they were handed across to the bank teller. If you wanted tickets, you texted Spike. If you needed expenses sorted out, Spike was the man.

One of my abiding memories is of him sitting beside us in a dressing room in Nenagh not long before his passing. As we were getting ready for the match, Spike joined us, but he was so frail and ill by then that he had to be carried in. We welcomed him into our circle and sat in silence with him for a minute or two. Subconsciously, we knew that we were saying goodbye to Spike and that he was saying goodbye to us, and to Tipperary hurling.

He was a man I had a really strong bond with. In an environment like that, there are not too many people you can trust, but Spike was one. I could tell him I was hurting. 'I know, but you need to keep the head down,' he'd say. It was sound advice at an incredibly difficult time.

I've never spoken to Babs, John Leahy or Tom Barry since that time. That's not for any particular reason, we just happen to move in different social circles. In Ballybacon, there's a mural on the back wall of the clubhouse, noting our contributions to Tipperary hurling. A blue and gold number 15 shirt celebrates the All-Ireland medals that Babs won in 1964, 1965 and 1971, with a white goal-keeper's jersey bearing the number 1 listing my two All-Ireland medals in 2001 and 2010 underneath. 2007 must have been such a difficult time for the old stock in Ballybacon. Many would have grown up watching Babs play, some of them hurling alongside him. I have absolutely no hatred or anger for Babs. Throughout that period, I maintained a huge inner belief in my ability and stuck rigidly to the processes and systems that had always enabled me to get the best out of myself. I couldn't change Babs, and even if the two of us sat across a table from each other in the morning, I wouldn't ask him why he dropped me. It was a huge decision, which I have no doubt was made from gut instinct.

I look at the paintings of those two jerseys on the wall and I'm proud of them. They represent my club, my people, Babs's club, his people. He brought so much to our club and I feel sorry that his second coming as Tipperary manager didn't work out. For me, it became a complete mental battle. I found myself in a situation where I had lost control. I was angry, and while my first instinct told me to lash out, thankfully I was mentally sound enough to resist that temptation. It should not be forgotten that Gerry suffered too – a good player who got caught up in a much bigger game. Sadly, that Wexford match in 2007 was to be his last championship appearance for Tipperary.

What also kept me going was the knowledge that new, young, vibrant Tipperary players were bubbling to the surface. Paudie Maher, Brendan Maher and Noel McGrath were busy winning All-Ireland medals at minor level and were the talk of the county. Liam Sheedy managed that 2006 crop to glory and Declan Ryan repeated the feat a year later. They were now ready to do something even bigger. I attended Loughmore-Castleiney's county final in 2007, just to watch Noel play. He was only sixteen years old at the time. 'Please be ready, please get stronger and bigger.' I'd heard about a young man from Templederry, Gearóid Ryan. 'Christ, you should see this fella playing' people would say. There was a lad in Lorrha, Patrick Maher, raw as bejaysus, but he'd go through a brick wall for you if you asked him to. Paudie Maher was from Thurles, and while he wasn't that big when he eventually joined the Tipp senior set-up, he was placed on a weights programme and turned out like King Kong.

I had spent a number of years feeling like I was banging my head against a brick wall as Tipp went through lean times, but seeing these young kids play and hearing about their exploits gave me hope. What we needed was a man to pull all of this emerging young talent together, merge it with experience, and try to get us back to where Tipperary hurling should be.

19

The Messiah

A familiar figure is standing in front of me in the queue for chips at Heuston Station. This is probably one of the last places you would consider to revive an intercounty career, but this is where it happened.

The sight of the Supermac's outlet is a godsend for a player who's denied himself one of the simpler pleasures in life for a number of months. Comfort food is in order after we've been knocked out of the 2007 All-Ireland senior hurling championship, on an afternoon when I twiddled my thumbs on the bench yet again. Some of the lads scattered like seeds in the breeze across the capital and beyond but I just wanted to get home.

Standing in the queue, waiting to order food, I wanted to remain as anonymous as possible. I'd heard enough of 'Ah, if only you were playing' and that type of nonsense. It wasn't fair on Gerry Kennedy either because he had enough to contend with himself. He was still just a young fellow and everything was new to him. In the blink of an eye, he'd been thrust between the sticks for Tipperary and the fact that I was dropped was all that anybody wanted to speak about when they met him on the street.

As fate would have it, Liam Sheedy was next in line for a burger and chips, or whatever his poison happened to be. At that point, nobody knew that he would succeed Babs Keating as Tipperary manager but, looking back now, maybe I had a sixth sense. Our planets had aligned. Liam hadn't spotted me yet as I leaned closer to whisper in his ear.

'Are you ready to come in and save the day on your white horse?'

Liam half looked over his shoulder but didn't fully turn to engage.

'Keep your mouth shut and your head down,' he replied. 'It will all be all right.'

'OK.'

Now, I didn't really know Liam in a lot of ways. Sure, I'd hurled with the guy, but I only knew him as a hurler. In general, players don't really know much about each other's personality traits or family backgrounds. You might have a few close friends on the panel but typically an intercounty panel comprises forty disparate personalities. Cliques can emerge as some lads gravitate to the ones they know or like, and one of the most important jobs any manager has is to get everyone to pull together.

Liam guided the Tipperary minors to All-Ireland success in 2006 and he was also a regular hurling analyst on local radio station Tipp FM. Sure enough, he was appointed as successor to Babs on 25 September 2007. In no time, Liam had appointed Eamon O'Shea and Michael Ryan as selectors.

I didn't know Eamon from Adam but I knew Mick. He had stuck up for me in 1996, and when Davy Fitzgerald scored that equalizing penalty against us in 1999, Liam and Mick were on either side of me on the goal line. Talk about the wheel coming full circle.

As a player, straw-clutching can begin when a new manager is put in place, particularly if you've had a disappointing time under his predecessor. My biggest fear was being perceived as bitter, that I was some kind of maniac stomping around looking for revenge for what had happened to me while all I really wanted was to play for Tipperary again.

There was no need to be paranoid about how I had played in 2007 because I hadn't played much.

'Maybe someone's saying something into Liam's ear, telling him that I'm going to be a right little upstart. Or maybe they think I'm a lunatic. Do they think that I was fighting with Babs? Do they think I was a problem? How am I going to get across to Liam in our first meeting that I'm not a problem?' The washing machine was in full spin in my head, thoughts churning, and fuelling fear to almost mind-bending levels.

There was only one thing I could do, and that was to lay my cards on the table when I met the new management team.

Our first meeting with Liam, Eamon and Mick took place at the Anner Hotel in Thurles. Liam was seated in the middle, Eamon to his right and Mick on the left. The room felt slightly claustrophobic, the atmosphere something like you'd experience on a first date. Liam had his serious head on while Eamon was sitting back, taking everything in. Nobody knew him, and he was very quiet. Liam spoke for the most part, and when I offered my tuppence worth, he took notes. It was all very formal and reminded me of how it was when Nicky took charge.

I sensed that these three men meant business and I was very keen to impress on them, more than anything, that I just wanted to serve the cause.

'Look, lads, I don't want to be friends with ye, I just want to make sure that I get an opportunity to play for Tipperary. I don't want to be all cosy with ye and I don't want to be on your side of the fence. I'm a player.

'Whatever message you have to give me, I want it between the eyes. I want to know what I'm doing right and what I'm doing wrong. I'm here to serve and I want to help you win an All-Ireland.'

That message was no different to the one I had delivered to previous management teams. I was there if they wanted my opinion on anything but I wasn't going to presume to volunteer ideas unless invited to do so. I wanted them to know that I was a player capable of taking responsibility and instruction, without taking things personally. We would quickly discover that Liam Sheedy was a manager with the X factor and someone very much focused on each individual player.

In his professional life, Liam is the Head of Sales and Revenue with Bank of Ireland. He's also an RTÉ analyst and a board member on the Irish Sports Council. In a previous job, he had progressed rapidly through the ranks at Proctor & Gamble. There's something exceptional about him.

When Liam speaks to you and looks you in the eye, he doesn't break eye contact. Liam was our leader, our inspiration. We knew that he was prepared to make the necessary personal sacrifices and that we could trust him. I felt that I could put my life in Liam Sheedy's hands, certain that he would honour that trust. Brian Cody is the same in Kilkenny. Why do the vast majority of his players commit to him without question or hesitation? The answer is quite simple. They know that if they commit fully to the Cody cause, he will make them winners and better people in return.

I've no doubt that Liam Sheedy made me a better player over the course of his three years in charge of Tipperary. He encouraged me to take more responsibility for my performances, while also feeding me a constant flow of relevant information that I could process quickly. 'We need to do this.' 'The game needs to go there.' 'It's too slow.' 'It's too fast.' The information deposited in my memory bank, allied to my experience and ability, made me a better player.

One time a few of us were in the gym in Clonmel's Hotel Minella on a dark winter's night when Liam arrived to see how we were doing. We were speaking to Noel McGrath and a couple of the other Limerick-based players later that same week, mentioning how Liam had popped his head in. 'Jesus, he was in Limerick as well that night.' That was Liam. He could appear anywhere at any time, and he helped to establish incredible lines of communication between the players. In a nutshell, Liam set up a system and a process that worked. Players were encouraged to communicate positively with each other. He'd instinctively know when to deliver a message that left you in no doubt that he needed something from you during the next competitive game. 'I need a little bit more for this match.' Message received.

That first meeting in Thurles was the starting point. With passion burning in his eyes, Mick also spoke about how things were going to change. Eamon's part was to observe. He sized up body shape, the quality of eye contact, posture, tone of voice. Studies have shown that the words streaming from your mouth equate to just 7 per cent of the entire communication package. The remaining 93 per cent, which is non-verbal communication, comprises body language (55 per cent) and tone of voice (38 per cent). Professor Eamon O'Shea is an expert in body language.

The mood in the room, after that initial period of awkwardness, struck me. It was a ten out of ten feeling. I saw a change. Across the table, I could plainly see the drive and sense of purpose in Liam's eyes. Eamon was more enigmatic. At that stage, little was generally known about Eamon other than that he had hurled for Tipp and was a bloody good player in his time, a wing-forward. He won an All-Ireland club medal in 1986 with Kilruane MacDonagh's, scoring 4–19 throughout the campaign. That's fair shooting, but Eamon never really got the big break at intercounty level, probably because Tipperary were going through such a lean period when he was at the peak of his game.

I was energized leaving the room that night and on the drive home. I was already formulating a plan. I had to 'wow' these guys, lay down an early marker. I needed to show them that I was serious. I needed to pound the roads and work hard on my aerobic fitness. I vowed that nobody in the squad would be as fit as me ahead of the heavy slog in November and December. I installed free weights, a treadmill and a bench at home. I'd cover six or seven miles on the treadmill, completing each mile at a six- or six-and-a-half-mile pace.

When my son Paul was born in January 2008, I was conscious of not making too much noise when I was training and so I moved the treadmill to the back of the house. That enabled me to run outside in the fresh air. When you're training indoors, the lungs don't open to full capacity, and to get through the season that was ahead of us I needed to be prepared.

But my work on the treadmill in November had me ready for our first big examination, a pre-season fitness test at University of Limerick towards the end of the month. That was where I first met Cian O'Neill, our new physical trainer. First impressions last, and Cian certainly made his mark.

For the first hour and a half of the fitness test, we concentrated very much on flexibility, which was never my strong point. I was never a Ryan Giggs, the Premier League footballer who credited yoga as the key to his longevity. Stretching was never really for me. I had conditioned myself into believing that I never had time for it but, in truth, I never made time. I'd rather hit the local ball alley than spend half an hour stretching, or put my toes under the sofa and clock in a hundred sit-ups while watching the TV.

As we were put through our paces, Cian watched intently,

offering instruction when required. He cut an imposing figure, and when he stood in front of us for the first time, we listened. Cian's a big boy and there was a certain tone to his voice that resonated instantly. He knew what he was doing.

I knew that the flexibility part of the test wasn't going well for me and it wasn't a surprise to learn that my scores were well below average. But that was OK because I knew there were better things to come. I was paired off with Benny Dunne for the sit-ups and scored well on that exercise. After a break, we were ready for the bleep fitness test. The time had now come for me to leave a calling card.

I knew that I had to run with Eamonn Corcoran to stay in the game because Corcoran was the fittest player we had and was always the last man standing in fitness tests. I slipped in beside Corcoran and off we went, up through the levels as lads dropped out. It was tough, but as the levels rose higher and the pressure intensified, I looked around to see that Corcoran and myself were the only two left. I blew up first but the applause for my efforts from the rest of the group was music to my ears. Goal number one had been achieved. I'd made a statement.

It was probably the fittest I ever was for the time of year and I was noticed without even hitting a ball. Most of my early paranoia drifted away but was quickly replaced by a fresh bout. 'What will my touch be like at training? OK, you're fit enough, but look, you're not a midfielder, you're a goalkeeper, so what are you going to do now?' Still, the new year brought with it renewed hopes and dreams, and the promise of a first start against University College Cork in the Waterford Crystal Cup.

I resolved there and then to keep my head down and avoid the media spotlight at all costs. The last thing I wanted was whooping and hollering cries of 'hip, hip, hooray' because Brendan was back. What would that achieve? Absolutely nothing, except heap unhelpful pressure on Liam. The last thing I wanted was to be viewed as a problem. Would I become too big a headache for Liam Sheedy? What if the media were constantly ringing him to find out if I'd be playing in the next game, and Liam began to wonder why he bothered his arse bringing me back?

I promised Liam that I would conduct no media interviews. 'Look, Liam. I'm talking to nobody, and nobody will know when I'm playing. I promise you.' He looked at me as if I was half cracked as I ran off towards the goals at Dr Morris Park on a cold January night. The first ball that came my way dribbled in under my legs. The very first ball. I suffered a complete dose of the jitters. These were only makeshift goals, bollards for Christ's sake. But my reaction was positive as I picked the ball up and quickly restarted play. 'Jesus Christ, Brendan. Calm down. Just play.'

It wasn't long before Eamon O'Shea was sprinkling magic dust over us. I found him a little eccentric at first, but once you started to understand what it was he was trying to get you to do, how he wanted to open your mind to creative possibilities in how you played, you were soon a different and a better player. Bland wasn't good enough. If you're bland, you may as well be a lemming running off a cliff with the rest of them. Socially conditioned to follow the pack rather than stand out from the crowd.

Eamon was the only guy I've ever trained under that never used cones on a pitch specifically for hurling drills. Lines of the field were his canvas. We played games within the lines of the pitch, often in confined spaces with the constant threat of blue murder hovering in the air. One of his favourite exercises was to play matches between the 65-metre lines. We were encouraged to operate within tight, confined parameters. Having trained between the 65s, opening up the full width of the pitch on matchday was a revelation. The extra space provided would allow us to fully express ourselves. People watched us train and I'd ask them what they thought. 'Fucking chaos! It's mad! Players are running everywhere. What are ye at?' But in the middle of it all, I knew exactly where the ball had to be. In a drill, I was completely in sync with everything happening around me.

I would compare what we were doing to the movie *The Matrix*. It's a complicated film full of symbols and numbers, but once you understand them, it makes sense. That's what Eamon was to us, the head of the Matrix. It took a while to decipher his messages but when you did, everything became clear. We could see his world, his game, his strategy. I understood Eamon relatively quickly but I don't think it's possible ever to fully understand him. As a collective, it probably took the team eighteen months to evolve to a point where we were fully in tune with how he wanted to play.

Eamon sees the pitch as a blank page. He knows the way he wants his team to play the game, by creating space and moving fluently. One of his great gifts is the ability to tailor a training session to the mood of the team. He would watch carefully and walk among us as Cian O'Neill warmed us up. Eamon would drift to the periphery of the group, arms folded, watching and gauging the mood and humour of the team. Was there energy present? Were the energy levels too high or too low? What was the temperature like? Eamon O'Shea is a human thermometer and he'll start a training session at the tempo that he deems appropriate. He might start it slowly if he thinks that the general mood is too giddy, to bring the group down. Liam would often say to us that the right level was always chest high, never too high or too low. And he'd point to chest level, below the chin. 'Right there, lads.' Eamon, too, always knew where the right level was. Unknown to ourselves, he'd always get us there, to a level where we were training optimally. So if he had to take us down, he would, and if he had to take us up, he'd do that too.

When he got us there, the quality came, space opened up, and he got the movement he desired. His training was a constant challenge, fresh and varied. He also understood one of the psychological traits that had scuppered many a Tipperary team in the past, namely the tendency to rest on our laurels. Having built up a big lead in a game, we would almost invariably lose our concentration and allow the opposition to work their way back into contention.

'Over here,' Eamon would command. 'Drill. Four against four.' The instruction could come during a water break. There was no time for standing around. That's one of the big no-nos in sport psychology. Simple, active drills were the norm and we were never on the pitch without our minds switched on. At any given moment, Eamon could dart to the other side of the pitch and begin setting up a drill. Subconsciously, this is a good time for a player to reach for the water bottles, while the manager is otherwise engaged. But Eamon would quickly realize that we were switching off and, boom, he'd get us moving again. 'Get four against four, quickly. Who are you with?' And we were organized in a flash.

'Happy? Yeah, good, good.' And then we could drink. Us watching him, him watching us. Always engaged. We drank with our heads moving, wondering where he would spring to next.

In the stand, Liam Sheedy sat back and observed.

The manager–coach axis spun beautifully. Liam was safe in the knowledge that Eamon was the man to coach the team and that allowed him to get on with the job of managing. I'm still not sure how they met but I hold a romantic idea that when the paths of two great people cross, a new star suddenly appears in the sky.

Because of his banking skills, Liam knew how to set up a process that would deliver success. The start of any process requires good materials and even better leaders. Liam cherry-picked the best. Cian O'Neill told me that after Liam had interviewed him for the strength and conditioning role with Tipperary, he got on board immediately. He wanted to because he knew that the set-up would be just right.

With Eamon, it was more a case of wanting to get involved because he understood what we had been through in 2007. He'd seen players suffer and he vowed that it wouldn't happen again. 'Men of honour' was a phrase he often used. First and foremost, Eamon knew what he wanted from players and he knew how to coach them.

At the very start, as I said, we didn't quite understand how we were being coached. We could spend fifteen minutes simply hitting a ball into the netting behind the goals. We'd been giving out previously about Babs asking us to run around Lucozade bottles masquerading as cones before hitting the ball over the bar, yet here we were, hitting ball after ball into a net after playing a 'one-two' with a teammate.

Eamon was all about rhythm, the rhythm of the strike, and the speed of the ball off the hurl. The heartbeat of the game of hurling. When you were in that rhythm, you expressed yourself like you were twelve years of age again.

An Eamon O'Shea team is designed for Croke Park and, as Nicky realized when he was in charge, there's a huge difference between how you play Munster championship hurling and how you play in the big arena. The Munster championship is blood and thunder, shouldering opponents out over the sidelines, thumping the ball as hard as you can towards the opposition goal. There's not a huge amount of structure there and games can be quite frantic at the provincial level. But when you get to Croke Park, you have that little bit of extra space and the game becomes more strategic, positioning players in the half-forward line to make a selfless run, following a move to its conclusion. A forward might make ten lung-bursting runs at Croke Park, for that one chance. That's why Eamon loved Larry Corbett so much. Larry could make three runs and get on the ball three times. He'd never make ten runs in a match because he could see the ball through a different pair of eyes, through Eamon's eyes. And that's why Larry was Eamon's joker in the pack. He was already out of left field. Larry was Eamon on the pitch, capable of seeing things that others couldn't, like that run in the 2010 final to pick up Noel McGrath's killer pass. That's why Eamon fell in love with Larry, because he made the runs that Eamon dreamed about.

Cian was also a massive cog in the wheel. After the first two months, he tapped into the movement that Eamon craved from his players. He used small-sided conditioning games, with space at a premium. Four players against three, five against two, with those outnumbered encouraged to take the correct options under extreme pressure. For the first couple of months after training, I would arrive home with my hands cut to ribbons.

There we were, sometimes two of us surrounded by six, out-numbered. But what they were doing was slowly extracting a much higher work-rate. You won't get anything simple if you're outnumbered; you have to work desperately hard for it. It reached a stage where, in your head at least, you always felt outnumbered. That was conditioned into us.

In time, I'd arrive home and Pam would comment on how my hands were bleeding again. 'Are they?' I wouldn't have noticed. It was part of the game. It was forged in January, February and March 2008. Liam and Eamon worked hard to polish their diamonds.

At a team-building camp at the Curragh army base, one of our exercises involved crawling along the floor of an indoor hall with a teammate on our backs. We went all the way to the wall at the other end, touched it, turned around and came all the way back. Even if it took you all day and all night to do this, it had to be done. Our hipbones never left the floor. Liam set about stripping mentally brittle players to the bone, before building them back up again. He knew what kind of animal he possessed when he'd see a guy's elbows bleeding through his jersey. But that same guy could be asked to go again. And he would do it. He would place that man on his back and go to that wall and back one more time. That's how you find out if you can go to war with this guy, if you can rely on him when you're cocooned in a trench in the face of enemy gunfire.

Remember, too, that Liam had beasts that had been caged in 2007. Guys like myself, Eoin, Shane McGrath, John O'Brien. Tipp had talent, but that talent had to be focused and channelled in the right direction.

Liam probably viewed me as one of the leaders in the group, but I'd been told right from the start that there would be no guarantees. 'I don't know what way this thing is going to pan out for you, Brendan. Everyone has a chance here.' That was fine. I didn't expect or want any special treatment because of what had happened in the summer of 2007. I had to earn my right to be there all over again.

I didn't need Babs Keating to drop me to discover how much I wanted to play for Tipperary. I had the ability to do it and all I needed was someone to provide me with a focus so that I could set my goals accordingly. If your mind is process-driven and you find that someone is jumping from Z to X, B to F, and finally back to A, it muddles the brain. You'll work through it and follow instructions but you'll know that it's not right and that it won't bring success.

Liam didn't talk to us a whole lot. He wasn't being rude. He was working every day of the week in a pressurized environment where at some point he might have to pull someone aside and tell them that they were surplus to requirements. That was just his professional life in the bank. So did he want to be friends with somebody he might have to have a tough conversation with?

Liam showed us respect, and that respect was reciprocated. I'll put it like this. A common rule of thumb in life is that you're not going to be liked by everybody. On a particular day you and I might get along great, but the next day things might not run so smoothly and there could be tension. Mutual respect is key. That's the way Liam operated. Liam often had to deliver bad news to a player, perhaps telling him that he was being dropped from the squad. That player might not have liked it but he accepted it. We all knew that Liam always acted in the best interests of the team, that there was a bigger picture which sometimes required tough decisions to be made.

He'd always arrive into the dressing room in good humour. 'Well, lads, how's it going? Ah, a great night for it!' It could be snowing outside, but Liam's enthusiasm was infectious and the atmosphere even more so. One of his first jobs every evening was to clear out the physio room. He saw this as a haven for softness. You could have lads sitting around the massage table, shooting the breeze as one of their colleagues was rubbed. Our masseur Mick Clohessy and physio John Casey were told to have the physio room cleared in time for a 7.10 p.m. start on the pitch. If you wanted to come in at five and get your rub, fine, but you were required to be on that pitch on time.

Liam was organized. Before training sessions, he ensured that every member of his backroom team was briefed. Reports arrived from the physios informing him who was fit and who wasn't. Liam then knew exactly how many players he'd be working with. This information was also passed on to Cian O'Neill.

It was a renaissance, and it gathered momentum when we finished the National Hurling League season as champions for the first time since 2001. Back then, Nicky put the trophy in a black bin bag and told us it would mean nothing if we didn't follow up with Munster and All-Ireland titles. This time it was a little different. Claiming meaningful silverware marked a major step forward in our evolution under Liam. But in Tipperary, teams are ultimately judged on championship performances, and it was no different for us. Were we just a spring daffodil or could we flower in the summertime? We were determined to find the answer, and the very next morning we boarded a flight from Cork for a training camp in Portugal. This was a real statement of intent. There was no time to bask in League glory as our minds were immediately refocused to the championship. Preparation was meticulous but still, neutral observers didn't fancy our chances as no Tipperary team had won a senior championship match on Cork soil since the 1920s. Then again, records are there to be broken, aren't they?

20

The Blackrock End

This is it, the moment of truth. We're wrapped tightly in a huddle as Liam Sheedy prepares to call out the team to face Cork in our opening game of the championship. I have my arm around Paul Ormond. To all intents and purposes, I shouldn't be worried. We're 2008 National League champions and I played well throughout the campaign, but I'm still nervous. 'Please God, let him call out my name.'

'In goal, Brendan Cummins.'

I drop my head and exhale.

'Congratulations, you're back in your rightful place,' Ormond whispers.

I was back, but anxious two days later as we made our way to Cork. At our Fota Island resort base, Liam had the tone of the meeting just right. He produced a flip chart and began ticking boxes on the paper. 'Have we the work done?' Tick. 'Have we the sacrifices made?' Tick. 'Is there anything more that we can do? No, so we'll just go out and play.'

Then it was Eamon's turn to tell us how we were going to play. 'Run here.' 'Run there.' 'Create space.' 'Keep moving.' 'Don't stop.' 'Don't stand still.'

Liam then showed us a video he had put together of the players in action, with Keane's 'Somewhere Only We Know' providing the soundtrack. It epitomized everything that we were doing – and we were doing things that nobody else could even realize or dream about. Evocative footage was cut brilliantly into the package – me bringing off a save, John O'Brien flashing the ball over the bar, Conor O'Mahony with his fist in the air, the white tape wrapped around his wrist shining like a beacon.

The bus journey to the ground the next day was special. We entered the ground at the Blackrock End, with Cork supporters banging on the sides of the coach. Liam played our song, the famous Johnny Cash number 'I Won't Back Down', and it captured the mood.

They might try to push us through the gates of hell but we weren't going to back down.

It's an incredible feeling, knowing that everything is done, the boxes are ticked and that there is nothing else humanly possible you could have done to get yourself to this point. I glanced at the people outside and promised myself that they would witness something today they could tell their grandchildren about.

Just throw in the ball – I've waited twelve months for this! Liam, Eamon and Mick have given me everything I ever wanted, and now it's time to perform.

The Cork supporters were massed at the Blackrock End like sardines in a tin. During the first half, I could see from the City End that it was becoming a little crowded down there, and some of the Cork fans were released from the Blackrock End on to the edge of the pitch behind Donal Óg Cusack's goal. At half-time, the gardaí knocked on our dressing room and asked if I wanted the overflow of people moved, but I was in such a good place that having them behind me really didn't matter. We'd come from seven points down in the first half to trail by just one at half-time and the wind was in our sails.

The Cork fans were eight or nine deep behind the Blackrock End goal and the craic began.

'Well, lads!'

'Well, Brendan boy, how's the going?'

'Grand day for it!'

' 'Tis boy, leave in plenty now won't ya?'

'I will, lads, no bother, I won't let ye down!'

I was in such a good head space that I truly felt I could have sat in the crowd while the game was on, and got up to stop the ball when it came my way. That kind of good-natured banter and humour was the hallmark of Cork supporters. I respected them, they respected me, and we got on great. While I was stopping the ball and causing them heartache, not once was I slagged or a smart comment passed. At full-time, it was more of the same.

'Thanks, lads. Good game. Sorry it didn't work out for ye.'

'No problem, Brendan boy. Good man, well done boy.'

Surely there's no other sport in the world where you could have that. It was certainly a lot different to the late Tony Reddin's experience back in 1950, as the great man once recounted to me.

Over fifty-five thousand people were at the game in Killarney and as Tony looked around him, he could see bottles, cans and sods of turf raining down on top of his net. One man even caught him by his jersey as he ran out to clear a ball. It was mayhem. On and on it went. Tony had a coat chucked at him as he went to save another ball. 'I looked around and the net was gone,' Tony remembered. 'They'd pulled the net off the goal! What could I do? I couldn't run, I had to stay there.

'Right at the end, a long ball came in and the goals were so rickety from all the pulling at them that the uprights were loose. I hit the post a shot of my hip and, as it wobbled, the ball went the wrong side of it and wide. I was lucky I didn't get killed!'

Tony and I laughed out loud as his eyes sparkled with the memories.

On their way home, the Tipp lads thought it would be best if they didn't raise the blue and gold flags until they reached the outskirts of Killarney.

That was Tony's abiding memory of a big Munster championship match against Cork. By beating them down on their home patch, we had made our own piece of history. It was a lovely contrast, and it took me back to 2001, when Tony came to watch us train in Semple Stadium. It was unbelievable to find yourself in the presence of a hurling icon. People might often refer to a good save that I made but there was always the proviso 'you'll never be as good as Reddin!' Imagine leaving that kind of footprint in the space of just ten years. I find it incredible that few people alive today can remember seeing him play and yet he's still spoken about in such reverential tones.

The victory over Cork was a seminal moment in our evolution. We had won the League and that was fine, but Tipperary's recent history suggested that if we won something, the chances were that we'd fall in a heap shortly after. The dressing room was alive with joy. We'd been there so many times, listening to the whooping and hollering next door, hearing opposition supporters in the tunnel outside yelping with delight as they made their way out of the ground. But this was our turn, and we were going to enjoy it. There was a problem though, the onset of another of those excruciating headaches I'd usually experience after big games. I went straight home to spend time with Pam and my son Paul, who was just a few months old.

Having him in my life provided me with a great grounding in 2008 and beyond. One of my favourite tricks was to rock him to sleep to the sounds of a Michael Bublé concert I had recorded on the TV. Bublé never realized what an impact he had on my infant child and this grown man's attempts to come to terms with the magnitude and challenges of fatherhood. Knowing that I was returning to Pam and Paul after games helped me to get through them. 'It won't be long until you're home, don't lose a second of this.' And I'd push on then. Those were just fleeting moments during the battle but a great way to erase any small doubts and stay in the present.

Victory in Cork set us up for a crack at old rivals Clare in the Munster final. They'd come through on the other side of the draw, beating Waterford and Limerick, and would provide tough opposition. Not having tasted provincial success since 2001, we badly needed to win a Munster title.

I felt really strong in the game once again, and when I was in that zone I'd often reach a point where everything seemed to be moving in slow motion. In the 2001 Munster championship against Clare, I pulled off a save to my left to divert a Colin Lynch shot and remember thinking that I should have done more with it, that the ball was travelling slowly. But when I saw it later I realized that the sliotar was really travelling, as it flew quickly off the base of my stick.

A question I've been asked many times is what's the best save I made in my career. It's probably the one from Henry Shefflin in the 2009 National Hurling League final, when I dived full length to knock the ball wide on my left-hand side. Typical Henry, he shaped as if he was about to pop the ball over the bar before arrowing his effort towards the top corner. The double-save in the 2004 Munster championship match against Waterford is high on the list. I parried a shot from Paul O'Brien, and when Paul Flynn doubled on the rebound, I dived to my right to knock the ball behind for a 65.

But I prefer to concentrate on the save that meant the most to me, and there's one clear winner in that category: it's the one from

Niall Gilligan's 20-metre free at the end of this 2008 Munster final against Clare.

The reason it's my favourite is because of where I had come from in a year. Losing my place on the team in 2007 was the Good Friday of my intercounty career; the 2008 Munster final was Easter Sunday. When I stepped forward, dived to my right and diverted Gilligan's shot over the bar, it was the first time that my head said 'don't' but my heart roared 'go on'. I let it all out, rising to my feet after making the save to pump the air with defiance, twice. Our corner-back Eamonn Buckley, who was standing on my right, patted me on the back as I released a torrent of pent-up emotion.

Shane Maher was another of my defenders on the goal line when we stood up to Gilligan's free. After I'd been dropped in 2007, Shane was at training one night and ran to the top end of the field to join the group I was in. He then realized that this was the place where the subs were and, almost embarrassed, hightailed it to the other end. Benny Dunne was standing beside me too when I made that save, one of my very best friends, and Declan Fanning was my full-back before I was dropped. In terms of where I was at that moment in time, and considering where I had come from, I couldn't have asked for four better men standing on either side of me.

RTÉ TV requested an interview after the game and their reporter was Clare McNamara, who's also from Ardfinnan. Reporters often get some of their best stuff from players and managers minutes after a game, when emotions are still running high. We are often an easy kill for them, but I could sense an ambush was coming. Clare tried to soften me up with a couple of straightforward questions before winding up for the knockout punch. She asked me if I felt I had proved a few people wrong.

I refused to answer the question directly but qualified my

response by pointing out that I'd just won a Munster final and was enjoying the feeling. The past was the past. I then let Clare know that I was ready to leave. She asked for one more question.

'As long as it's nothing to do with last year, I'll give you any answer you want,' I told her.

I shook Clare's hand when the interview was concluded, but the message was clear: 'I'm sorry, but I can't deal in the past any more. That's gone. Over.' I understood that she had a job to do and it was a fairly obvious question for her to ask in the circumstances. The exiled goalkeeper had returned to win a Munster champion-ship medal – a terrific angle for any journalist. Perhaps she wanted me to unload with both barrels, something like 'Yeah, I proved him wrong. Are you watching now, Babs?' But there was no way I was falling into that trap.

Gerry Kennedy was still involved in the set-up and he didn't need any of that either. In recent years I've got to know Gerry better than when we were actually together in the Tipperary squad. I've great time for him, he's a good lad. I had nothing against him at all, and while we would have chatted, there was never any talk about the year before. Liam eventually brought Darren Gleeson, who was also from Portroe, into the panel as sub goalkeeper and that was the writing on the wall for Gerry. His senior intercounty career was over. I rated him as a goalkeeper, no question. But when you're in what was effectively a trial period, you feel that you have to take chances, to make a statement. It's something I identified early in my career, not to go chasing a game, to let it come to you.

I see it with some of the current goalkeepers in hurling. They want to be involved all of the time, coming 10 yards out to meet the ball rather than positioning their defenders smartly. I always felt that prevention was better than cure. If your defenders are organized, there's no need for you to go on a mad dash from goal.

Proper communication will allow a defender to do that job for you.

Gerry felt that, having been given the shirt in 2007, he had to prove himself. That was only natural. He felt he had to do something that would be remembered. That creates extra pressure. When I reclaimed the shirt, I never went chasing a game. If I had nothing to do over the course of seventy minutes, that was absolutely fine because it meant my teammates further out the field were in total control. When the next day comes, the ball may be in your vicinity more and you need to be ready for it.

Our Munster final victory set us up for a crack at Waterford in the All-Ireland semi-final. They'd come through the qualifiers while we tried to bridge a five-week break. It was new territory, not just for Liam and the backroom team but also for us as players. We hadn't experienced anything like this since winning the All-Ireland in 2001 and there weren't too many survivors from that year still knocking around.

In the hotel the night before the game, Liam showed us a video he had put together, with messages from our families. They were asked to say how much it meant to them to have their son or husband playing for Tipperary on All-Ireland semi-final day. It almost reduced me to tears. Perhaps we were too emotional going into the game, wanting to win so much. That impacted on our performance because we slightly deviated from the processes that would ensure a result.

Waterford were filleted by Kilkenny in the final. It was like a Lada trying to keep pace with a Ferrari. Waterford were stuck to the ground, emotionally spent after beating us in the semi-final. After that game, I remember Waterford player Eoin Kelly's partner whizzing past me at full-time and greeting him with a massive hug. While that was fine and she was naturally excited, I remembered my first All-Ireland final in 1997 and how, after beating Wexford in the semi-final, we had fellas on the team who could bring some of us right back down to earth very quickly. 'Hey now, that's only the semi-final. The cup is given out after the next game.' Waterford were happy just to be at Croke Park, and that's not a slight on them in any way. Limerick were the same in 2007.

It's like a boxer preparing for a big fight. He's surrounded by his entourage telling him how great he is and the trash talk fuels his ego. But when the lights come on and the bell goes, ding-ding, he's on his own. When it's All-Ireland final day and over eighty thousand pairs of eyes are peering in on top of you, Croke Park's a scary place. I'm sure some of those Waterford players had a quick look around and thought, 'Holy shit, we're playing in front of all of these people and millions more are watching around the world. And now we're on our own.' This is when the mental game begins and you have to shut out the visions you have of Monday night parades and back-slapping for weeks, months and years to come. 'This could probably be the only opportunity in my life to win an All-Ireland, and if I win this, I'll be remembered for ever.' That's a huge thing to get your head around.

Our semi-final defeat had taught us another huge lesson, one that our Eoin Kelly referenced on numerous occasions afterwards. Before the throw-in, Waterford goalkeeper Clinton Hennessy ran from his goal to have a go at our corner-forward Seamus Butler, and he found support from his clubmate Declan Prendergast. With that, it seemed like the whole of Waterford arrived to the scene of the crime, but nobody from Tipp came in to help Seamus. Loads of white jerseys were there, telling Seamus to get up off the ground. They had laid down a marker. It was a game for the big boys now, but we were found wanting. We couldn't cope with it and their manager Davy Fitzgerald had done a number on us with his tactics.

Waterford had our number from early in the game. It was a

sobering lesson, but one not lost on one of our younger players, Shane McGrath. Shane was convinced that we would learn from that experience. We had come from well down the pecking order to win two big trophies, the League title and Munster championship, and Shane's rather prophetic words were incredibly mature for a guy who was still only twenty-four at the time. 'We'll get that chance again next year,' he insisted. 'And we won't make the same mistake again. We'll be better.'

21

The Cats

On the night of the 2007 All-Star function, I remember training alone.

I was angry, not because I wasn't at the event in Dublin but because I'd never put myself in a position to be there. I hadn't even entered the starting stalls, for Christ's sake. I was never in the race for one of those bronze statuettes and I couldn't watch anybody else collecting one on the TV. So I picked myself up off the couch and punished myself on the local pitch for an hour.

When I'd finished, I stood in the middle of the field and promised myself that I'd be wearing a tuxedo in twelve months' time, in front of the camera and not a hundred miles away like I was now, sweat dripping from my brow. I couldn't have just sat and watched Limerick's Brian Murray collecting the All-Star for the year's best goalkeeper as my mind collapsed.

When the All-Stars were handed out on 17 October 2008, it was a year since I'd run around that pitch at home, with only streetlights to guide me along my path. But this time was different. I had one of those bronze statuettes in my possession.

I arrived home late on Saturday evening. Pam and Paul were both in bed so I pulled on my training gear, placed the All-Star award on the passenger seat of the car, and drove down to the local pitch. I trained there, with the statuette perched in the middle of the field. When I came back home, I slipped quietly into bed after a shower. Mission accomplished.

We had won League and Munster titles in 2008 but it was an All-Ireland medal that I craved now. Experience tells you when you have a good crop of players, a good set-up, and you know that you must win when those ingredients are present. I had been through enough lean patches to recognize when we had good stuff and when teams weren't good enough to win. This team was good enough.

One of Liam's great traits was his ability to leave you in no doubt that he was the boss. Our first pitch session in 2009 was at Dr Morris Park and I was ready to go in the new training gear that had been supplied to us before Christmas. But a few of the lads were late, and a few others arrived not wearing the training gear. That kind of behaviour drove me scatty. A player arriving late or not wearing the correct gear hadn't been thinking about the group all day. His head was somewhere else instead.

I felt that I had to lay down a marker, that I couldn't allow this to happen. I signalled to Cian O'Neill that I wanted to have a chat with the group before we kicked off. Cian had no problem with that and I had my say. 'Look, lads, fellas were late, fellas are wearing different coloured tops.' Some of us were wearing Tipperary training tops that, for some reason, had the Kilkenny colours on them, just under the arm. Black and amber. Mad. But the tops had the Tipp crest on them so that was fine. It was just the style of them. 'When we meet these lads wearing these colours later on in the year,' I continued, pointing under my arm, 'we need to be together, and it starts now, not later in the year.'

I was anxious to get that point across because during all my years, I always found that any more than two 'crisis' meetings in the season was a surefire sign that the show was over. You could have a meeting in January and that was fine, to map out goals and targets for the season ahead. Maybe another in March. But no more after that.

The other lads took on board what I had to say. There were some mumbled apologies and, to be fair, they could understand where I was coming from.

Togging in after training, Liam called me over. 'Excellent,' I thought. 'He was impressed by what I had to say to the group.' Not so.

'Come here, you. If you ever again address the group without my permission, there will be murder.'

'OK, sorry, boss.'

'Yeah, just don't let it happen again.'

I didn't, and Liam was right. We were dealing with a new Tipperary here, a Tipperary that Liam was in charge of. He had a clear vision for where he wanted the team to go and didn't need me sticking my oar in where it wasn't wanted.

Everything that Tipperary did in 2009 was focused on becoming a better team. Kilkenny remained the team to beat, and when we played them at Nowlan Park in a League match in March, they whipped us by seventeen points. I wasn't great on the day, and that's putting it mildly. They were twenty points ahead at half-time and received a standing ovation as they left the field. We had built up that game in our heads as a defining moment for us. They had hammered Waterford in the All-Ireland final but we weren't Waterford, they couldn't do that to us, we thought. Our heads were wrong, and they wiped the floor with us.

At half-time, Liam tried to deflect some of the heat from us. 'I'll take the flak for this,' he said. 'This will be on me. Just go out and play the second half, don't worry about the consequences. Play the game, don't worry about anything else. I'm big enough and bold enough to take it.'

Liam's tone was different when we met at training the following Tuesday night. His tongue-lashing stripped us naked. We felt like children who had let Daddy down. We had the best set-up any of us had ever seen but we had let him and each other down by not performing. That was unacceptable, particularly in a game that we had built as one in which we were going to show that we were no soft touch. We were putty.

We had done plenty of talking about being better than Kilkenny, how we were certainly better than Waterford. What happened to them wouldn't happen to us. But it's about more than words. Action was required, Liam said, and we needed to believe in what we were doing and get stuck into it. We were lackadaisical, believing our own hype, taking things for granted. Thinking that we were a match for Kilkenny meant that we were set up for a hiding. There's no better team to punish vulnerability.

The group was introduced to Declan Coyle, a former Ulster football championship winner with Cavan and a motivational speaker I had met before. Declan is the author of a book called *The Green Platform*, in which he explains his philosophy. On the green platform we interpret even negative events as creating positive opportunities. On the red platform, which is the enemy, we would interpret those events as a complete disaster, resulting in a feeling of powerlessness, that life could never have a positive meaning again. If we are on that green platform, we will ask questions to help identify better outcomes. We also ask questions on the red platform but with negative connotations. This feeds into a belief system that is positive on the green platform but negative in red. Ultimately, the quality of our lives will depend on whether we believe in the green platform, or continue to operate in the red. It's fascinating stuff. A good example of the green platform is when an athlete takes his time and chooses the positive energy he needs to use to respond to a particular situation. If you're on the red platform, you'll react out of anger, blame or shame.

Declan explained how our biggest, most important goals must become more purposeful, powerful and real in our minds than our doubts and fears. People grow best from their areas of strength, so they need to work from their strengths rather than focusing too much time on fixing weaknesses.

I wasn't a regular visitor to Declan for one-on-one sessions because I usually got so much from him that it would fill me for a month or two, sometimes even three. His philosophy mirrors mine – live in the moment. He's also very big on the power of the ego and how it drives and influences what we do. The best way to make sure that the ego doesn't run riot is to dampen it down and manage the thoughts in your head.

Declan wouldn't know a huge amount about hurling but he's an expert in developing mental strength. At intercounty level, ability is a given so it's about how you use that ability and stop your mind from putting obstacles in the way of maximizing it. If you marry ability with mental strength, then you can be yourself in the way that Eamon O'Shea encouraged us to be.

We found ourselves back in a League final in 2009, in a game billed as the clash of the champions. All-Ireland champions Kilkenny against League champions Tipperary. What a game it was. We were fully tuned in right from the start and our warm-up in Littleton had a part to play in that: small-sided conditioning work that Cian had drilled into us, five versus two, dog eat dog in the middle third of the pitch. That's where you can beat Kilkenny: win that battle between the two 65s and get the ball inside quickly.

The night before the game, we met in the Horse and Jockey. Liam called Larry and me to one side. 'Need a big one tomorrow, lads, need to lay down a marker.' We weren't going to take any backward step. There was no way we'd be bullied again.

Kilkenny were masters of it, capable of mentally and physically dominating opponents before the ball was even thrown in. What really epitomized our display was Paudie Maher's job on Henry Shefflin. Paudie put no real stock in reputations and for the carefree young hurler that he was, just twenty years of age, Shefflin was a challenge he would relish.

Brian Hogan was taken off injured after Seamie Callanan opened him up with a shoulder and Martin Comerford was brought in for Kilkenny. 'Gorta', as he's known, is a great character off the field, and as he sprinted on to the pitch it looked as if he was about to hit Declan Fanning a belt of a shoulder – the usual getting-to-know-you kind of thing. Declan sensed the oncoming danger and turned Martin upside down. Two big statements in the space of a few minutes.

We took Kilkenny to extra-time in a pulsating game, but more than that, we now believed that we were physically strong enough to match them. A year and a half into Cian O'Neill's conditioning regime, we were on the right track. Even though we didn't win, we'd helped to erase the memories of Nowlan Park, and Liam had a real platform to work from heading into the summer.

Each and every one of us believed in what he was doing. There was no need for a code of conduct or anything like it. When it's right, you don't need any of that. In a conversation with Tyrone football manager Mickey Harte, I asked him once what he did to keep players numbered 21 to 30 on a panel interested and motivated. 'These fellas were trying to win something that hasn't been achieved in Tyrone before,' he began, 'so it was very easy to motivate them.' The problem arises in years two and three, especially if a fringe player has tasted success. Number 22 or 23 on the panel is now being told that he should be on the team, and frustration grows. That player will now question the true worth of any future success if he hasn't been directly involved. Also, that player will insist to supporters who are wondering why he's not playing that he should be, and he'll start to lose it a little bit. The other end of the scale is the difficulty involved in managing the so-called 'star' players. Because of how they are perceived, it's very hard for a manager, fearing a public backlash, to drop them.

Liam kept in touch with his players via one-on-one meetings. You never really knew where you stood with Liam and that ensured that you could never assume that you'd arrived. That's why I loved his management style. You might have achieved something but then he'd place another challenge in front of you. 'You did that, grand, this is what more looks like.' The bar was always raised higher, out of reach, and you were always stretching to get to where his expectation of you was.

A stretch for one player might be a huge thing, not so much for others. It was all relative. But it kept us on our toes. You were constantly chasing something. For the regular starters, the chase was to hold on to their positions; for the subs, to break through; for the rest, it was to put themselves in a position where they had a chance of coming on in a game. If you dipped below the standards set for you, you not only let yourself down, but Liam too.

This was a guy who would go to the ends of the earth for us. Working with sport psychologist Caroline Currid, there were a number of sessions where players were encouraged to share their feelings with each other. In order to progress, they had to let themselves be vulnerable, and that's a difficult skill for most men. Liam and Caroline created an environment where players could be vulnerable but also feel safe.

Some of the other guys shocked me with some of the issues they had to deal with in their lives. Here was I thinking that I was messed up at times. I respected the people in the group a lot more as human beings after those sessions, which provided a glimpse into their souls. Caroline was good at her job. Players who wanted to talk to her did so of their own volition.

Our Munster championship campaign would culminate with victory over Waterford in the provincial final. It was another Munster medal, and the first time since 1989 that Tipp had put back-to-back titles together. It was a nice year to win it too as the GAA was celebrating 125 years in existence and the final was played on home soil in Thurles as part of the overall commemorations. Collecting the trophy in the New Stand, I looked down on the crowd and drank in every precious second. I wasn't taking success for granted any more. We had to earn it. Training was what I lived for. Medals were the reward.

Just like 2008, we faced a five-week gap before an All-Ireland semi-final but management wouldn't allow any looseness to set in. Normally after a championship game I didn't try too hard the following Tuesday night at training. It was more a case of flicking the ball around, working relatively hard and everything would be fine. Eamon spotted this. 'Hey, hey! All-Ireland semi-final in five weeks. We're starting tonight. Come on, come on! Not good enough!' I began to attack the ball, even in the puck-around, and that was a change.

There was just one small logistical problem that I could see: a planned training weekend clashed with a U2 concert at Croke Park, an event I was really looking forward to. I didn't tell Liam that I was going to miss it but I did mention it to Ger Ryan, our ultra-efficient logistics man, and he organized a couple of tickets for another of U2's gigs.

On the morning of the Limerick game, Liam asked three of us to speak about a theme with the rest of the group. Declan Fanning's was 'sacrifice' and he mentioned how I'd sacrificed the first U2 concert to attend the training weekend, and how this was a sign of commitment. I responded by saying that I couldn't wait for Tipperary people to see what I'd been looking at for the previous month in training, how they would marvel at our passion, technique and the style we now possessed, how the scoreboard would tick over at a rate of knots. We were shown a video of us doing our stuff on the pitch and I felt as though I was back on that bus again in Cork, outside Páirc Uí Chaoimh before Liam's first championship game in charge.

The All-Ireland semi-final against Limerick was the day when Eamon's 'Matrix' finally clicked into place. The fifteen players that started and the five subs that came on were all in perfect sync with each other. This was our moment of clarity, a moment I had not experienced since 2001.

22

Heartbreak

I understood the Matrix quicker than most because I was standing in a static position in the goalmouth. I was watching this thing unfold for a long time, blurred vision at first, but with every visit to our Carton House base, the fuzz cleared. This was Nirvana, the most sensational feeling on a hurling pitch, a consciousness that you're fulfilling your potential with each and every one of your teammates doing likewise at the same time. We knew it when we met in Portlaoise, when Eamon gathered the team together, when Liam addressed the subs, when we went out on the pitch. We were one unit with clarity of purpose, an unstoppable force.

Limerick were annihilated. We won by 6–19 to 2–7. The job was done and we were through to our first All-Ireland final in eight years. Kilkenny stood in our way, but we believed that hard work and continuous improvement were the keys to success. The middle third had to be won if we were to stand a chance. Get the ball through that area as quickly as possible and get at their full-back line with fast deliveries. That's where we felt Kilkenny were vulnerable, and we had to believe that there were chinks in their armour. We knew that they committed bodies to the middle of the field but logic suggested that when they did that, they left space in behind, which would allow our forwards to do their thing.

Any inside line with room to exploit should do well, no matter how good the full-back line is. Waterford had taught us that lesson in 2008, isolating our full-back line and targeting that area with deliveries that bypassed our half-back line. That was the model. Davy Fitzgerald had unlocked us then, but that was how we wanted to play and, in 2009, that's how we operated.

It was my first All-Ireland final since 2001. The game had evolved so much in eight years. We knew that Kilkenny would go for the jugular right from the start, like they had against Limerick and Waterford in previous finals, with Henry Shefflin on the edge of the square. If there are any early jitters, they will manifest themselves in that 10- to 15-yard radius around the goalmouth and, sure enough, Henry broke through for an early goal chance. He expected me to go to ground and that would allow him to flick the ball over me. But I stood tall and that left Henry with a decision to make. Stick or twist time. His eyes flashed to my left-hand corner and that allowed me to get down and flick the ball around the post. First battle of the day won.

Seamie Callanan took a fierce frontal charge from Jackie Tyrrell, but we expected that. We felt that Seamie would come in for some special treatment after the challenge that had broken Brian Hogan's collarbone in the League final. Seamie was fair game. We were coming to fight and all was fair in love and war.

We were well in the match and what we wanted to achieve was slowly but surely coming to pass. What undid us on the day was the lack of a killer instinct in front of goal. Kilkenny's goalkeeper PJ Ryan produced a once-in-a-lifetime display and we lost Benny Dunne, who'd been making serious contributions coming off the bench, to a red card. I was very close to Benny and my heart went out to him. Tommy Walsh, who was struck, got up straight away in fairness to him, considering the belt he got. Benny and Tommy were marking each other when Brendan Maher sent a line ball into the Kilkenny half of the pitch. Benny pulled wildly and caught Tommy at chest height. I'll never forget Liam's reaction. He offered Benny a consoling pat on the back as he made his way back to the substitutes area he had vacated just minutes before. If that was another manager, he could have turned his arse, walked in the opposite direction and pointed the finger of blame at Benny for costing the team. But he didn't, he went out to meet him as he was coming off. It was as if Liam was saying 'right, it was a mistake, but I have your back, you're one of ours'.

I hadn't considered that refereeing decisions might influence the game and, while Benny could have no complaints, we were fuming when, shortly afterwards, Diarmuid Kirwan awarded Kilkenny a penalty. I'd always thought that the Kilkenny forwards would be the ones I'd have to worry about but the next thing you know, Kirwan has his arms spread wide for what he saw as a foul by Paul Curran on Richie Power outside the large rectangle. I'm waving my arms as well, in sheer disbelief, because I saw it completely differently, and I'm shouting: 'No way! Look at the big screen! No! Have a look up! Look up!' There is always a sense of indignation when a referee makes a decision with which you don't agree.

Henry struck the penalty over my left shoulder and I got a stick to it, thinking that I'd diverted it over the bar. Goal. But we were still in the game. Before Henry's penalty, I'd sent a pinpoint puckout to Noel McGrath and he'd stuck it over the bar to put us two points ahead with less than ten minutes left.

That score was just one of many plays in the game but it was born out of hours and hours of practice. It's one of my favourite memories as the hard work that had been put in, far from prying eyes, came to fruition on the biggest day of the hurling year.

It was all down to Eamon O'Shea. He had immensely improved this key aspect of my game. He gave me clear instruction, which was exactly what I wanted. He told me where the ball had to be hit, and he didn't just tell me that I had to hit it better, he showed me how to do it. 'Come here and I'll show you what to do. This is where I want the ball, this is the height I want it at, and this is the speed of delivery.' We worked on this every single night, and he allowed me the space to seek perfection. Eamon knew that I was obsessive, and after training in Thurles I'd travel home to the hurling wall in Ballybacon. I scrawled circles on it, one at the height of Paddy Stapleton's catching hand, another for Michael Cahill, another for Paul Curran and so on, each one representing a potential recipient of a short puckout. Striking, striking, striking. Night after night.

The rugby player Ronan O'Gara used visualization techniques throughout his career. I've heard that before he stood over a kick at goal he would visualize a circle between the uprights, and always aimed to kick the ball through the circle. The thinking behind that was that if Ronan viewed the posts as his target, and he was a foot outside, he's missed. But if he's a foot outside the circle, he still scores. I put my own slant on this form of psychology, using hula hoops stuck on the tops of wooden canes. Like the circles on the hurling wall, each cane represented the height of a defender, in the positions where they would stand on the pitch, and I'd work on fizzing ball after ball through the hoops. That was my own personal thing that nobody else knew about because if anybody saw me doing it they'd think I was off my head. When I was finished, I'd throw the canes and hula hoops into the ditch and fetch them out of there when I practised next.

That delivery to Noel McGrath was a stock puckout from my artillery, to hit between the two 65-metre lines, waist-high all the way. The ones that went to hand like that were honed in Dr Morris

Park and Ballybacon. We caught Kilkenny out with that one when Declan Fanning was down with cramp. Kirwan allowed play to continue, and with ball in hand I was looking for Noel, watching him moving. He could see my eyes as I looked towards the other side of the pitch, beckoning for a path to be cleared. I had to wait until Noel was in position, and with Declan receiving treatment, I had the perfect excuse to delay for a few seconds. Noel was set and I hit him on his right-hand side so that when he caught the ball, he could effortlessly turn and put the ball over the bar.

Eamon had given me that level of control because when he told me what he wanted from me in training, he wanted it better the next night. Eamon looks you in the eye and asks with that questioning tone in his voice – 'yeah, yeah?' If there was a night I wasn't present for squad training, I was at the hurling wall. I even had lights installed there so that I could get my work done when Pam and Paul were gone to bed. And that's the way it had to be, because on matchday it had to be perfection, or as close to perfection as was humanly possible.

Remember that we were dealing with Kilkenny here, trying to draw their wing-forwards 20 yards closer to our goal, to prevent them from shielding their wing-backs. It had to be pinpoint. If it went wrong, we just reset and went again and again, and kept on trying to win the match. 'On a given day it might not go right,' Eamon would say. 'But you keep trying to win the match.' If I didn't try something, he'd run down the sideline and ask why I hadn't.

At the other end of the field, our forwards moved into positions to collect longer puckouts because they were encouraged to take risks and not to fear mistakes. You went out and played more freely, more creatively, because nobody was going to give out to you. They would only give out to you if you didn't take a gamble.

On the training pitch, Eamon created makeshift boxes with cones. Then he'd tell me to hit the ball into the box. Darren

Gleeson and myself worked on that every night for ten or fifteen minutes. Then he'd place a player in such a way as to block our view of the box so that we had to hit the ball over that player's head and into the box.

What I had to get right was the pace and timing of my swing. I videoed myself in training, my phone stuck to a goalpost. As a goalkeeper, you're allowed a free strike of the ball and if you don't have a stock swing that you can call upon when needed, like a golfer, then you're not doing your job as far as I'm concerned. I studied the footage, listening to the sound of the ball off the hurley, watching the rhythm of the swing and where the hurley finished. When I swung, I followed through all of the time. My stick had to finish over my left ear, the same as a golf swing. I had to adapt and change but I was provided with an environment in which I could. What happens in many teams is that the collective is trained but the individual never, or rarely, is. But Eamon worked with me individually because my puckouts would be crucial to implementing the style of play he wanted. He identified that I would have the ball in my hand at least twenty times per match, with an uncontested free hit. So it made perfect sense to devote time to how I would deliver it. After all, you can't just tell a guy three days before a match where you want him to hit the ball. That could take a month, six weeks or even two months of practice and forward planning.

But despite all our good work, a goal against Kilkenny would prove elusive. I'm convinced that just one goal would have opened the floodgates, and we would have walked home. I still don't know how PJ saved Callanan's shot, and Eoin slipped when he had a real sight of goal. There was surface water at the Canal End as areas of the pitch had been re-sodded after the U2 concerts. When Martin Comerford scored a second Kilkenny goal after the penalty, we were spent. The tank had been emptied, but it still wasn't enough.

The full-time whistle brought sheer desolation as some of our shattered bodies collapsed on the turf. Paudie Maher was inconsolable. 'Come on, lad, get up. You can't be seen like this. We'll cry inside in the dressing room. Be proud, stand big. Don't show any weakness.' I had a feeling that we'd meet these fellas again and I didn't want a picture in the paper the next day of a Tipperary player with his face down in the dirt. That was not representative of the performance we had delivered, and certainly not representative of the season that Paudie had had.

In the dressing room, beside mirrors and washbasins, Shane McGrath was sitting up on the counter. I'd togged off under the hand-dryers. Shane had tears flowing down his face. The cynic in me has seen young fellas after losing big games and while you know that they care to a certain point, you wonder if they really, really hurt. I've been in dressing rooms where the odd one or two fellas cry because they're upset about the whole thing, and that's fine, but this was the end of the world as far as these lads were concerned. I'd never experienced this level of raw emotion. When we lost the 1997 All-Ireland final – and maybe it was because there were more experienced lads in the dressing room – I certainly didn't get that sense from them. But this was the end of two years of hard slog and we knew we could have won. Declan Fanning spoke about Benny and he spoke about family, and he vowed that our time would come again.

Benny was OK, though naturally down in himself and upset because he'd been sent off. In his own mind he would have felt that his sending off was the losing of the game. That wasn't how I felt. Not then, not now, not ever. We had enough to win that match even without Benny Dunne. We lost concentration, thought about where we were and the finishing line fast approaching. We had a little bit of the 'oh shit, we should be out of sight here' and we lost sight of the process.

When that happens against Kilkenny, one of their players is always likely to make an angled run, like Comerford did, and it's a goal. It was a little bit of history repeating from 2002, when DJ Carey cut through the middle of our defence in the All-Ireland semi-final and offloaded a pass to the goalscorer, Jimmy Coogan. In that second or two, and that's all it takes, they'll punish you if you switch off. Every single lapse of concentration is pounced on. That's why they win so many All-Ireland titles.

We had died with our boots on, and Tipperary supporters recognized that. We were afforded a round of applause by a line of them when we arrived at the Burlington Hotel later that night. Some of them were in tears but they were so proud. Liam spoke about our disappointment and his words nailed how we felt. He vowed to return twelve months later with the Liam MacCarthy Cup. He didn't say that looking for the big cheer, he said it with matter-of-fact pride.

We drowned our sorrows, and when next we saw some of those Kilkenny players in the flesh, blue and gold and black and amber had been replaced by casual attire as we socialized together on the All-Star tour to Buenos Aires in December 2009. PJ Ryan and I captained the respective teams and Kirwan refereed the exhibition match at the Hurling Club in Hurlingham. Kirwan was presented with his All-Ireland medal at a function there and the Kilkenny players gave him a standing ovation as he made his way up to collect it. We gave him one on the way back down. He didn't know where to look.

On those trips, players from rival counties can let their guard down, and have a laugh with each other. A few of the Tipperary and Kilkenny lads went drinking together and it just so happened that Comerford, a really funny guy, and Lar Corbett were in the mix. Larry mentioned the picture of Comerford after he scored the second goal in the final, looking up to the stand with the mad head on him. 'Martin, Jesus, the cut of your face,' Larry piped up. 'You're fair ugly in that picture! You must be gutted! This is a picture of you after scoring a goal in an All-Ireland final and your face is all over the place!'

Gorta was quick as a flash with his response. 'Look, Larry. Henry's on the telly all year warning ye . . .'

'About what?' enquired Larry.

'He was on that Lucozade ad telling ye about the last fifteen minutes, and ye didn't listen! That's not our fault, Larry!'

We all fell about the place laughing, and Larry wore a grin from ear to ear. Touché, Larry, touché.

As two distinct groups of players we got on well, but our rivalry had intensified. We knew that we had a team good enough to beat them. Kilkenny knew it too. They had won the four-in-a-row but they knew that they weren't guaranteed All-Ireland success on an annual basis any more. Peace was declared for a few days in the Argentine capital but it was a bit like the Christmas Truce in 1914, when British and German troops crossed trenches and played football with one another.

There was one night when my conviction that we would beat them was copper fastened. On the Monday after the final, a huge crowd greeted us on our return to Thurles. Liam delivered a message that reminded me of US President Barack Obama's first inauguration speech in January 2009. In it, Obama mentioned the ideals of renewal, continuity and unity. Liam's words stirred huge emotion in me. His temperature gauge was spot on. He knew not only what needed to be said to soothe our pain, but also to keep us in a position where we were ready for the next battle.

We disbanded to meet and greet family and friends before convening again in Noel Ryan's later that evening. A section of the pub had been cordoned off for us, and again, this was a new departure. This was our time. Players, family members and a few close friends only. Not many supporters, no crush. We drank and sang songs, all thirty players and backroom staff together as one happy family. It was a really special night, and we were comfortable in each other's company. But the pervading sense was that the job wasn't done. Sure, it was only right to celebrate the year the way we knew how, together. But I just knew, right there and then, that we were going to win the All-Ireland in 2010.

23

Joe

I took a phone call from a woman after we won the Munster hurling final in 2009. She was ringing on behalf of Joe Bourke, 'a very sick' boy in Templemore, and enquired if it might be possible for me to call to see him with the trophy. She told me that Joe was a big supporter of mine and a visit could brighten up his world. I was only too happy to oblige.

I called to my local hurley-maker, Jim O'Brien, to get a stick made for Joe before I made the trip. It was a small, autographed goalie's hurley, and I brought a signed sliotar for him too. When I arrived to the house, there were cars assembled in the driveway. My visit had been flagged well in advance but I didn't mind that: the locals who had obviously been alerted to my arrival had called to see the trophy too.

Nothing could have prepared me for the effect that this little man would have on my life. Joe was suffering from a condition known as neuroblastoma, a rare form of childhood cancer. It was plain to see that Joe was very ill as he had visible tumours protruding from his head. Apart from that, he seemed just like any other young child. He could walk and talk, though I noticed how he was bumping into furniture in the sitting room. Not only was Joe suffering from cancer, he was also blind.

Because he couldn't see, he didn't believe that it was Brendan Cummins who had called to see him.

'No, it's not Brendan Cummins.'

'It is me, Joe. I brought you a hurley and ball.'

I felt a little bit silly after saying that because Joe would surely have no use for these items. What I could do for Joe was simply to spend some time with him, and he sat beside me on the sofa in the sitting room of his house for the duration of my visit.

'Joe, you'll be hurling with Tipp some day,' I told him, because that was his dream. He wanted to be a full-forward, his favourite position.

It was a humbling experience as we had pictures taken with the cup and I left Joe's house that night with a collection of precious memories in tow.

I didn't hear from the family after that until Christmas time, when I was told that Joe had suffered a setback and that his outlook was bleak. He died in January 2010, and I called to the house again to pay my respects. Another queue of people had formed outside but for a very different reason this time. Just a few months earlier we were there to celebrate Joe's bravery and the Munster hurling trophy but now we had gathered to say our goodbyes to him.

Joe's brother, Tom, who was five or six years of age, met me at the front door. I told him that I was so sorry about what had happened and how he was so brave. I turned a corner to enter the room where Joe was laid out, and the sight that greeted me is forever etched in my mind. In the coffin alongside Joe were the hurley and ball I had given him on my summer visit. Tears began to flow, and meeting his mother and father again was incredibly difficult. I had my own young boy, Paul, and these two wonderful people had lost their son. It was awful. The day of Joe's wake also happened to be Paul's birthday. He probably wondered why I was hugging him so much when I arrived back from Joe's house.

Joe's parents have had another child since, healthy and well, but his memory will never fade in their minds. Catherine and Mike named their daughter April, after the month in which Joe was born. What struck me most about him was that, despite his sickness, he wasn't afraid of the dark.

I told my story about meeting Joe at a team get-together in Carton House in April 2010. Our sport psychologist Caroline Currid had recognized that the group was still carrying the hurt of our All-Ireland final defeat from 2009, hurt that had to be lanced. I just about held it together as I recounted meeting Joe for the first time, and being present in his house for the wake. The reason I spoke about him was to provide a sense of perspective. This was hurling, and each and every one of us in that room was blessed with an ability to play it. Having been offered a glimpse into Joe's world, and the cross that he had carried all of his short life, I knew we were extremely fortunate and, having been blessed with the skill and opportunity required to play for Tipperary, it would be a travesty to waste it. At times of doubt, I thought about Joe and how he wasn't afraid of the dark. That's quite a big thing to get your head around, when you find yourself consumed by trivial matters that seem overwhelming. If I closed my eyes for five minutes and attempted to walk around I don't think I'd manage too well, and from the moment I met Joe, the sense of adversity I felt before a championship match paled into insignificance. Sadly, Joe would never get the chance to play for Tipperary as his life was cut short, long before it should have been. What I could do for him was carry his spirit into battle. The symbol we wore on the backs of our 2010 championship jerseys neatly summed up everything that Tipperary hurling stood for that year. At shoulder height, neatly stitched into the fabric, was a circle containing the letters F and R. F for freedom, R for redemption.

The dictionary definition of 'freedom' describes it as the power or right to act, speak or think as one wants, the state of not being imprisoned or enslaved. That summed us up. We were free to express ourselves on the field of play.

Redemption is defined as the action of being saved from sin, error or evil, the action of regaining or gaining possession of something for payment, or clearing of a debt.

The only error we had made against Kilkenny in the 2009 All-Ireland final was not winning the game, but we did have a debt to clear. We owed it to ourselves to go one step further and to be redeemed, to atone for what had happened and bring ourselves to a state of deliverance.

On the Los Angeles leg of our team holiday in January 2010, I trained on both mornings. It was glorious there, with the famous Ferris Wheel and people gliding past on roller-skates.

In San Diego, I went for a run with Benny Dunne on our first day there, around the marina and back to base via the beach. In the evenings, I took it up a notch. After finding a quiet area on the beach, I drew lines in the sand with the heels of my runners. Shuttle runs and accelerations until I nearly dropped. 'Don't break the line.' When I had finished, there was no mark where my foot had stopped before the line.

What I didn't realize was that Eamon O'Shea was walking the beach. A couple of years later, in a quiet moment, he said to me, 'I saw you training in San Diego.'

It was gorgeous in the evenings, cool with the sun going down and the sound of waves breaking on the beach. It was murderous stuff but the voice in my head was in overdrive. 'We're not finished. I want those last few minutes against Kilkenny back, and when we get them again, we'll be ready.' There was something burning in each and every one of us.

Clever, subtle messages were the order of the day. Johnny Cash's 'Redemption Song' was played on the bus to matches. It seemed like the tune was everywhere. Mick Clohessy was humming it as he got to work on tight muscles on the massage table. That song was effectively embedded in our DNA. This was about more than just playing for Tipperary. This was our life.

Liam Sheedy recognized that we couldn't afford to peak too soon and so, like a trainer would do with a good racehorse, he held us back. That might be a reason why we were hammered by ten points against Cork in the first round of the Munster championship at Páirc Uí Chaoimh. Mentally, we were steeling ourselves for other challenges that would come further down the road. Only when the pressure was at its most intense, with the spectre of championship elimination hanging over us, would we really perform.

Our first game of the New Year was a Waterford Crystal Cup fixture against Clare in Borrisoleigh. We were not long back from holidays and merely fulfilling a fixture, still coming to terms with our All-Ireland final hangover. Clare beat us by a couple of points with a fine bunch of hungry young players.

It wasn't the end of the world, far from it. It showed growing maturity on our part that we could contextualize a defeat like that. The Waterford Crystal Cup was a big deal for us in previous seasons. We won it in 2007 and 2008 at a time when players felt they needed to perform well to ensure they were in contention for the National League.

We lost heavily to Dublin in our opening League match in February but we beat Kilkenny in a rearranged fixture at Semple Stadium a week later. The game had been postponed twice due to adverse weather conditions. On the first night we were due to play them I was particularly nervous and actually pleased when it was postponed. The match was called off for a second time on 20 February and management used the opportunity to put us through our paces with a savage training session.

This was an evening when fresh battle-lines were drawn with Kilkenny. They trained at the other end of Dr Morris Park, with no more than 40 yards separating the rival camps. Nobody could know how the year would pan out but we knew that if we were going to reach the Holy Grail, we would have to go through them.

The League fixture finally went ahead at the third time of asking, on 7 March, and this was another opportunity to show Kilkenny that they were playing a new Tipperary. No longer were we a team that was complacent, we wanted to win every game – a mirror-image of Kilkenny.

Liam clashed with Brian Cody on the touchline and there was no backing down. We won by four points.

In the dressing room, the air was one of contentment, but there was a certain emptiness too. We'd won, and that was great, but Kilkenny weren't hurting next door like we had been the previous September. It was just a League game after all, and that wasn't enough. We hadn't exorcized any real demons.

We finished our League campaign with four victories from seven outings – not enough to finish in the top two and thereby qualify for the final. Bar that Kilkenny game, the League was largely an irrelevance in the greater scheme of things. Championship was the be all and end all, but our planned warm-weather training camp in Spain was cancelled in April because of the volcanic ash cloud. We went to Carton House instead, a familiar haunt. The atmosphere was good.

That was when I spoke about Joe, to get across a message about what bravery really meant.

One of our players was a very quiet character, a guy who would rarely display outward emotion. You would know in his eyes that there was something different about him by the way he played the game and held his position. He knew that he possessed ability and dogged determination, he just didn't express that too often. He spoke about how he felt he had let his best friend and teammate down on the day of the All-Ireland final.

Now I knew that these two lads were close, but I didn't fully comprehend until then just how tight the bond between them really was.

Tears ran down his face as he described walking into the Burlington Hotel and seeing his friend's mother there. The word he used to describe that moment was 'shame'. He could see the effect that defeat had had on his friend's mother, who was also in tears. This woman's tears were born primarily out of pride, but after losing an All-Ireland final, players become introverted, reflecting on what they did wrong in a match. Emotion wavers somewhere between pride and hurt – pride that you did so well and hurt that the guys around you lost.

I felt that my teammates were hurt and that, as one of the more senior players, I needed to protect them. I compared myself to an army officer in the trenches when a grenade is thrown in and kills three of his troops. There is nothing the officer could have done to prevent that from happening but he thinks that he could have fallen on the grenade to save his men. I had enough ability, enough experience and had done enough training to influence what went on out on the pitch.

In truth, there was nothing more I could have done, though maybe I could have helped our players to relax after Kilkenny scored the penalty goal because within a minute, Martin Comerford stuck the ball in the back of our net for their second goal.

What I had learned from the motivational speaker and author Declan Coyle helped me to cope with these thoughts. He explained to me that even if you're sitting alone in a dark room, the human mind will generate a problem because the mind is a problem-solving machine. That's why it's so important to stay in the present, allowing your mind to solve problems for you that may surface at that very second. It needs to be trained to work forward, because looking back is not helpful. You can look back, sure, but don't dwell on it.

It was a difficult circle to sit in. Liam, Mick and Eamon spoke too, and it was a draining experience. Every single person in the room was obliged to talk but this wasn't a problem because we were so comfortable with each other.

It was a feeling I hadn't experienced since 2001, and another good example of Liam's management skills. As an older player, I was so clear about what I was looking for and how I hoped to achieve my goals. This was individual to me, however, and it was difficult for me to focus the minds of other players. But that's a hallmark of a control freak and, besides, it wasn't my job, it was Liam's. Everybody would get there, some quickly, others slowly, and Liam's one-on-one work with players ensured that.

Before our first championship fixture against Cork we wore GPS trackers in training, an idea that Liam had floated as far back as November at an event in Dungarvan, where I received the 2009 Munster GAA Hurler of the Year award. A number of Premier League soccer clubs had been using this technology, which allowed managers to ascertain how much effort players were putting in at training. It was still a relatively new concept in the GAA but Liam was a visionary, and if it could help us to become better, he was all for it.

Wearing the tracker acted as a psychological spur for everybody. I ran everywhere. Due to illness, I missed one of the training sessions but took the opportunity to sit in with the guys monitoring the results on their laptops. This technology could show in visual form a player's effort levels, moving from blue to amber to orange, and finally into the red to represent high work. The quicker the bar returned to blue, the fitter the player because his recovery rate was swift.

There was a wealth of other useful information to be mined from these devices. Two weeks after the Munster championship defeat to Cork, I asked for Paudie Maher's stats from the first half. The information showed that the vast majority of runs Paudie made were into the D, that 13-metre area of semi-circular space outside the 20-metre line, were at top speed and in the red zone to indicate high effort.

I knew there and then that we had been caught out badly by Cork, whose tactic was to place long deliveries into the D, allowing their full-forward Aisake Ó hAilpín to start his run from outside that area, and collect the ball there. That was Cork's gameplan, and in fairness to them, it worked a treat. We applied little pressure within 40 yards of their goal, which allowed a Cork defender to collect a short puckout and bypass our strong half-back line with a long ball. Paudie had played at full-back at underage level but he was uncomfortable in this position as a senior player and was cleaned out by Ó hAilpín. We were only two points down at half-time but Ó hAilpín scored a second-half goal and Cork cruised to victory.

It was one of those really shitty days at the office, and we met at the Horse and Jockey a couple of nights later to sift through the wreckage. There was plenty of talk but most of it was hot air as far as I could gauge. Some players insisted that this was a one-off, and that it wouldn't happen again. The general mood was that we had been in an All-Ireland final in 2009 and that we'd get back there again.

I let it go for as long as I could but I couldn't hold my counsel all night and decided to speak.

'We're about as far away from winning an All-Ireland as Carlow are,' I said.

One of the lads, who should have known better, responded, 'We're only amateurs,' and I almost cracked up.

'Are you feeling OK?' I hit back. 'Am I in the right place?'

A man I'd seen crying in that dressing room last September was now hiding under the 'amateur' cloak.

I wasn't happy either with the socializing in Cork on the Sunday night. Not many of us were on the bus on the way home to Tipperary and I was led to believe that some of our lads were drinking with Cork players. I brought this up, and made my feelings clear. I was unhappy that some players were nursing hangovers on Monday when I was training.

Call it the moral high ground if you like, but I was right. I had trained on the Monday while others were nursing hangovers.

My words had the desired effect because the meeting changed from a problem-based gathering to a more solution-focused one. The rest of the group took what I had to say on the collective chin. I had come out swinging and connected with a knockout punch. They understood that I had spoken the truth and sometimes when you do that, it doesn't really matter how people take it initially. The important thing is that the truth is spoken.

It wasn't the case that our standards had slipped. We were more caught up in chasing results and scoreboards rather than focusing on the process that would allow us to achieve those numbers. Get a performance first and foremost and the results will invariably follow if it's good enough.

Liam remained calm. 'Look, we don't know who we'll be playing next but we're going to hit this with everything we have. It's knockout from now on, no second chances.'

In our first qualifier against Wexford in Thurles, I came out to a ball in the second half, went to pick it up but made a mess of it. I followed that up with a loose handpass, and even though this was at a time when we were well in control of the game, Liam came storming down the line to let me have it. I waved a hand in acknowledgement. It was unacceptable.

Patrick 'Bonner' Maher made his championship debut in the Wexford game, and many will remember how Eoin Kelly and Lar Corbett very publicly admonished him on the field of play for not giving a pass to one of his better-placed teammates. Some might have felt that was harsh treatment at the time for such a young player but I had no issue with it. It was corrective and necessary. In the dressing room after the game, Eoin and Larry sat on either side of Bonner, both of them explaining that when we got to Croke Park, we might only get one or two of those opportunities in the entire game, and that we had to make them count.

Declan Fanning spoke about the next game in two weeks' time and urged the lads to refrain from alcohol. 'We'll go home tonight, recover tomorrow and train on Tuesday,' he said, bearing an ugly battle wound on his ear that required twenty-five stitches.

Offaly were next on the list, in Portlaoise, and while we never hit the real heights, we won by six points and the team was moving. Almost everything that we did appeared athletic and purposeful. Players were now hurling with a freedom, working off instinct and not over-thinking it like we had against Cork, which was almost mechanical in nature. With those first two hurdles negotiated, the stakes rose higher as the All-Ireland quarter-final draw pitted us with Galway. We were now off the life-support machine.

Joe Canning scored a penalty goal, a rocket to my right that hit the net like a steam train. Entering the final minutes, we were two points down and in serious danger of elimination. But there was still hope. Eoin had spoken about all of the times he had seen

Tipperary supporters drift out of Croke Park when that familiar 'bing bong' came over the tannoy as the public address announcer urged stewards to proceed to their end-of-match positions. That was normally the signal for our supporters to head for the exits, but it would be different this time. 'The very minute that bing bong comes,' Eoin began, 'we put on the turbo.' And every time I saw those men in the hi-vis jackets circling the perimeter of the pitch, I sensed that something special was about to happen.

Eamon passed by the goals when we were two points down and nodded. 'We're going to win this,' he said, and kept moving. I must admit that I had my doubts because we were in a serious hole. I knew that we had the ability if we caught a break, and we did when Galway's key defender Ollie Canning went off injured after Eoin caught him with a late swipe at the Canal End. Eamon continued his lap of the pitch, filling every player that made eye contact with a renewed sense of confidence.

I hit a puckout to John O'Brien, who'd given me the nod, and Johnno swung it over the bar. Pa Bourke was on and his first contribution set up Gearóid Ryan for the equalizer. Pa was at it again for the winner, teeing up Lar Corbett who manoeuvred himself into position to get his shot away. We held out in a frantic finish, and at the final whistle I fell to my knees. We'd finally beaten Galway, a team I rarely felt was good enough to win the All-Ireland but who could scupper your own ambitions. Despite Galway's annual shortcomings, we were rarely good enough to get over them, but we'd jumped this fence and it was a massive breakthrough. How many times can you recall a championship game over the past twenty years when a Tipp team scrambled out of a situation like that? I've only been involved in two, that Galway game and the victory over Clare in 2001. It's a great feeling when you hit that finishing line and dip your head just before your opponent.

It's not a fluke when you win a match by a point. It boils down to a collective spirit and consciousness to do the right thing, at the right time. We didn't have that for years, and that was the gap that separated us from the rest. As individuals we possessed good skills, but collectively we didn't knit together. John O'Brien's great fielding wouldn't knit with the killer pass that Larry looked for. But now we were in sync.

There was still one hurdle to jump before returning to an All-Ireland final, a Waterford team coming in as Munster champions. A young player named Brian O'Halloran was drafted into their starting team and I smelled blood from the start. I looked him in the eye and sensed that it was over for Brian before it had even begun. He was a kid thrown in at the deep end and was substituted in the twenty-second minute. His eyes were glazed over and I prayed that Paul Curran wouldn't touch him, to knock him out of the trance he found himself in. If Brian was hit, maybe that would have made him angry and he would have performed, but from a Tipp perspective, he was fine the way he was. It's different when it's a Kilkenny player: you take up position before throw-in and they'll look straight back at you, intent burning in their eyes. We beat Waterford comfortably, and our puckout strategy was on the money. We decided to go with short ones because Waterford were expected to sit back, which they did. Eamon trotted in ten minutes into the second half and we opted to go long with the puckouts, to see how they would work. At that stage in the game we were well in control.

I was drug-tested after the game and it took what felt like for ever to produce a urine sample. Dehydration was one problem but stage fright was another. I had my pants around my ankles as the tester watched my every move until I delivered what he was looking for. After one aborted attempt I walked back on to the pitch, sipping water, but having failed to provide the sample initially, there was more paperwork involved, as I had to effectively 'sign in' again. For an amateur player, I found this a little extreme. Eventually, I got the job done.

We retired to Thurles that night and it was time to celebrate, which was important. There is a time for socializing during the course of a season but only in an organized and sensible fashion. This was another hallmark of Liam's reign and stemmed from a team-bonding trip to Wales shortly after his appointment. I had my initial reservations at the time about a group of boisterous young men leaving the country for a weekend away on the tiles but the lads behaved themselves; nobody was swinging from hotel chandeliers, downing shots or tearing their clothes off.

A question went round the group on that trip, one that seemed simple enough but required some thought: 'Why are you playing for Tipperary?' Some guys spoke about the excitement that pulling on the Tipperary jersey generated in them, what it did for their parish, the people around them, their families. It came to my turn. 'The reason I'm here,' I began, 'is that when the time comes for me to go back up into the stand and look on as a spectator, I can look down at ye guys on the pitch and still feel part of it, because in some small way I'll have helped ye to develop into players whose deeds will be remembered for ever.'

For me, the prospect of winning another All-Ireland title was a huge motivating factor but I didn't want to leave a group with massive potential without trying to shape them in some way. Far too many times I had seen a promising young player make the same mistakes that had stunted the progress of those that had gone before him, so I tried to lead by example. If I set the bar high for myself, they would have no choice but to strive to reach it. It's why remaining unbeaten in those 20-metre sprints during fitness tests was so important to me – though it was about much more than that. It was about respect for yourself and, more importantly, respect for the man beside you. If you conduct yourself in the correct fashion off the field of play, there's a good chance you'll carry those values and beliefs with you on a Sunday afternoon when the ball is thrown in.

In the heat of battle, the guy beside you is all you have. Standing there in front of eighty-two thousand spectators and millions more tuned in around the world, the three lads in the full-back line were all I had. If they didn't hear me, and I didn't hear them, we were alone, and that's the last thing you want. There's safety in numbers, feeling that you're doing something for the guy beside you. Eoin Kelly had a great saying, that if you were nervous before a game, you were thinking about yourself. It's a good way to look at things. You should think about the man beside you instead and that helps to shift the attention away from yourself.

We needed to look after each other because the biggest challenge of all awaited us in the 2010 All-Ireland final: Kilkenny, hunting a fifth successive All-Ireland title, the team labelled as the greatest of all time.

The pre-match talk centred on their star forward, Henry Shefflin, and that suited us just fine. Henry had torn the cruciate ligament in his left knee in the semi-final against Cork but, remarkably, it seemed there was a chance that he would play against us. Still, this was talk that we had to steer clear of, and in reality, what Kilkenny were or weren't doing at their Nowlan Park base was of absolutely no relevance to our preparations. Holed up in our Carton House base, the comedian Pat Shortt was on hand to provide some light entertainment, with his sidekick dressed in a Kilkenny shirt as Pat gave him the occasional kick in the backside. We needed that touch of escapism, that stimulus, and Shortt provided it in his own unique style. It wasn't a case of trying to take the power out of the Kilkenny shirt in any way. To me, they were the team standing in the way of me winning an All-Ireland, and as I had said to the lads in Wales, this was an achievement that could set them up for the rest of their careers.

On the training pitch, Eamon gathered the goalkeepers and defenders together for a chat about Kilkenny. He wanted to talk about the challenge that lay in store. It was an exercise in visualization. 'Eoin Larkin will stand here, Henry, for however long he lasts, will be here,' he explained, pointing to the areas of the field where our Kilkenny opponents would be situated. Eamon had Kilkenny pretty well figured out, to the point where he could almost second-guess their intentions.

We had a feeling that Henry wouldn't go the distance. Dr Murchin's medical opinion was that he was unlikely to last much longer than ten minutes, given the severity of the injury. We took that as reliable information because if Dr Murchin tells you that you're going to die in ten minutes, it's probably wise that you grab your phone and say goodbye to your friends.

Apart from that, there was very little talk about Henry. It was more about the overall threat that Kilkenny posed. We talked about Kilkenny as a collective rather than as individuals. We had to bring their house of cards tumbling to the ground, and the way to do that was to attack their main pillars, wing-backs Tommy Walsh and JJ Delaney, at numbers 5 and 7. We had to get Bonner Maher into the game, and if his marker, Walsh, was turning in the opposite direction, facing his own goal, we were in business.

As we pucked around on the training pitch, Eamon shuffled over to me.

'Listen, can you hear it?'

'Hear what?'

'Nothing, silence. There were fifteen thousand people in Nowlan Park watching them train.'

Classic Eamon, and Kilkenny were set up. I always felt there would come a time when we had them on the edge of a cliff, but to make sure that they were terminated, we had to follow them down. Previously we would have talked about pushing them over the edge, and while we did that in 2009, they somehow grabbed a foothold and clambered their way back to the top. This time we must push them over and follow them all the way down to make sure that they hit the ground first. We knew we were going to die, metaphorically, but they had to die first. That's real commitment, but it was the only way we would arrive back to Thurles on the Monday evening after the final with the one thing that was missing twelve months earlier, the Liam MacCarthy Cup.

Pre-match preparation was so forensic that we even managed to address a psychological issue that had haunted us for some time. We generally struggled to manage big leads in games, allowing teams to catch up after we had put ourselves in seemingly unassailable positions. The reason why I felt we didn't hold on to leads was that when we pushed ahead, the crowd went quiet, and we were so used to playing in feverish atmospheres that when the voices died, our minds dipped. It was as if, subconsciously, we thought the job was done because nobody was shouting any more. When the opposition scored what looked like a consolation point, an almost sympathetic ripple of applause greeted it, but before we knew it, an eight-point lead had been whittled down to two and we were on the ropes.

Driving by Semple Stadium in the weeks before the All-Ireland final, you'd have heard recorded crowd noise from a football match between Dublin and Kerry at Croke Park blaring over the public address system as we trained. This was Liam's idea. The noise was so loud that my full-back, Paul Curran, would struggle to hear me when I shouted, no more than 10 yards away. What the noise did was allow us to operate in an environment where we couldn't hear ourselves think. Liam would raise his hands to the press box in Semple Stadium and that was the signal for the volume to crank up a notch or two.

It was powerful stuff because it was noise that I recognized instantly. The hairs on the back of my neck stood up and my senses were alive. I was in Croke Park, and in those training matches I never played badly. Liam would turn off the noise for spells and the players were told not to speak when the game was in progress. On one occasion, Seamus Callanan burst through and drove the ball wide from 30 yards. It was the kind of situation that Seamus relished but it opened our eyes to a realization that when crowd levels dropped, our minds followed. If the roar was there, Callanan would have ripped the net in half. Liam usually played the crowd noise for twenty or twenty-five minutes before the silent game, when you made decisions based on instinct alone. The trick was to have a teammate moving into a position where he was in your peripheral vision because unless he did that, he wasn't in the game as far as you were concerned.

The quest for excellence was collective but also very much individual. It's what made me place a fruit bowl over the fridge in the kitchen, instead of indulging in my number one vice, chocolate. It's what made me go to the gym three times a week when I didn't want to; it's what made me practise for hours on end in the ball alley. Kilkenny made me do all of that because I didn't want to end up meeting them and making a show of myself. To face down Kilkenny, they have to see you as equal to, if not better than, them.

After our final training spin in Thurles on the Thursday evening before the final, we converged in a huddle on the New Stand side of Semple Stadium. We spoke a few words about ourselves, hydration, how the tickets had been distributed to family and friends. The boxes were ticked and now it was up to us. Our kitman, John 'Hotpoint' Hayes, ran across the pitch and dipped his head to join the circle.

'Lads, I have something to tell ye. I don't want to tell ye but I'm going to now. Last year, I walked into the medical room in Croke Park after the final and I saw Eamon O'Shea crying. That man can't cry again this year.'

My head almost exploded. It cut me to the bone to think that Eamon could be that upset. It would be like somebody going down to my son Paul's bedroom and giving him a kick – that same repulsive feeling in the pit of my stomach. Hotpoint left the circle and ran back to finish what he had been doing.

Eoin Kelly broke the silence. 'Lads, that can't happen again.'

24

Seamie

Seamus Callanan should have been an All-Star in 2008 or 2009, take your pick, but after two incredible seasons that announced his arrival as a star of the future, he was now coming to terms with the fact that he wouldn't be starting in the All-Ireland final against Kilkenny. It can happen that way sometimes for a young player who blazes a trail but isn't rewarded with individual accolades. He can doubt the process, and when that happens he loses himself somewhere along the line and it can take a while for top form to return. I suspect that's what happened to Seamie but his reaction to being left out of the team was sensational and told me everything I needed to know about his character.

As we togged off in the dressing room after our final training session, Seamie took the opportunity to address the group. 'I know that I'm not playing,' he began. 'But I don't care that I'm not. I just want Tipperary to win and I'm telling you that when I come on, I'm going to give this team some lift. I'm behind everybody all of the way from now until Sunday at 3.30 when we start the job. I'll be coming on to finish the job and I can't wait to pass the fella who's coming off, wrecked from trying so hard. And I'm going to go in and finish it.'

It was the perfect note on which to go our separate ways, and from that moment until I saw the lads again in Portlaoise on the Sunday morning, it was time for mental preparation. On the Friday, I took a half-day from work and went for a walk in the afternoon at 3.30, to get a feel for what the light was like at that time of day. Bear in mind that we trained in the evening and the afternoon light bounces a different kind of glare on the senses. It's not that much of a difference, mind you, but in a world where a fraction becomes a slice and then a chasm if you're not careful, every little detail helps. I gazed skywards and looked at the clouds drifting across the sky, wondering where the sun would hit me from on Sunday. The grass was cut at home, just like that freshly cut grass I'd walk on at Croke Park.

Sunday morning brought with it the hint of evening promise. It's All-Ireland final day. After meeting in Portlaoise, we boarded the team coach that would ferry us to Dublin, a place of freedom and redemption. The motorway to Dublin reached gridlock when Kilkenny supporters came off the M9 to join the Tipperary hordes making their way to the capital on the M7. A garda escort took us up the slow lane as the rain trickled down the window panes. Rain wasn't what I wanted to see but I reassured myself by thinking that I normally played well in wet conditions. It was a time for positive thinking. I told myself that I loved the rain when, in truth, I hated it. Kilkenny and Tipperary fans beeped their car horns, waved or uttered expletives, depending on whether your vehicle was decked out in our own blue and gold or black and amber, the Kilkenny colours. I listened to The Script on my headphones on the coach and that relaxed me.

When we reached our base at the Radisson Blu St Helen's Hotel in Dublin, I walked out the back of the hotel and rang Pam. 'What's the atmosphere like around town?' I enquired. It was a brief chat before Pam wished me the usual 'best of luck'. The phone went on airplane mode after that – my trigger to shut out the rest of the world. I was here to perform now.

Lactic acid built in my forearms as I paced a circuit outside the hotel. I moved my fingers, kept walking, took in the air and looked skywards, feeling the rain on my face. My tracksuit top was zipped up to the last, just how I liked it, that feeling of it around my neck providing a sense of security, like I was locking in everything until 3.30 and then it was time to release.

Two weeks before the final, Liam had asked every player to describe each of his teammates in two words. We duly completed the exercise, handed the sheet of paper back to Liam and thought no more about it. On the bus from the hotel to Croke Park, we were handed an envelope with a card inside signed by Liam, Eamon and Mick Ryan. There was an individual message for each player, and mine read: 'We believe in you, just be yourself.' The envelope also contained an A4 page with twenty-nine comments from teammates. I looked around the bus and witnessed a chain reaction as envelopes were torn open and players read what their peers had said about them.

Those moments created an inferno of emotion that felt like it could almost blow up the bus, but emotion alone was not going to win us the game. I remembered what Eoin had said about being nervous, that if you were it was a sign that you were thinking about yourself. Suddenly, I was thinking about everybody else on the bus, about the responsibility I had to those people to concentrate and be the best that I could be – unbeatable. 'Leader', 'father figure' and 'best trainer' were some of the words the lads had used to describe me, words that really mean something when they're written down by your teammates, all of them younger than me.

There was a real sense of destiny about what we were doing. All roads led to Croke Park, and we were ready to be there. I knew that we were going to win the All-Ireland. It wasn't a cocky feeling. We had reached a point where it was almost inevitable. Everything was right, and when that's the case in Tipperary, we win. If we don't, it's because something is wrong somewhere along the line. It's why Kilkenny win so much because, in their camp, every-thing is right nine times out of ten. In other counties it might be six out of ten, and in a year when they win an All-Ireland that figure might rise as high as eight. If it's nine out of ten, you win multiple All-Ireland titles, like Kilkenny have. We had that feeling now.

I'd said to Hotpoint that I wanted to sit in the dressing room before the game this time. Normally I'd tog out in a more private area because my preparation was designed to get me ready for the battle between me and the ball. I wasn't like an outfield player, who would be facing a direct opponent, so I needed to be outside the group, getting myself right. The group will ultimately win the game, but what the individual brings to that group is a vital component. The way I saw it, if I was in that dressing room for too long and looking at a guy who I suspected was not 'on point', that would affect me in a negative way. In Thurles, I was always in the dressing room with the group because it was like walking into my sitting room at home – there was a familiarity to and comfort about the place. At other venues I focused on my mental preparation separately, before joining my teammates.

Lar Corbett smiled as I sat down beside him.

'What are you doing in here? It must be a fucking big occasion if you're togging off with us!'

I pulled on my gear and went outside to watch some of the minor game. It was good to feel the fresh air on my face because for the last few hours I'd been breathing in air from the bus, the hotel, the dressing room and the tunnel. There was a quick realization looking out that this pitch was bloody small on matchday, the crowd almost in on top of you, the stands feeling like a vast dome above your head.

Seven days before the final, Croke Park was the furthest thing from my mind. When we'd returned home from Carton House, I was sitting at home thinking about the match and it was one of those rare moments when I felt uncomfortable in my own skin. I dragged myself off the couch, pulled on my training gear and went for a run up the mountain – purgatory in November but a joy now.

At a particular point on the run you hit a crossroads, and I met Thomas O'Leary there, our club chairman. I had the headphones on but I could still hear Thomas shouting over to me, with a broad grin on his face.

'Are you playing midfield on Sunday or something?' he roared.

'Yeah, I can't wait! Hanging for it!'

On I went, and a stretch in the road that would really test me in November came into view. It's where you really have to grit your teeth and avoid the temptation to walk for a bit, but while you're having the argument with yourself, you're over the hump and away. What a gorgeous day that was. As I ran, I felt a power surge inside me, a crystal-clear sense of place. This was my home, where I put in some of my hardest training. I couldn't wait to represent the people of my parish.

Coming down the mountain, I was moving particularly well, but that meant I was going faster and my feet weren't so much running, more stopping me from falling over. I reached the bottom and pushed on a bit more, in full flow as I listened to the music on my earphones.

Back home, I towelled the sweat from my brow, showered, and

emerged from the bathroom feeling energized. Despite my aching feet, I had savoured each and every step along that stretch of terrain. I knew I was ready for what was coming.

25

Freedom and Redemption

A few things make me feel at home at Croke Park. I run out on to the pitch and hit the ball three times in the air and catch it each time, feeling the sensation of my body leaving the ground as I rise in the air. My feet hit the ground as I return to earth and the thud reverberates through my feet and up through my shins. Senses are activated, and that works for me.

Another one is the double blink. When I do something well in training, like a good save or an accurate puckout, I blink twice. That locks in the good feeling, and with ball in hand before taking a puckout in a match situation, the double blink rolls the happy film in my head.

In the latter years of my career with Tipperary I also became aware of the trails aeroplanes left in the sky. At Páirc Uí Chaoimh, for example, the planes flew over the uncovered stand, heading for Cork airport. At Croke Park they travelled behind Hill 16, bound for Dublin airport. When training in Thurles, I'd often tune in to the sound of a plane between 7.30 p.m. and 7.45 p.m., and when I heard another one later I'd know that there were roughly twenty minutes left in the session. In the cauldron of a heaving stadium I often looked to the sky to catch a glimpse of these plumes left by aircraft. They provided me with a moment of escapism, gave me a sense that there was more going on in the world than just this game I was immersed in.

These are little quirks that are very individual to me, but they make me feel good. Hopefully they'll work today. We're just minutes away from throw-in as I adjust the collar of my goal-keeper's jersey to make sure the Manchester United top is tucked in underneath. I don't want it sticking out because that would just look stupid.

I'm standing beside Paddy Stapleton, my roommate when we're cooped up in hotels, and that familiarity is good as we prepare to meet President Mary McAleese in the pre-match formalities. The parade starts, and I extend my two arms straight out as my fore-arms have filled with that damned lactic acid again. The extension provides immediate release. The parade passes by the Cusack Stand but, while I will be told later that we really looked like we were 'in the zone', all I can think about is how sore my bloody feet are.

I glance quickly across at the line of Kilkenny players walking alongside us in single file, two tribes separated by just a few yards. And I'm thinking that none of them, this time last Sunday, were running 6 miles up and down a mountain; none of them have that kind of commitment this year. By fuck, they're not taking this off me, not today.

I focus on our captain Eoin Kelly, number 14 on his back and that symbol between his shoulders, freedom and redemption. Together, we slowly pulled our jerseys on in the dressing room before the game, reaching halfway before Liam urged us to stop for a moment.

'Look at the circle, boys, that's us. That's what we're bringing today. Freedom and redemption. If ever you have any doubt today, and some of you will have doubts, you'll look at the back of your friend's neck and that will tell you why you're here.'

Eoin's our captain, our on-field leader, and he's always been very good to me. A few weeks before the final, he asked me why I wasn't taking any of the frees. 'I've seen you putting the ball over the bar from almost your own 20-metre line in club matches, why don't you do that with Tipp?'

'Conor O'Mahony takes frees from our own half,' I reminded Eoin.

'I've been saying for a while that I can't believe you're not having a go,' Eoin chirped back.

I shrugged it off. 'I suppose you're right, maybe. Look, Conor takes them and that's not my job. I'm a goalie.'

But twenty-seven minutes into the All-Ireland final of 2010, I put Eoin's theory to the test. We were awarded a free deep inside our own half and I reached for what I thought was the hurley I used for puckouts. Walking towards the ball, I glanced to Liam on the touchline, and he pointed his finger forward, urging me to go for it. I gave it plenty, and as the ball soared towards the Hill 16 end goal, the wonder grew. The further it travelled, the louder the roars became until they reached the top of the crescendo as the sliotar dropped over PJ Ryan's crossbar.

A minute later, a similar opportunity presented itself, and while it wasn't as far from the Kilkenny goal this time, my effort dropped short. I looked at my hurley and wondered why, because it was a clean strike and I felt I had nailed it. For the first free, and without knowing it, I had picked up from the net my free-taking hurley that I used at club level with Ballybacon. That stick usually enabled me to get 20 yards of extra distance because it was half an inch longer and heavier too. It's amazing when I think back on it: I managed to score my one and only championship point, in an All-Ireland final, with a hurley I had picked randomly from the goal. For the second free that fell yards short of the Kilkenny goal I'd used my puckout hurley, a lighter stick. There was an inch taken off this hurley so that the ball would travel faster from puck-outs, and with a lower trajectory. Eamon's plan was that we would play around the Kilkenny 65-metre line, not their 45-metre line. It wasn't until after the game that I realized I'd used two different hurleys for those two frees. These things are just written in the stars, I guess.

Henry had gone off after twelve minutes, as we believed would happen, and what an ovation he received as he limped off. Tipperary people stood to applaud him. But Henry's absence required even greater focus on our part. Kilkenny could catch you in a blink of an eye and we needed to keep attacking the game, just like Liam had urged us to do.

At half-time, defenders and forwards split into groups to dissect the first half. Liam then addressed the group and reminded the subs that they were the ones who would come in to finish the job that we had started. I looked at Seamus Callanan, and his demeanour told me that he was ready. Benny Dunne was waiting too, like a caged animal. Liam produced his loser's medal from the 1997 All-Ireland final. 'Do you want another one of these?' he asked. No way.

I'd been beaten by Richie Power's goal before half-time. It was a good strike by Richie. Otherwise, I was pleased with my contribution, and I vowed that Kilkenny would not score another goal.

We scored three more. The floodgates opened, and that famous passage of play when Lar Corbett scorched on to Noel McGrath's defence-splitting handpass is one of my favourite memories from that day. Gearóid Ryan fizzed a ball to Noel, and from my vantage point I could see that Larry was already on the move. I knew that Noel would spot his run because Noel is blessed with fantastic vision. Larry bore down on goal and unleashed the shot when he could see the whites of PJ Ryan's eyes. We'd learned from our experiences in 2009 and were ruthless this time.

I lobbed in a long free at an angle for one of our players to tip it down to an in-rushing forward. Noel was on the end of it, and we had our third goal. I didn't get much to do in that second half but one error handed TJ Reid a point, after John Tennyson sent in a long delivery. I took the ball comfortably into my chest and sent a handpass to Michael Cahill but, when it left my hand, Reid pounced and flashed it over the bar. I got away with one there and scolded myself for carelessness.

Seamie came on, and what a lift that was! I didn't want the game to end. With five or six minutes remaining, I reached for my yellow towel in the corner of the net, complaining to the umpires that I was sweating like a pig.

'Brendan, it's raining.'

'What?'

I hadn't noticed.

What an impact our subs made that day. Seamie knocked over two points, and in stoppage time, Benny's moment arrived. David Young, another man in, drifted a ball into midfield and Benny collected it before getting a shot off under pressure. It seemed like an eternity but Benny's effort fell over the crossbar. If my point in the first half was fate, this took it to a whole new level. Benny, the fall guy in 2009, had come on to exorcize his demons. He was free, redecmed. Seamus Hennessy, another sub, added a point before Larry struck his third goal. We were home.

At full-time, I made a beeline for Gearóid Ryan. 'You fucking beauty, I told you!' I'd had a few chats with Gearóid in the build-up to the game. He was a player who thrived on confidence and, at training, I'd tell him that he didn't realize how good he was. I believed totally in his ability, Michael Cahill the same. I'd told Michael at Carton House not to worry about the game. 'We'll win, just play.' And he did.

I ran towards the sideline, looking for Pam. A steward let me through and I shared a hug with her before returning to the pitch for more celebrations. The traditionalists might think that something has been lost since spectators have been stopped from coming on to the pitch after the match, but I didn't feel that way. This was a time for the players, in that twenty minutes or half an hour, to look at each other and say thanks, without even uttering that word. When you see players hugging, each knows what the other has gone through, the trials and tribulations of the previous twelve months. Sacrifices have been made without knowing if it's all going to be worth it in the end. It's complete selflessness.

I was determined to soak up every last precious second of this. I knew how it could be the last time I'd climbed up the Hogan Stand to accept the Liam MacCarthy Cup. I was hanging over the metal railings that led up to the podium when Eoin hoisted the silverware aloft. If God had a pause button, I'd have asked him to press it right there and then.

The lap of celebration around the pitch was simply incredible. My feet still ached but adrenalin compensated. Gazing at the happy faces of Tipperary people, a thought struck me that many of them could have been in Thurles on that Monday night twelve months ago to welcome us home even though we hadn't finished the job. If ever a group of supporters helped to become part of a common cause, it was then.

My mind finally quieted. During the game it was a constant stream of 'we haven't won it yet, focus, concentrate, next ball, keep attacking the game', followed by those double blinks for reassurance. The exam was finally over – and that's what it is, a searching examination of everything you've done over the previous twelve months to bring you to this place. No, it's more than that: it's where you bring everything you've done since the doctor slapped you on the arse and you cried for the first time.

Even in defeat, Kilkenny still had class. Their manager, Brian

Cody, had attended the Canon Hayes sports awards in Tipperary town in 2008, and that was the first time in my life I had spent some proper time in his company. We were seated at the same table after he had travelled with his wife Elsie to collect the national award. I found him to be a really nice man who almost instantly transformed my perception of him. I thought I was about to meet some kind of Darth Vader character who would shut me out and not engage in conversation. That's Brian's on-pitch persona. The man I met that night was immensely likeable and open. We developed a healthy respect for each other, and after the 2009 final, Pamela sought out Elsie to offer congratulations. Now it was Elsie who looked for Pam to repay the compliment. Brian found me in the players' bar after the game.

It's an awkward place for winners and losers. If you've lost, you'd rather be somewhere else, but you still have to face the hotel, the meal, the trip home the next day, and the people you feel you've let down. When you win, it's the complete reverse. You want to scream, shout and go mental, but you must be respectful of the players huddled in the opposite corner of the room who have just lost an All-Ireland final.

Brian came over and couldn't have been more gracious.

'Congratulations, ye deserved it,' he said. 'Today, ye were better.'

'Thanks very much, Brian.'

That short exchange summed him up. A fiercely competitive man, he was able to put his disappointment to one side to offer his congratulations.

Traffic had eased by now and it was time to leave Croke Park. The respective team coaches were ready to pull away, Liam MacCarthy perched proudly on our dashboard.

Freedom.

Redemption.

26

Mountain Tops

Human beings, especially males, crave structure, discipline and challenges. The three are distinctly aligned, but if you fall down in even one of these key areas, you won't pass the test as an intercounty hurler. When skin and hair are flying, and all looks lost in the bear-pit that is the championship, cool heads are required.

Dr Liam Hennessy, one of my earliest physical trainers, was once a young aspiring pole-vaulter who dreamed of competing at the 1980 Olympic Games in Moscow. He'd say that you couldn't launch a rocket from a canoe, that you needed a ship to do it. But you can only build a ship good enough to win an All-Ireland by running up mountains, thinking about performance and having control of your emotions, by having a plan, setting goals, assessing yourself with rigorous honesty and by having others who you trust do likewise. Two questions I asked myself were why and how. Why had I performed poorly, and how was I going to fix it. I'd go home after a bad performance, write down why I was bad but also how I was going to solve the problem. I looked forward to the new me, like the young snake that sheds its skin as it goes.

In his All-Ireland victory speech, Eoin Kelly referenced how

Liam Sheedy had taken over a sinking ship in 2007 but now we had sailed to the Promised Land and our reward was celebration, which comes in many forms. I saw tears of pride and sadness replaced by tears of joy in the eyes of my neighbour Liam Myles at the Burlington Hotel on that Sunday in 2010. He grabbed me by my shoulders and uttered one word: 'Thanks.'

The banquet was a sight to behold, with local tailor Val O'Gorman present in case of any wardrobe mishaps. Spare suits were available if anybody needed them – yet another example of Liam's attention to detail. The job was complete but the standards would remain high. Wives and girlfriends were seated as we made our way to the function room through the Burlington Hotel kitchens, and we were greeted by a standing ovation as we made our way to the tables.

It was a great night, but winning an All-Ireland final didn't make me immune to the blinding headache that would always come in the aftermath of a championship match. By eleven o'clock, all I wanted to do was sleep, but this was a night we had waited a long time for so I stayed up a little bit longer. I lasted until 12.30, chatting in the bar with Liam Barrett and Derek O'Mahoney from home. Shane Mason from the local club and his wife Yvonne were there too, like they've always been, through thick and thin.

I was happy, of course I was, but my body was shutting down. I felt like a shell. I'd reached the top of the mountain but now it was time to zip the tent and get some rest. Back in my room, just before I closed my eyes, the enormity of what we had achieved began to sink in. My ears were ringing as a blur of images raced through my head. I was back on the Hogan Stand steps again, holding the cup, lifting it skywards. I wouldn't say 2010 was better than 2001 – the two were on a par with each other – but coming near the end of my career, and having seen how much it took to build this one, I felt a deep appreciation for what we had achieved.

A garda escort to Heuston Station the next day heralded the arrival of the new All-Ireland senior hurling champions. Twenty minutes from home on the train, a sense of joy returned as I realized that I would soon see my son Paul again. He was there with Pamela's mother, Margaret, to greet us on the platform – a big boy now, not the baby I had rocked to sleep in my sitting room listening to Michael Bublé.

Thurles was alive and hopping but we didn't get into the heart of the town until after ten o'clock, having spent time at Semple Stadium mingling with supporters. I signed so many autographs, and while some lads might have found that a chore, it never was for me. I remember Nicky English and Declan Ryan, my child-hood heroes, presenting me with medals and signing autographs when I was a young boy. Their generosity left an indelible mark and I felt it was only right that we continued to carry the flame. The education I'd received from Ken Hogan on that bus ride back in 1993 infused me with a sense that the Tipperary jersey really meant something, and that each and every player who gets to wear it has a responsibility to pass on good values and beliefs to those who will follow in their footsteps.

Six days after we won the senior final, our U21s demolished Galway in the All-Ireland final. It was a turkey shoot in Thurles and we looked set to dominate the hurling landscape for years to come. There was no reason to think otherwise. Everything was positive. We were addicted to the Liam Sheedy drug, fuelled by good doses of Eamon O'Shea and top-ups from Mick Ryan.

The Liam MacCarthy Cup was on a tour of Tipperary, stopping in various towns, villages and clubs as our people shared in the glory. I even made the front cover of *VIP* magazine. They paid a visit to our home for a photoshoot. It was a perpetual celebration, and after the visit to Ardfinnan we jumped into our cars and headed out to Ballybacon. Travelling over the bridge into my home parish was paradise. A generator provided for extra lighting hummed as I delivered a speech to the local people, with the practice wall I had hammered hundreds of sliotars against providing the backdrop, and the mountain on my right. I was home and happy, but I felt that the journey had only just begun. Tipperary had wasted previous opportunities to build on All-Ireland success but with Liam, Eamon and Mick steering the ship, we'd surely be back here again next year. 'Tipperary, 2010 All-Ireland champions' had a lovely ring to it, and with every-thing in place again for the next year, I felt that more of these glory days were just around the corner.

Sport, of course, has a habit of throwing up surprises. Nothing could have prepared us for what happened next.

27

Legacies

'Why are you doing this? What's going on?'

I'm pleading with Eamon O'Shea on the phone but there's no turning back.

'It's not me, it's Liam.'

It was a Wednesday night in early October 2010 when my phone buzzed with the sound of an incoming text message. It was from Liam Sheedy, informing the players that the management team was stepping down. I was standing in the kitchen, by the window, and almost fainted with the shock. It was like hearing the news that somebody had died – and if that sounds like an exaggeration, it's not.

I felt physically sick. I had invested everything into this and finally we had a manager who was investing everything into us. I had a coach in Eamon O'Shea who was a miracle worker and we wanted more of the drug. Rumours had surfaced in the weeks after the All-Ireland win that Eamon wouldn't be sticking around but I refused to believe them. I wouldn't let myself.

I rang in sick the following morning because I couldn't sleep. I contacted a few of the other players and apparently what happened was that Liam contacted the county board first to inform them of his decision, before sending out a group text. Liam cited work commitments as the reason for his decision and I understand now why he had to step down. The way Liam operated was at 100 per cent; even if it was 99.9 per cent, it wasn't good enough. It was perfection or nothing, and there was no turning back. This was final.

We met a few nights later in Thurles for a commemorative squad photograph, which would be sold to generate funds for a team holiday. The atmosphere was funereal. We walked into a dressing room that had been a sacred place for the three years that Liam was in charge. After we were annihilated by Kilkenny in the 2009 National League, Liam spoke there a couple of nights later with a passion that had the hair on the backs of our necks standing to attention. My God, if the walls could talk they would have some stories to tell. The feeling that room gave us was similar to the one you experience when you walk into your own sitting room, a real comfort, but it was more than that. It was a place of work. In preparation for the photo-shoot, jerseys hung from hooks like they normally would on matchdays. It all seemed so normal. The elephant in the room was Liam's decision to leave the job.

When the formalities were complete, we derobed and the realization hit home that this really was it. We would never have this again. Liam addressed the group and tears rolled down my cheeks. The sheer anguish of it all was on a par with what I had witnessed in the Croke Park changing rooms after the 2009 All-Ireland final. It really was that bad. We were mourning what we once had.

The selfish part of me felt utterly cheated. I had a manager that I respected, and that respect was reciprocated. All the while I knew that if he had to drop me at any time, he would, and I'd have nobody to blame for that but myself. There was no favouritism, nor hidden agendas. Nobody was elite or different, the collective won or lost together. I always felt that Liam would be with us for ever.

By the time we embarked on our team holiday to Jamaica in January 2011 a new manager had been installed, but that raging fire no longer burned inside me. I didn't have the same anger I had carried with me in 2010. I went for a run on the treadmill in the hotel gym and stopped after ten minutes. When I got back to my room, I was angry with myself for not committing to it. It was a drop in standards but, having won the All-Ireland, the voice inside my head was telling me it was time to relax. 'Look, you did that, you need to rest up now.'

There were so many excuses not to go hard at it. Liam was gone, and lack of continuity has been a recurring theme in Tipperary. We had a good man at the helm and more success, I'm sure, would have followed. Even though he was familiar with the players involved, there would have been no favouritism shown in terms of team selection. If the sky-high standards that character-ized his three years in charge dropped, he would also have taken appropriate action. It's a competitive world that an intercounty player inhabits and if he can't step up to the mark, he'll be deemed surplus to requirements, and quickly.

The passing of time will look fondly on Liam Sheedy and what he achieved as our manager because his achievements were quite staggering. As a hurler, Liam wasn't blessed with fantastic natural ability but what he did have was massive work-rate. He ticked all of the boxes in training. He wasn't a legend in the eyes of Tipperary supporters but, when he became the manager, he left as one. He wasn't a player who had songs written about him, a hero like Nicky English, whom people naturally gravitated towards. Liam had to generate something that would make people follow him, and while that's difficult, his people skills and attention to detail were the reasons why he quickly won the support of the players. It wasn't because he slung a winning ball over the bar in an All-Ireland final, with blood pumping from a head wound like a modern-day Cú Chulainn. Liam had to earn the respect of the Tipperary hurling public, and he did that by winning an All-Ireland title.

It was the little things that made the difference, like the evening when he turned up at separate gym sessions in Clonmel and Limerick; like the time he flew to Spain to have a look at our training camp before we travelled out there. He wanted to know what the facilities were like, how the food tasted, the size of the pitches, how many the gym could hold. He'd even asked our team sponsors for money to buy iPods for the players, and we were provided with footage of opposition players to study. But now he was gone, and things would never be the same again.

I'd see him again of course, and the time we spent together on the 2011 All-Star tour of San Francisco is precious to me. Two years earlier we were in Buenos Aires and passed each other in a shopping mall.

'Well.'

'Well.'

I was a player, he was the manager. That's how it had to be, a very definite and necessary divide. San Francisco was different. We toured like brothers, eating breakfast together, travelling everywhere, cycling across the Golden Gate Bridge and touring Alcatraz Island.

'We could never have had this back then,' I said.

'No, we couldn't, Brendan.'

I was delighted that we had it now.

On that trip, I gained an insight into how he thought and how he had made Tipperary successful. Following in his footsteps would prove too big a task.

28

Declan

Why I'm doing this again I'm not too sure. The last time I had to go down this road it didn't end too good. But I have to put down the experiences somewhere, so this is it.

I was back in diary mode again in February 2011. My first entry was penned on the 18th, and looking back now through the prism of hindsight, I understand why I put pen to paper. My mental state at the time wasn't too clever. I'd damaged my hamstring early in the year and had played just one game before the National League, a challenge match against Wexford. And our first meeting with the new management team had set alarm bells ringing in my head.

Declan Ryan, my hugely respected former teammate, was confirmed as Liam's successor in November 2010. Joining Declan was another of my former playing colleagues, Tommy Dunne (as coach), and selector Michael 'Glossy' Gleeson from Thurles Sarsfields. We met for the first time at a fitness test at University of Limerick and this was a chance for Declan to lay down a real marker. Irish people tend to form an opinion of a person almost instantaneously. First impressions last, so if you don't make a statement, you're on the back foot right from the start. I knew Declan, of course, from my playing days but I had no idea how he would adapt to the role of manager.

Tommy was a guy I really looked up to. He'd captained our 2001 All-Ireland winning team and was always one of my role models. He was a year older than me but I always wanted to be like Tommy because of the way he trained and conducted himself. In that room in Limerick, Tommy was now the trainer and I the footsoldier. The reality of this dawned on both of us before the start of a run. I was standing beside a cone, ready to go, when our eyes met. We smiled at each other. It felt strange, because for so long Tommy and I had begun pre-season together as teammates. Our working relationship had changed.

Tipperary hurling had reached another crossroads, and history suggested that when All-Ireland success was achieved, it was rarely followed by another title. After all, Tipp hadn't won back-to-back All-Ireland senior titles since 1965. But this new management team brought good pedigree. Declan was manager, Tommy the coach and Michael the selector when the minors won the 2007 All-Ireland title, following in the footsteps of Liam Sheedy, who had presided over the 2006 win. The challenge for the three of them now was to repeat Liam's feats at senior level. I knew that this could end in one of two ways: either we decided that we wanted to win it again or we'd take a little break. Stepping off that treadmill in Jamaica suggested that the latter might be the case.

In 2011, I can only compare us to a ship coming in to dock. The engines were still powerful enough to keep us ahead of many of the other vessels but as we approached port, they shut down. The last plumes of smoke spluttered from our ship when we overcame Dublin in the All-Ireland semi-final. We thought we could pour more coal on the fire in time for the final but it never happened and the new, improved Kilkenny model with Captain Brian Cody at the wheel steamed to glory.

I had been worried about us right from that very first meeting at UL, when Michael Gleeson said that he was unsure about addressing the group. He mentioned how we had won All-Ireland medals but that he had not. Declan had three of them, Tommy one, but the message that Michael sent out was that he didn't feel he belonged here. His words were humble and self-deprecating but in a room of high achievers he needed to be far more confident and self-assured. He had walked into a room of winners and, in that scenario, the players held all the aces. Any hint of weakness would be immediately recognized. The biggest problem facing the new management team was that they were on a hiding to nothing. If success was not replicated, casual observers would reason that it was their fault. It's a far more complex dynamic, of course.

As players, our bad habits slowly crept back in. The training schedule wasn't as organized as it should have been and some players arrived late to our sessions. Declan was addressing the team on a sporadic basis. During these early days in charge, it seemed to me that he was trying to find his feet in his new role. The question I asked myself was whether I would address the situation by saying something to him or hold my counsel. I decided on the latter because I had to take into account that Declan was still settling into the job and that things might change.

I had come back from injury in time for the start of our National League but Declan told me that I would be given some extra time to recover and that Darren Gleeson would play in goal in our opening League fixture against Kilkenny. It was our first competitive game of the season and we should have turned in a performance that sent out a message that we were in it for the long haul, but Kilkenny won by seven points. When Dublin beat us a week later at Croke Park, our hopes of progressing to the knockout stages of the competition were further dented.

From the moment we were late leaving Portlaoise, I think it set the tone for the rest of the evening, I wrote in my diary as I reflected on that Dublin game.

I could talk all day and night about standards because they refer to a level of quality or attainment. When they begin to slip, it's a bit like the first rust on a piece of metal. If left unchecked, the rust grows and eventually the metal is unfit for purpose. I was always a stickler for time-keeping; I hated it when players turned up late for training or team meetings. At the team hotel on the afternoon of the Dublin game, our pre-match briefing was due to start at 2.30 p.m. I know because I wrote it down. I arrived into the room at 2.29 and just a handful of players were present, along with team management. The meeting got underway at 2.37 and, after studying some video footage of our opponents, Declan spoke about the importance of the game and how Dublin would bring a huge physical presence.

When we arrived at Croke Park, our players were dressed in various tops and tracksuits, but Dublin were uniform, wearing official team gear and really looking the part. Again, another bugbear of mine, because research has suggested that clothing has a powerful influence on how people are perceived. If you looked at Dublin and ourselves that evening as we paced the Croke Park pitch before a competitive game, you'd have thought they were the All-Ireland champions, not us.

Darren was picked in goal again and I took the opportunity to daydream out on the pitch, reliving memories of the previous September. It was probably the highlight of the entire night for me. Our players wore expressions you might see on the faces of condemned men as we togged out before the game. The atmosphere was flat in the dressing room, energy levels even more so.

That lull continued on the pitch during our warm-up and I mentioned the flatness to our trainer Cian O'Neill. He agreed that our body language was poor, shoulders were slouched. Paul Curran had spotted it too and he attempted to rally the troops, reminding them that this was the venue where we always played well. Paul's words were from the heart, as always, but didn't have the desired impact. Dublin won by a point and the mood after the game was one of total dejection. Declan said that the performance wasn't good enough and that we would have to up the intensity levels in training. Brendan Maher, to his credit, referenced the time-keeping issue and how it had to improve.

We were short a few bodies on the way back to Tipperary as some of the lads stayed in Dublin and a few others were arranging their night out on the bus journey home. I was angry and frustrated when I arrived back to Ardfinnan, partly down to the fact that I hadn't played, but my emotions were more focused on those slipping standards. I rang Conor O'Brien for a chat the next day as he was desperately unhappy when his name was omitted from the squad list submitted for the matchday programme. I urged 'Foxy', as he's nicknamed, to remain positive and to get himself ready for training on Tuesday night, where he could release his frustration. But Foxy never got that chance because he was one of four men dropped from the squad after that Dublin game, along with Hugh Moloney, Paddy Fanning and Timmy Hammersley. I rang Foxy again and he was devastated. Players being dropped is a consequence of the natural rate of attrition in any panel but I felt that Foxy was hard done by. His commitment was unquestionable.

Foxy would be recalled for the 2012 season, but when he was dropped it came as a shock. At our next training session, Foxy's enforced departure impacted on the eighteen or so players who were there. We were down bodies due to college commitments

Above: Clear and present danger. Goalkeeping isn't always about getting the hurley in the way. Any part of the anatomy will do here as I face up to Offaly's Rory Hanniffy.

Below: In the trenches with two of the greats. Philip Maher is on my right and Paul Curran on my left. I couldn't ask for two better wingmen.

Left: Standing firm. Here I am, benched, during the national anthem before the Munster senior hurling championship replay against Limerick in 2007. Moll is in my thoughts.

Below: The benchmark. Sharing a moment with Wexford's great Damien Fitzhenry after the 2007 All-Ireland quarter-final.

Below: The Blackrock End. Making a save during the 2008 Munster championship match against Cork in front of the iconic terrace at Páirc Uí Chaoimh.

Above: You cannot be serious! Nine months of hard slog boiled down to Diarmuid Kirwan's decision to award Kilkenny a penalty in the 2009 All-Ireland final.

Below left: My ball! Rising highest in a crowded goalmouth against Clare.

Below right: Understanding the 'Matrix'. Eamon O'Shea opened my mind to new possibilities in hurling.

Above left: We've done it! It was nine years coming around again but here I am at full-time in the 2010 All-Ireland final.

Above right: The Holy Trinity – Michael Ryan, Liam Sheedy and Eamon O'Shea had this ship sailing all the way to Liam MacCarthy Cup glory.

Below: What dreams are made of. Sharing the Liam MacCarthy Cup homecoming in Thurles with my little man, Paul.

Above: Visiting Our Lady's Hospital for Sick Children in Crumlin on the Monday morning after the 2010 All-Ireland final. It's a place close to my heart.

Right: The spark that ignited my goalkeeping dream. Here I am with Connie Naughton, who I idolized as a kid.

Below: Soaking up the sunshine. A recent family holiday in Lanzarote. There's more to life than hurling, you know!

Above: There are times when a picture tells much more than a thousand words. I unleash a torrent of pent-up emotion after we beat Dublin in the 2011 All-Ireland semi-final.

Left: I was never far from home on championship day when I saw this banner unfurled.

Below: Superman! This catch against Cork in 2012 made me feel invincible – but there's always a sting in the tail.

Top: The final curtain. Walking off the Nowlan Park sod in July 2013. Stepping into mortality was a difficult moment.

Above: King of the mountain! Poc Fada sponsor and great friend Martin Donnelly (*left*) is proud as punch as I accept the trophy in 2014 from National Poc Fada chairman Humphrey Kelleher.

Right: Marathon men! At the start line with Jackie Cahill before the 2014 Dublin City Marathon. We both got around safely!

Above: A man of faith, in so many ways. Fr Tom Fogarty gave a young man from Ballybacon-Grange a second chance, when others might not have.

Below: The backroom team. I was deeply honoured in January 2014 to receive a civic reception from South Tipperary County Council. Pamela, Paul and Sarah are with me on a proud night.

but the lads present trained with heavy hearts. Foxy was an extremely popular guy in the dressing room. Declan explained his reasons for letting the four players go. Complacency was put forward as the main one; he wanted to send out a message that no player on the panel should take his place for granted.

Declan was quite forceful in his view but I felt that he needed to be more vocal at training, a more constant presence rather than skirting around the edges. Tommy was hands-on in his coaching, which was excellent, but Declan and Michael sometimes seemed detached from the group. As players, had we become too used to Liam Sheedy, who always took total control? We would have to adapt to this new way of doing things.

In round three of the League, I finally played my first competitive game of the year, a five-point victory against Waterford. Declan was pleased with the result and praised our effort but also mentioned that the players who hadn't performed well would have to train harder. I was happy with my own display but felt low before throw-in. When the game got underway, the negative thoughts disappeared but the final whistle brought them flooding back again. I really didn't know where I stood. Declan provided some reassurance when we returned to training, telling me that I had played well, but it seemed to me that there were always little niggling problems along the way. Cian had to call the group together to demand more effort in our runs. Lads weren't hitting the line like they should have been, slowing down before the finish. This was not a good sign.

I played against Offaly in round four and preparations for this game were much better. We were shown a video of the Munster rugby set-up, with some of their players talking about the bond that exists between them. We increased our work-rate in the game itself and our use of the ball was of a much higher standard. I was now feeling much more like my old self, due in no small part to the fact that I was back in the team, but also because Declan praised my performance again. He seemed to be finding his feet and lines of communication were open. Slowly but surely we were getting there. But Brendan Maher broke his ankle towards the end of March, and when we drew with Cork at Páirc Uí Chaoimh, our League hopes were snuffed out.

Our penultimate League match took us to Galway, but Declan told me that I wouldn't be playing. He qualified that statement by insisting that it had nothing do with form, he wanted to give Darren a game, and this was more good communication on his part. It certainly left me with a good sense of where I stood – a nice contrast to the earlier stages of the campaign. In my head, I wrote off the remainder of the League and started to focus on the championship, but I worried if this was softness on my part. I desperately wanted to play but I tried to focus on the positives instead, reasoning that management knew what they were doing and had decided that I would play in a specific number of League games to tune me up for the championship. I couldn't be too selfish either. Darren was playing well and deserved his chance.

The reality of not being involved hit me when we reached Galway. My diary entry a couple of days later summed up my mood: *I am the worst sub in history.* And it was true because I had spent the entire weekend beating myself up over the fact that I wasn't playing. *I think it's part of my make-up, that feeling of not being in control or not being the one with the responsibility.* From now on, I would concentrate on the following key concepts, which I wrote in bold letters:

SHUT YOUR MOUTH, SPEAK WHEN SPOKEN TO.
TAKE THE TRAINING AND GAMES AS
PREPARATION FOR THE CHAMPIONSHIP.
MORE CONCENTRATION ON THE JOB AT HAND.

These are the values I had always lived by, and when I focused on them, things usually worked out just fine. I had spoken to team management over the weekend in a private meeting and commented that the team wasn't as self-assured as it should be, that the average age of the group was twenty-three and the young players needed to be challenged more. I also brought up the puckout strategy that Eamon O'Shea had devised so that they could look at it if they wished. This information was volunteered with good intentions, but it was time to let them get on with it. The control freak in me had bubbled to the surface – I wasn't the manager of the team.

Our League campaign concluded with a draw against Wexford at Semple Stadium and, hey presto, I was back in the team. I played well, and although I hadn't been involved in as many League games as I would have liked, my form was very much up to scratch.

A trip to Carton House was organized at the end of April in preparation for the championship and my training stepped up a notch. I lifted weights at home and devoted extra time to core work. I felt fitter and stronger than I had in a while and our dietitian Aoife Hearn remarked on how my weight had come down. On our first night at Carton House, a team meeting discussed our championship opponents, Cork, and how we needed to heed the lessons of the previous year, when they knocked us out of the Munster championship. Overall, the three-day camp was a success, but I still felt that there were further gains that could be made if the team was challenged more, in terms of movement around the pitch and general play. A lot of our work was based around training cones and that brought a huge degree of structure. It was a contrast to our coaching under Eamon O'Shea, where everything felt off the cuff.

On the Friday night before we played Cork, I wrote: *We have to be on our game, which I think we are. I feel good but again, I'm on my guard. Looking forward to it as usual but in a nervous sort of way. Wish it was here but looking forward to the rest over the next two days before the off. Hopefully I'll be happy reading this on Monday morning!*

29

Ring

*I*t's Monday morning and I'm happy. We won.

Our 2011 championship campaign began on 29 May with a 3–22 to 0–23 victory over Cork at Semple Stadium. We were off and running, with Eoin Kelly, Lar Corbett and Benny Dunne scoring the goals. I had been troubled by a knee injury sustained in a club match before the Cork game but twenty-four hours before throw-in I ventured up the mountain and soothed the problem with a dip in the stream. It definitely helped me and I felt nice and calm for the remainder of the day. Then Manchester United lost 3–1 to Barcelona in the Champions League final and that disappointed me.

Earlier in the day, Leinster had come from 22–6 down at half-time to win the Heineken Cup, and while my rugby allegiances would naturally lie with Munster, I was hugely impressed by Leinster's character and resilience. It sent a strong message that, even if we found ourselves in a difficult situation against Cork, we had to fight until the bitter end. Leinster were down and out yet still managed to salvage what had seemed to be a lost cause.

The day of the Cork game didn't start well, however. We

warmed up in Littleton, but the bus that ferried us there from the Horse and Jockey was too small. I ended up sitting on a step when I always tried to ensure I was seated in the back right-hand corner. I remembered then how the former Munster and Ireland rugby player Alan Quinlan, a Tipperary man, had written in his book *Red Blooded* about how little issues crop up along the way to challenge a player's routine. In Quinlan's view, how you dealt with these issues was important. You mustn't let the little things get to you. As chance would have it, a bigger bus arrived in Littleton before the end of the warm-up and I almost sprinted on to it to grab my usual spot. This might seem trivial, but this was a red line issue for me on the day of a match. Once I was settled on the bus, everything was OK.

The League hadn't worked out how I'd planned but championship is the real deal and I felt ready. Management had provided us with an extra nugget of information that would prove useful. We were told that all the Cork players would be wearing red helmets. This uniformity was a potentially clever move on Cork's part, but we were prepared for it.

We were still jittery in defence from the start. Paudie O'Sullivan had an early chance that I managed to get a stick to. Patrick Horgan flashed an effort past the far post. Having survived those scares, I felt we would be able to push on, and that's exactly how it panned out. We won by eight points, a good result considering that Cork had beaten us by ten a year earlier. Our post-match stats were incredibly detailed. We were rated out of ten on different aspects of the game – concentration, discipline and so on. Mine related to the number of puckouts that we'd won and lost in the game. We held up well in this regard.

Our Munster semi-final was fixed for three weeks later, 19 June, and we won by nine points having survived a mini-revival by Clare in the second half. It was more nerve-racking than Cork but that might have had something to do with the atmosphere around the ground, which was far less tense than what you might normally expect from a match between Tipp and Clare. Perhaps we took them for granted a little bit because I did notice that the lads were laughing and joking on the bus journey to the game, more than they normally would be.

The game started in the worst possible fashion as Conor McGrath drilled home a goal for Clare in the first minute and we were in fire-fighting mode for the first twenty-five minutes. Our full-back line was being dragged out of position by Clare's good movement and our half-back line also lacked structure. Three first-half goals from Eoin, Bonner and Larry helped to steady the ship, and at half-time, Tommy told us to stay quiet for five minutes and allow our minds to process what had happened. This seemed to work because a sense of calm descended on the dressing room, and in the second half we did enough to get over the line, with Seamus Callanan scoring our fourth goal. Stephen Lillis and Paddy Stapleton came on at half-time and they brought more solidity to our defence.

Normally, beating Clare is a time for celebration, but the lads seemed very downbeat in the dressing room after the game, even though our stats were very good once again. Thoughts quickly turned to champions Waterford and the challenge they would present in the Munster final, with Davy Fitzgerald in charge. The fact that I would equal Cork legend Christy Ring's all-time championship appearances record of sixty-five dominated the pre-match talk.

It was probably the strangest game that I ever played in. The signs were there that we were primed to produce something big because training had gone really well in the week leading up to the game. We had subconsciously clicked into championship mode and were relaxed and focused on matchday. The warm-up in

Carrigtwohill before we made our way to Páirc Uí Chaoimh was ferocious. We had a drill at the very end where players swarmed around each other, launching body hits with bone-crunching ferocity.

In a six-minute spell before half-time, we scored four goals to lead by 5–10 to 0–8 at the break. I was psyched for a big performance and expected that I would have plenty to do but it was game over at half-time. I wondered how on earth I would keep myself ticking over during the second half. I knew what the lads were going to do further out the field, flicking the ball over the heads of their opponents and keeping the scoreboard moving, but it was a nightmarish scenario for me as a goalkeeper. Concentration levels could naturally drop with the job already done but I had my own personal pride and targets to meet, and I needed my back men to help preserve a clean sheet.

We kept the foot on the pedal and it was one of those days when nothing went right for Waterford, as we hit a particularly good moment. Larry was moving so well and Eoin was fired up in the full-forward line. I caught a glimpse of the Eamon O'Shea era. Was it a carryover from 2010, or had we taken our game to a whole new level? Our minds were operating at a much higher level than the Waterford players'.

With seven minutes of normal time remaining, the fourth official's board signalled for a substitution: number 1 would be replaced by number 16. I felt somewhat embarrassed. Declan knew that I was equalling Ring's record, and while I received a lovely ovation from the Tipperary supporters as I trotted to the sideline, I was almost blushing. I'd been struggling with all this talk of records. I wasn't some kind of dinosaur that needed a pat on the back for matching the great man's achievements.

In truth, given how fantastic a player Ring was and the fact that we played in different positions, I was very much in the ha'penny place compared to him. It was difficult answering questions about the record after the match as Ring was a real legend of the game and I was just some fella from Ballybacon who happened to play in sixty-five championship games. The bigger question burning in my mind was whether or not it would be my last time playing in a Munster final. On the TV match commentary, the former Offaly player Michael Duignan remarked on how it was a fine achievement to equal the record but proffered the view that this was grist for Kilkenny's mill. The suggestion was that we were operating with an over-inflated swagger, and taking me off was sneering at Waterford. Still, there was a nice symmetry to our victory. In my first senior championship game back in 1995, we beat Waterford by twenty-one points at Páirc Uí Chaoimh. On the day I equalled Ring's record, we also enjoyed a twenty-one-point victory over the same opponents, and at the same venue.

I was interviewed by Newstalk radio on the Monday night about the appearances record, but when the dust settled and life returned to something approaching normality, I realized that I hadn't really enjoyed the previous few days. I was obsessed with the All-Ireland semi-final to come, and the thought lingered that this year might well be my last. But if it was, I should be enjoying it rather than letting all of these little worries affect me in a negative way. It seemed like I was the only one not basking in the massive performance we had delivered against Waterford. Perhaps worrying about what might lie in store for us further down the line was making me edgy. Whatever was troubling me had to stop because when I was enjoying my hurling, I would always play better. But I was finding it increasingly difficult to quiet my mind. I dreamed one night that Kilkenny won the All-Ireland and I experienced the vivid sensation of looking at them lifting the cup and wondering if I would ever get my hands on it again.

The annual Poc Fada event was held in early August and that

provided a welcome distraction. It was the fiftieth anniversary of the event and I was desperate to win it. I covered the 5-kilometre course in the Cooley mountains in County Louth in fifty pucks, with Graham Clarke from Down finishing second on fifty-four.

The Poc Fada is a competition very dear to my heart. It takes place on the August Bank Holiday each year and has been running since a man called Vincent Godfrey from Limerick won with fifty-two pucks in 1961. I'm proud of the fact that I hold the record for the least number of pucks, forty-eight in 2004, and I've also won the competition a record nine times. Some great people are involved, like the event organizer Humphrey Kelleher and sponsor Martin Donnelly. The nearby Carrickdale Hotel, run by a good friend of mine, John McParland, becomes a hive of activity for the weekend, and in 2011 it provided calm before the storm that Dublin were ready to brew in the All-Ireland semi-final.

There were some really good moments in the lead-up to that game, including one gym session that Cian described as the best he had ever seen in his four years working with us. I spoke to Eamon O'Shea on the phone, and that was a huge boost to my confidence. Just hearing his voice was enough to get me focused on the job at hand. He was in good form and had a few tips on how Dublin operated. I rang Tommy to ensure that we got a look at Dublin's forward play at a training camp that was planned for Fota Island in Cork. Tommy obliged, and we had a productive weekend there. The lads were moving well but needed to be aware of an opponent drifting off the shoulder. From our video analysis, we could tell that Dublin's biggest threat was that man running from deep, and Liam Rushe was particularly good at this.

Kilkenny had booked their place in the final and now it was our turn to fulfil our part of the bargain and set up another of those 'dream' finals.

There were times when I felt anxious about the Dublin game,

but other times when I was really energized, just thinking about playing at Croke Park again. There were little things to contend with along the way, including the botched booking of a family holiday to Lanzarote that cost me a few bob. But that minor issue was nothing compared to what was coming down the tracks.

30

Tears for an Unborn Child

D r Vijay's solemn expression gave the game away, and our world crumbled. Before she delivered the bombshell news, Pamela and I were full of the joys of life. We'd travelled to South Tipperary General Hospital in Clonmel for the first scans of our unborn child, happily reminiscing about how we had been down this road before, with Paul. 'I'll be as big as a house,' Pam remarked with a smile. It was all so exciting as we looked forward to the little person that would be joining us at the end of February 2012.

Pam sat up on the bed and Dr Vijay applied the gel for the ultrasound. We were greeted by what I can only describe as a black blob on the screen. Sadly, we didn't see what we were hoping to. Dr Vijay took a few measurements and we could sense that there was something very wrong. I made eye contact with Pam, trying to reassure her that everything would be OK, but fearing the worst.

Dr Vijay brought us upstairs for another scan which confirmed her suspicions. Pam had suffered a missed miscarriage. We believed that she was three months' pregnant, but the foetus hadn't developed beyond nine weeks. I was praying that we would wake up soon and realize that this was all just a bad dream, but no, this was devastating reality. I was angry, hurt and extremely worried about Pam. She wasn't just sad, she was petrified, and in floods of tears.

As Pamela got dressed privately, I asked Dr Vijay if there was any hope.

'I'm afraid not,' she replied, gently.

'What happens next?'

'We have to take what's left inside out. We'll perform another scan next week and then we will perform a D&C.'

Also known as dilation and curettage, D&C is a surgical procedure often performed after a first trimester miscarriage.

'If there is anything in there,' Dr Vijay added, 'we have to give it to you.'

'What are the chances of something being in there?' I asked.

'She is gone a bit in the pregnancy, I won't know until I go in.'

The little life that we created hadn't made it. At the time, I didn't realize that anywhere between 10 to 25 per cent of pregnancies will end in miscarriage. We would later discover a secret society of people who also carry this pain. I would mention what had happened to us to close friends and some would tell us that it had also happened to them. I could see the relief in their eyes, that they could talk about this too.

But right there and then, it was without doubt the worst experience of my entire life. Expectant parents are supposed to skip through those hospital doors and emerge with a little picture of their future son or daughter as a souvenir. They'll smile at other people in the waiting room and everything is so right with the world. But when Mammy and Daddy come out of that first room with pained expressions, and then go upstairs, there's a serious problem. That's exactly where we found ourselves.

I still struggle with the memories of that mid-August morning. We drove back to Ardfinnan with tears in our eyes. At home, we sat on the sofa and wondered why this had happened to us. I was far more concerned for Pamela's wellbeing as I don't think any father truly connects with his unborn child until he feels it kicking for the first time. I was sad that I wouldn't get to experience that sensation again but, my God, imagine how Pam or any other woman feels in that situation. And in the back of my mind, I was thinking what on earth would happen if Dr Vijay did find something during the D&C procedure.

I was also dreading the conversations we would have with the people close to us when we broke the news. To make matters worse, I was due to play in the All-Ireland semi-final in forty-eight hours' time – but that game was a distant dot in my consciousness. In fact, it didn't even exist.

My left eye was killing me because I'd taken a terrible whack at training the night before. Towards the end of the session we had a drill where a forward would run in from the 20-metre line before hitting a shot at goal, with a defender applying fierce pressure. Bonner Maher was tackled hard and he threw up the ball to swing one-handed. The sliotar penetrated the bars of my faceguard and struck me flush in the eye. There was a little bleeding but I got it iced before leaving Semple Stadium and again at home that night. When I woke the next morning, my eye was almost closed but I didn't think it would present any major problems come Sunday.

What had happened in the meantime rendered a game of hurling utterly insignificant. The prospect of playing or not didn't cross my mind because it wasn't something I was even thinking about at the time. And yet, despite everything that she was going through, Pamela insisted that I had to. We decided that I would, but that it should all be over as quickly as possible and I would be back home in a safe place on Sunday evening. I would now represent much more than Tipperary hurling. I would play for Pamela, for Paul, and the memory of that little light that had been extinguished. Somehow I had to switch into match mode because nobody sitting in the stands at Croke Park would have any idea about what had happened to us. Even if they did, their only real concern would be whether Tipperary would win against Dublin – and if I couldn't handle that, I couldn't play.

How I got through the rest of the weekend I'm not quite sure. Had I grown so mentally strong that I could become emotionally cold, even in the face of such personal adversity? I channelled my anger, temper and frustration towards the match, and what really helped me was the fact that my routine was so strong. No matter what the circumstance, I could still go to Croke Park and execute what I needed to. What also filled me with inner strength was the thought that if I didn't play well, it would make Pam feel guilty, and she had enough on her plate without me piling that on top of her as well.

Pamela tried to keep life as normal as possible. Her friends were brilliant over the course of that weekend. Sinead and Marcena called to visit and Lizzie made the long journey from Monaghan to spend some time with her. On Sunday, Pam went to her Aunt Christina's house in Dundrum with her mother Margaret, and Paul. Christina's husband, Mickey, travelled to Dublin with Pam's father, Jim, to watch the match.

With a heavy heart, on Sunday morning I made my way to the Midway Hotel in Portlaoise to meet the team bus bound for Dublin. Benny Dunne stayed close to me and Darren Gleeson was brilliant too, in the way he spoke to me and helped me along. I broke the news to Cian O'Neill when he enquired about the scan and how it had gone. At our regular pre-match base in Dublin, the Radisson Blu St Helen's, I rang Pamela. It was different this time, no talk about the buzz in the city. I knew that at home she was putting on a brave face but she was upset too because she wasn't in Dublin. I was desperate to do well for her.

That really helped to focus my mind. I didn't care what happened to me any more and, from a game perspective, that was a good place to be. I played games on my mobile phone to pass the time and it seemed to pass quickly; even the journey to Croke Park felt quicker than usual. In the dressing room, the lads were in good form and there was a tension in the air, which is always good. I was ready to go and safe in the knowledge that Barry O'Gorman, one of my Ballybacon clubmates, would meet me outside the stadium straight after the match to bring me home. I told myself that this would only take an hour and a half and I was out of there.

'My friend,' Cian O'Neill began, 'that little one is looking down on you now, and you'll be fine. A clean sheet today.' That was just brilliant from Cian and he remains a true friend of mine. I attended his wedding last December. Sometimes we might not talk for two or three months at a time, but when we do it's like we were never apart. We get each other as friends, professionally, in every way. It just works.

Lar Corbett scored a goal early on but Dublin pulled a man back and I took a lot of short puckouts during the game. I felt confident with them, almost carefree, because after the couple of days I'd been through, puckouts were the least of my worries. We were level at half-time and the dressing room was quiet. The outfield players were sore because Dublin brought huge, but fair, physicality to the game and the hits going in were massive. I remarked that we had to take the remainder of the game second by second, and warned the other players that they should not fall into the trap of thinking that just because we were Tipperary we would pull away from Dublin. We discussed how our defenders would deliver the ball into our forwards after collecting my short puckouts because their spare man was positioned in the middle of their defence, providing extra cover. We needed to attack them around the fringes rather than go through the centre and we decided to take long-range frees quickly, which would prevent their spare man from slotting into position.

It was a tough battle in that second half but in the end we won by four points. I had ball in hand when the full-time whistle went and I belted it towards the upper deck of the Cusack Stand. I didn't know that I was being photographed at the time but I saw a picture later that captured the moment when I released a torrent of pent-up emotion. I looked like some kind of mad man, hurl clenched in left hand, right hand raised to the heavens, my black eye clearly visible through the faceguard.

To the naked eye, it looked to all intents and purposes like the reaction of a man relieved to have come through such a tight game, but there was so much more to it than that. It was as if nobody was in the stadium and I was there alone. My mind had been with Pam through the entire game, and when I cleared that final ball, I knew she would be happy. I'd even broken a hurl that day, fizzing a ball to Seamie Callanan head high, not realizing it was cracked until half-time. I switched sticks, something that would normally spook me, but not this time. On this day, a piece of timber just didn't matter.

My next thought was to get out of there as quickly as possible but the TV presenter Hector Ó hEochagáin wanted to speak to me about breaking Christy Ring's record. The Waterford game had seen me equal it but now I was out on my own on sixty-six. I was almost in tears but I managed to pull myself together for a couple of quick questions with Hector, who's a decent guy. My focus had been on 3.30 and getting through the game and now I felt like a deflated balloon, like one you'd see at the end of a party. I had hit rock bottom again. But I could understand where Hector was coming from and, of course, he had no idea what I was going through. I'd broken the record and he simply wanted to mark the moment.

After fulfilling that obligation, I sprinted off the pitch. I can only presume that the man above was sending a break my way because a friendly face was there to greet me. Sr Annunciata, a Tipperary woman based in Kilkenny, would often wander into the AIB branch where I worked in the city for a chat, especially before a game. She'd ask me if we were going to win at the weekend, the twinkle in her eyes reminding me of my grandmother Moll. Sr Annunciata truly cared and I always thought that she would love to drape a protective blanket over me before I went out to play. I thanked her for her support but my mind was racing and only the relative sanctity of the dressing room would provide refuge from the storm.

I made a beeline for the toilets and let it all out. I sat in the cubicle and had the cry I'd needed for two days. I hammered the door with rage. It had been tough to be out there, pretending nothing was wrong but burning up inside with all these emotions, not quite knowing what some of them even were.

Declan and Tommy had heard about what happened on Friday and they were unbelievably good to me. I told Declan that I was leaving immediately. He had no problem with that so I pulled on my tracksuit to cover my jersey and togs and walked out of Croke Park alongside the thousands of supporters still streaming out of the stadium. Just another face in the crowd.

Barry O'Gorman was waiting for me. His car was full, but they'd all squashed into the back to leave the front passenger seat for me. I climbed in.

'Barry, please get me out of here.'

31

Challenging Times

Wednesday. Jesus Christ, Wednesday. We are back in Clonmel Hospital for another scan. Hopefully this is the end of the nightmare for Pamela, but my mind is a complete mess. What if we have remains to deal with? Where do we bury them?

That stuff rattled through my head on Monday and Tuesday. After spending the night in hospital, Pamela faced the D&C procedure on Thursday morning. Thankfully, we didn't have any further issues to deal with. There would be no remains to bring home.

I knew there would be good and bad days. I studied some information relating to miscarriages on the internet, but I had to stop because the frustration and heartbreak of it all would have been enough to drive me crazy if I let it. Sometimes the enormity of it hit me like a train, but at other times I think the defence mechanism in me blocked it out and allowed me to look forward.

Declan let me have that Thursday night off training. This was one evening when I didn't want Pamela to be alone. I was off work too, and that little bit of breathing space was important to try to process the week we'd had. I didn't want it to appear that I was moving on too quickly, for Pam's sake, but in the weeks leading up to the All-Ireland final I realized just how much of an effect it had had on us. Training was a release, and I began seriously to consider, for the first time, what life would be like without Tipperary hurling. It probably wasn't the best thing to think about before such a big game but it was now on the agenda. On 22 August, I wrote the following in my diary: *Walking away would be hard but maybe I have enough. All that would happen next year is the same old crap in this diary. Again I find myself thinking, is this going to be my last ever game for Tipp? It's mad, there's always bloody something with me coming up to games.*

On the weekend before the final, we returned to Fota Island and I found it such a coincidence that Paul Curran brought retirement into the conversation. I had a feeling that it would come up at some point because Paul and I always talk openly and honestly, but it was as if he could read my mind. It was nice of Paul to say that it would be a stupid thing for me to do. I find it amazing sometimes that despite my self-confidence, it takes somebody else to provide me with assurance.

When I look back on it now, I was in a daze in the few weeks before the game, doing things I wouldn't normally do. I agreed to get a jersey signed for a raffle but forgot to drop it into Cahir House Hotel for collection on the Thursday evening before the game. The man who was looking for it rang the house.

'I'm in Cahir House, there's no sign of the jersey.'

'Ah, shit.'

I told this man, with whom I'd had no previous connection, that I would meet him in Ardfinnan. I was on high alert and desperate to help. What if this man's family was going through something like we were?

It was such a contrast to 2010, when nothing else in the world mattered but winning that final. Then life throws a curveball in your direction, an experience that allows you to cut through the bluster to what really matters. I see life as a giant roulette wheel sometimes, and when that little white ball lands on your number you must decide what you're going to do before the next spin. I felt I had dealt well with the hand of fate but the truth was that I would carry a bucketload of baggage for the next six months at least.

Not even listening to my favourite tunes could lighten the mood. I was snappy and irritable. We went to the cinema in Dungarvan, and this was another break in routine because we would always have visited the Clonmel Omniplex. But *The Inbetweeners Movie* was the one we wanted to see and the nearest place showing it was Dungarvan. We still went to McDonald's beforehand for a McFlurry, in keeping with time-honoured tradition. A few kids were there, shouting about how Kilkenny were going to beat the shit out of us and what Henry Shefflin was going to do. I was hearing them. In Clonmel it would have been just Pam and me, happily chatting in our own world, but now I could hear every jibe and murmur. I muttered an obscenity under my breath. Life had tampered with my filter system.

Pam and I were in each other's company that evening, away from home together for the first time since our tragedy, our minds subconsciously drifting back to the hurt and heartbreak. When two people are sitting opposite each other, as husband and wife, they can connect without even talking. Each knows what the other is thinking just by looking the other in the eye.

Approaching the Croke Park harbour, the good ship Tipperary was leaking water, and I was ready to jump on the lifeboat. I travelled to White's Hotel in Wexford and opted for cryotherapy over the thermal suite. That's how it had to be – I needed to shock myself. Maybe then I could switch on. But I wasn't living in the moment. My mind told me that I was preparing just I had in 2010 but we were a year older now and the Kilkenny players that we would face on Sunday had nothing else in their minds except revenge. The hunted were now the hunters, and we were fully aware of that. The intensity at training wasn't what it should have been between semi-final and final. The team was settled and we had fifteen players who knew they would be starting on the first Sunday in September. That's a comfort zone, and while the subs had accepted their fate, some of them were bitching about it. We were slowly unravelling. But the fabric was coming apart so slowly that we didn't really notice.

On 2 September, two days before the All-Ireland final, I penned what would turn out to be my very last diary entry: *Yesterday was very stressful. I was all over the place. Pam said I was even talking in my sleep last night, the whole works. Nerves there but that is good, trying to keep them under control as best I can. Stay relaxed and let it flow when the time comes. They are talking about rain on Sunday so that is going to make things a little trickier. I feel good though, that's the main thing, and looking forward to the next few days. Eamon O'Shea texted last night. 'Brendan, you will be the difference. Keep everyone in the now.' That sums it up. It has given me great confidence. I still have the nagging feeling in the back of my mind that this could be the last one, but hopefully it will be the best one. Next time I write into this, hopefully I will have another medal.*

32

Lost Opportunities

I'm convinced that I had an out-of-body experience in the dressing room before the 2011 All-Ireland hurling final. It felt so real, like I was looking down on myself getting ready for the game. Maybe it was a sensory overload, I'm not quite sure, or perhaps it was a consequence of personal trauma. I didn't feel right, that much is certain.

It was wet on the pitch and the floodlights were switched on. This seemed so surreal to me and I became overtly conscious of my environment. Hell, I hadn't even noticed it was raining a year before. Paul Curran dug me out of a hole in the first half when a long ball broke behind myself and Kilkenny's Eoin Larkin. There was Paul, the old reliable, roll-lifting the ball on the goal line before clearing it out to the side. I drove a free wide from more or less the same area I'd pointed from in 2010 and I was now in full thinking mode, no longer playing off instinct.

Michael Fennelly fired home a fine goal on the stroke of half-time and we were in big trouble. It got worse in the second half when Richie Hogan rammed in an unstoppable goal, controlling the ball on his stick before lashing it into the top left-hand corner of my net. I didn't even see it. Pa Bourke pulled a goal back for us but I was in a state of mind where I was fearing what would happen next, and telling myself what to do with the next ball that came my way. I was almost paralysed with fear, and when Fennelly broke through again, he struck a shot that bounced a few yards in front of me. I controlled the sliotar and cleared it, not quite sure how I'd managed to execute that piece of play. When Michael hit the ball, I was sure the back of my net would ripple again.

While at times we looked like making a fight of it, Kilkenny pretty much controlled the game from start to finish and claimed a four-point victory. It wasn't a wide margin, considering how poorly we played. We were three points behind in stoppage time when Eoin Larkin popped over the insurance score and Kilkenny were heading for the winners podium, just how I'd dreamed it.

When I commiserated with Tommy Walsh after the 2010 final, he was still wearing that trademark red helmet. Here was a man with four All-Ireland medals in the previous four years but tears were rolling down his face. In fact, his face was contorted with the sheer pain of defeat. Did I cry like that when we lost? No, because my life had been turned upside down in other ways. I was numb, for sure, but the hurt wasn't the same, certainly nowhere near what it was like in 2009.

There was a reason for that from a hurling point of view. Our players, if they searched deep inside their souls, could not claim to have ticked all the boxes. The box marked 'Intensity' certainly wasn't. The rawness and manic desire that stems from your sub-conscious wasn't there in 2011. I never woke in the middle of the night with a burning sensation, a longing to be with the group, at work. We had every excuse under the sun to shield us from whatever criticism would come our way. Liam wasn't there, Eamon wasn't there, we had a new manager. Bullshit. Between the white lines on All-Ireland final day, responsibility ultimately lay with the players, and we hadn't delivered. The biggest regret of all was that a Kilkenny defeat could have signalled the end of a dynasty rather than the beginning of a fresh period of dominance. Where would two successive All-Ireland final defeats have left Brian Cody? It was a lost opportunity to plant serious doubts in their minds and we were capable of doing that, more than any other opponent they had faced in that period from 2009. It's a testament to them that they didn't allow that to happen.

That All-Ireland final certainly didn't mean as much to me as the previous ones. I felt sad about losing but I now knew what real sadness and heartache felt like. I knew what it was like to sit on a sofa with my wife and mourn the loss of an unborn child. We sat on that sofa night after night knowing that nothing would fix this, only time, but it's never been fixed really. I looked upon it as an act of God, and tried not to feel bitter. It was OK to have a sad thought. We have been blessed with our daughter Sarah since then, and when I gaze into her eyes, I think about how lucky we are that all of those cells connected and made her. It's a mad, mad thing when you think about it, that something the size of your fingernail can develop into a fully grown adult.

After the 2011 season, a team holiday was mooted but there was no real appetite for it. We settled on a trip to Lanzarote but not everybody travelled, myself included. Players knew they hadn't fully committed to the cause and it's difficult to look each other in the eye over drinks knowing that was the case. A culture had developed in our team under Liam Sheedy based on real honesty, but when that core value is undermined, accountability is a difficult concept to get a handle on.

Cian O'Neill had decided that his time with us had run its course. He was a football man predominantly and he left for James Horan's Mayo revolution. Could Cian have gone another year with us? Yes. Would we have been better if he was there for another year? Perhaps. Without fear of contradiction, I can say that Cian is the best physical trainer I have ever worked with.

In an attempt to bring some kind of meaning to the year, I met with Declan Coyle in Dublin. I had so many doubts about where the team was heading and, after the year I'd had, I wondered if this was the end. I'd played OK in the All-Ireland final but there was more to life than hurling. We met at the Louis Fitzgerald Hotel and the initial plan was to spend an hour together. We hired a room containing two chairs, a table, and ourselves. Three hours later, we had spoken about the various elements of my psychological make-up that were preventing me from playing well. Metaphorically, I had provided Declan with a spool of thread representing the 2011 season, but the spool was knotted. He enabled me to wind the thread back, feed a piece through here and there, untangle the knots and spool the thread back to its original state. I entered that room problem-focused but left with solutions.

'Yeah, the thing is knotted, but there is no better man in the world to unknot it than you,' Declan told me. 'Here are the tools to do it. Read this.' Declan handed me some of his work to read through, and one particular line resonated with me above all others.

A lot of training can be like putting Post-it stickers on people that will simply blow away with the first gust of wind, unless work has been done to embed the changes inside.

It has just been a bad year. I can do this again.

33

Meltdown

Well lads, I'm sorry to say that I have withdrawn from the Tipp panel. I know this may come as a shock but, after careful consideration, I know that I cannot give the 100% commitment that is required.

I did not want to give this news by text but I could not ring everyone. I hope my decision will not affect the friendships I have made over the years. This decision was one of the hardest yet. I do not have all of the panel members' numbers so can you please pass on as I want you, the players, to be the first to know. I look forward to the second Sunday in September when I will be shouting on the players and the team I love. Larry.

Lar Corbett dropped this bombshell on Monday, 7 February 2012. He was leaving the Tipperary senior hurling panel. Hurler of the Year in 2010, Larry declared that business commitments at his new pub in Thurles would not allow him the time to commit fully to the squad for the year ahead. The news was greeted with widespread shock. I thought the situation was a complete shambles, and I suspected that there was more to this story than met the eye.

It was a significant blow to the group, and to our chances of winning something in 2012. This was the guy who had scored three goals in the All-Ireland final, a player capable of pulling a rabbit from a hat at any given time, a free-scoring machine. Larry struggled with injury and needed to be managed properly. Liam Sheedy was brilliant at that, playing Larry more often than maybe Larry himself thought he could. Because Larry is a different type of character, he was labelled as soft, the kind of player who would sit on his arse until the ground got hard. But Larry's hamstrings were a constant source of worry to him, and if you have a thoroughbred racehorse, it makes sense not to run him on soft ground if he has tight hamstrings.

Life moved on. The guys left in our dressing room were training five nights a week to get their hands on a jersey, and with one man gone that was one less obstacle in the way of a player determined to force his way on to the team. That's how players think. There was no mourning period and we didn't hang a number 15 jersey on a single dressing room peg as a mark of respect just because Larry was gone. His absence was referenced on a regular basis, but his name was never mentioned inside the group.

I had texted him back to tell him that I understood his decision but I also let him know that I wasn't happy. I suspected that the real reason behind his decision was increased frustration with the inner workings of the team, compared to how they once were. Sure, he had business commitments, but so did almost every other player. If you're involved in a county panel where everything is 100 per cent right, you will sacrifice everything else to be there. If it's not 100 per cent, you'll question that sacrifice, and I believe that's where Larry found himself.

He sometimes gave off a laissez-faire attitude but I knew that, deep down, Larry cared more about Tipperary hurling than people gave him credit for. He's eccentric, views the world differently and, while that makes him a genius in many ways, certainly as a hurler, he's also a frustration. You have to look at the world through Larry's eyes before you can connect with him. He's the only player I know that would have made that decision. I can't think of another member of our squad who would have made that decision, but then Larry was always his own man and I suspect he always felt that he could come back into the squad if the circumstances were right for him.

It was yet another example of how the Tipperary hurling team was now a runaway train. After meeting with Declan Coyle before Christmas, I had resolved to concentrate solely on getting myself into peak physical condition again. Control the controllables.

Declan Ryan had decided on a change of team captain and, while I felt that I was worthy of consideration, the honour passed to Paul Curran. He also informed me that Darren Gleeson would start in goal for the opening League match of the season, against our old friends Kilkenny at Nowlan Park. I was placed on standby because Darren's wife Naoibh was heavily pregnant, and on the morning of the game, Declan rang to inform me that Naoibh had had the baby and I was back in. For the one and only time in my senior career with Tipperary, I played with the number 16 on my back as the team list had been submitted earlier in the week for the match programme. We lost by eight points, but it was a start and we were off and running. Where the journey would take us, only God knew.

Training was difficult, and needed to be, but the set-up was buckled out of shape like an old bicycle wheel. Lads were narky with each other on the training pitch – the wrong kind of intensity. When we were asked for more effort, a fight would break out. When more intensity was demanded, a misplaced pass or shot at goal would result in a tirade of criticism. The player delivering the insults felt that he was showing intensity by pointing out what his teammate had done wrong, and that a better standard was required. But this only causes bitterness because the guy that made the mistake in the first place will wait patiently for his accuser to make an error, and then he can retaliate. I'd hit a loose puckout and hear shouts of 'Ah for fuck sake, Brendan. Come on, will ya?' Negativity ruled the roost.

We stumbled our way through the League campaign but still ended up in a semi-final, where we lost to Cork. Tommy was unhappy, tearing off his 'Maor Foirne' bib and throwing it in the dugout. At our next training session, he apologized for his outburst.

Larry returned to the panel in the middle of May, and was greeted with real fanfare in the media. There was even a security presence at Dr Morris Park on our first night back, presumably to prevent people from taking pictures. Some people were worried that hundreds would turn up to see the return of the prodigal son. The reality was far different, although I do recall a photographer present to capture the moment.

Less than two weeks later, our first championship outing of the season pitted us with Limerick, and we rallied from seven points down to win at Semple Stadium. The cavalry came roaring off the bench to turn the tide in our favour, with Seamus Callanan and Bonner Maher making big impacts. As a collective, I compared us to a punch-drunk boxer chasing past glories in the ring, swinging wildly and hoping that one would connect. Further looseness set in after the Limerick game and I feared there and then that the year was over. We had a dressing room of thirty lads who all thought they had the answers to our problems. The foot-soldiers thought they could do things better than management.

My own game was suffering. I was extremely careless in the Munster semi-final against Cork, having bought into my own hype. In the League semi-final, when a high ball came into the square I came through a crowd of players to catch it. The referee had blown for a square ball in any event but I felt great. I saw a photograph of that catch some time later and you'd swear that I was some kind of mythical character soaring towards the sun. I was one of them all right, hurling's version of Icarus, the boy from Greek mythology who attempted to fly with wings made from feathers and wax. The problem with Icarus was that he flew too close to the sun, the wax melted and he fell into the sea. Hurling's equivalent of this tragic theme occurred in that Munster semi-final, when Cork goalkeeper Anthony Nash launched a long delivery into our goalmouth. I came to meet it but got to the pitch of the ball too early and fumbled the ball into the net. I was lucky, because referee Brian Gavin had signalled for a free out. I got away with one.

That mistake bugged me on the way home. On another day, a lapse in concentration like that could have been fatal. Softness had crept into my game. We weren't due to train until the following Wednesday, but at lunchtime on Monday I went to the gym and put myself through the wringer. Six miles of running on the treadmill and three circuits of strength work later, I had resolved never again to drop the ball.

We beat Waterford to win another Munster title but Kilkenny were waiting for us once again, this time in an All-Ireland semi-final. The build-up to that game was actually quite good; training was aggressive, but in the right way. Then we went to Bere Island for a training camp in early August. Bad idea.

34

Islanders

Bere Island lies at the entrance to Bantry Bay, guarding the deep-water harbour of Berehaven in West Cork. The local people are rightly proud of the island, a haven for families, walkers, cyclists, and yacht and fishing enthusiasts. A picturesque and beautiful place, Bere Island is home to archaeological sites dating from the Bronze Age through to medieval times, including ring forts, standing stones, wedge tombs and burial sites. The British had their own particular interest in the island and at various times they constructed towers and a military barracks.

We left our dignity at the door when we visited Bere Island for that exhausting training camp in August. It was a place of hardship, where the failure of your team to win a sprint exercise was punishable with forty press-ups. Another exercise saw two men fighting it out for a medicine ball, with the spoils of battle returned to the winning team. But watching two of our lads grappling on the ground was like a bad episode of World Wrestling Entertainment.

I retreated to Mick Clohessy's massage table. Mick rubbed his hands in preparation.

'What are you doing, Mick?'

'Do you want a rub?'

'I don't want a rub at all, I just want to stay away from that shit.' I smiled.

One of the more troublesome exercises saw the group walk to the beach with empty sandbags. The idea was to fill the sandbags and then bring them back to the training pitch, where they would be used during army-like manoeuvres. We went back to the beach later and returned the sand but that wasn't the end of it, as we were ordered to strip down to our togs for the *coup de grâce*. The task was only fully completed when each team member had walked into the water to touch a rope some yards away. We had been training for an hour and a half at this stage and it's fair to say that everybody was tired. I was contrary too but, as team leader, I made sure that every one of our team went out and touched that rope before returning to shore.

One of the army officers barked, 'Hey, ye didn't all touch that rope.'

'We did touch the rope,' I replied calmly.

'He didn't,' the officer retorted, pointing at James Woodlock. 'He didn't fucking touch it.'

'He did touch it.'

'Well I'm fucking telling you he didn't. Go out and touch it again.'

It was schoolyard stuff but, to keep this man happy, we all went back out there and touched the rope.

Bere Island is also home to two hills, Baby Hill and Daddy Hill for our purposes. Baby Hill was probably 3 miles up from our base before you met Daddy Hill, with a big cross at the top. I got to know one of the army guys a little better on our way up because it was probably best to stay onside with him. I was feeling pretty strong on Baby Hill, even though my togs were still wringing wet from the sea. We were now two hours on the go, with nothing to eat and very little to drink. We stopped to devour some Jaffa cakes along the way but most of them had been eaten on the bus on the way to Cork, and poor old Hotpoint couldn't get to a shop as we'd taken a ferry to the island.

'Right, we're moving out!' We were at the top of Baby Hill, thinking that we were heading back down. 'No, we're going up here! Now, ye got to an All-Ireland final last year and didn't win it. That was yer All-Ireland final, but now we're going to go the extra step and win it this year! We're going up that mountain!' The army officer, the man who I thought was my friend, was sending us up Daddy Hill.

It was like gazing up at Mount Everest. I couldn't see the top. Three mouthfuls of Lucozade and the smell of a Jaffa cake wasn't enough fuel to get me up there. My togs had dried out but I felt like I was wearing a nappy because the bicycle shorts I was wearing underneath were heavy, having absorbed water.

Thirty yards up Daddy Hill, my engine blew. Paul Curran was slightly ahead of me.

'I'm finished with this shit now, this is it,' I moaned. 'I'm too old for some fella to try and break me.'

I walked for a bit before returning to something resembling a light jog. A gate leading to the top appeared like an oasis. We had made it, or so we thought.

'Is everybody here?' the army man enquired.

'No.'

'Who are we missing?'

We looked back down the hill and there was Shane McGrath, just a dot, maybe a mile away. Shane couldn't go any further and fell into a thorny bush. He was like a beetle turned upside down with his legs kicking. A couple of the lads decided to head back down and rescue him, and this suggestion met with the army man's approval. Team building, he thought. Now we're talking!

A tourist car came into view and we moved out of the way to let it pass.

'Hey, stop that car!' I shouted.

The lady in the passenger seat rolled down her window.

'Look, do you see that fella down there in the ditch? Will you do me a favour? Will you go down there, collect him, and bring him back up, please? We're on an oul' team-building thing here and he's in bits. And can you please collect the two lads who are gone running down after him too?'

This lady kindly agreed, and as the car made its way down the windy road, it passed Bonner and Paul Curran as they raced to Shane's aid. Shane was piled into the back before the car collected Bonner and Paul on the way back.

When McGrath fell out of the car the army man didn't appear best pleased. 'Who the fuck sent that car down there for them?'

Silence.

'I want to know who sent that car!'

'Hey,' I chirped up, 'I did it.'

'Do you know what? That was a fucking brilliant idea! Well done!'

The cross at the top of Daddy Hill was still half a mile away and I couldn't feel my legs. Hotpoint arrived in the jeep with some Lucozade Sport, and sucking on those bottles provided the sugar rush we desperately craved. It was time for the final assault on Everest, but we couldn't go straight at it because the ground underneath our feet was too soft and rocky. We travelled down into a ravine instead, muck above our shinbones and looking behind after every step to make sure our runners were still on, and hadn't lodged in the mud.

We finally reached the top, and I sat on a rock to rest my aching legs. Tommy Dunne was nearby.

'You're fucking mad,' I told him, smiling.

'This is great,' Tommy replied.

'No, Tommy. This is fucking madness!' I grinned.

Tipperary jerseys were handed to each of us at the summit. The point of the exercise was that we started at the bottom of the mountain wearing our club jerseys but came down wearing the blue and gold of potential All-Ireland champions.

When we returned to Bere Island village, the locals gave us some quizzical looks. I was running without bending my knees. Hotpoint drove by in the jeep. 'Brendan, you have to get in.' Finally, I caved in because we still had one more hill to negotiate before we were back at the army barracks. The sun was going down when our torture was over, after four and a half hours.

We had a recovery session the next morning at seven at the beach and we chatted about the challenge Kilkenny would pose in a fortnight. We agreed that the Bere Island experiment was a good idea but too fatiguing, and possibly too close to the game. Some players had club games to play when they returned home on the Sunday and the bus back to the ferry was a chance to catch up on some sleep, before a three-hour bus journey back to Tipp.

We played Moyle Rovers in a club match on the Sunday and I wore compression tights and a tracksuit in goal. I was freezing cold. When I arrived at the pitch, one of the lads had asked if I was OK. I looked like death warmed up. 'Training camp last two days,' I mumbled. 'Don't know where I am. I'm aching.' A stray blow caught me in the second half and the impact left what I think might be a piece of floating bone in my elbow. The ref waved play on, and I was so low at this stage that I felt like crying. When I got home, I crashed on the sofa.

At training a couple of nights later, Declan wandered over with a smile on his face.

'Well, what did you think of the weekend?' he asked.

'Declan, you are mad! I slept for two days after it.'

In fairness to Declan, he hadn't realized the severity of what we would endure on that weekend away.

'I know,' he conceded. 'I didn't think that was going to happen.'

I'm all for hardship, and those mountain runs at home are incredibly difficult, but Bere Island was extreme, and unnecessary on a weekend when club activity was scheduled. One of our players, Brian 'Buggy' O'Meara, was flat out asleep in the aisle of the bus on the way back to Tipperary. But that weekend wasn't the reason why we lost the All-Ireland semi-final. Maybe if I had been ten years younger I would have revelled in that Bere Island torture. Was it just me, with the passing years, becoming more cynical about these things?

35

Collateral Damage

'What's that roar about?' I ask our defender Conor O'Brien.

'Oh, here's Larry out.'

'What the fuck is he doing?'

We're almost a minute into the second half of the All-Ireland semi-final and Lar Corbett has finally emerged from the tunnel. I thought there was a streaker on the pitch. 'That's the best one I've seen,' TV analyst Michael Duignan had said at the start of the half. 'The ref threw in the ball and Tipp have only fourteen on the field. Lar Corbett hasn't come back out, wherever he is. He probably knew that Jackie Tyrrell would be waiting at the tunnel for him. I don't know where he is, but he's not out on the field.'

We were a point ahead in the game but ended up losing by eighteen. It was an embarrassment. I only learned what had really happened with Larry later that evening and the fallout at home was vicious. He had become involved in a bizarre tête-à-tête with Tommy Walsh from the start, following the Kilkenny man around the pitch. This was not a tactic that I could recall being mentioned in any pre-match team meeting.

I'd had a feeling that something was wrong from my very first

250

puckout. Normally when a goalkeeper looks out before sending a delivery down the field he'll see small numbers, the ones etched into the front of players' jerseys. But I saw big numbers. It seemed that everybody in the Kilkenny half-back line area of the field had their backs turned. All hell had broken loose down there but, far removed from this, I had no idea what was going on.

'I don't know what was going on at that match,' somebody would remark to me later. 'That was a disgrace.'

'What are you talking about?'

'Did you see Larry?'

'No, why? What happened?'

'He followed Tommy Walsh around the pitch.'

'Ah, no, you're exaggerating.'

Larry had also been given the licence to pen a weekly column for the *Irish Independent*. I spoke to Tommy Dunne about this, wondering why it had been allowed and expressing my concerns. Management didn't like it either, Tommy confirmed, but they were left with no option. There was also a feeling that by agreeing to Larry's request, he might play better. Was the tail now wagging the dog? Would Brian Cody have allowed this to happen in Kilkenny? Discipline is the core value of any group that aspires to winning anything; if it's not there, the show is over. You might fluke success but never in my twenty years of intercounty hurling did that happen.

I was angry with Larry. I was out to play an All-Ireland semi-final at Croke Park and nobody had told me anything about this 'tactic'. If I had a puckout strategy for Croke Park, and none of my teammates knew about it, how would they feel? In reality, there was no gameplan for Kilkenny that day. Looking at the DVD of the match later, one question repeated itself over and over in my mind – why? Paul Curran ended up being cleaned out because of the messing that went on further up the field. I wasn't immune in the general malaise because I should have stopped Aidan Fogarty's goal. 'Taggy' hit a shot and I felt that I'd done enough to deflect it to safety but the pace of the ball wasn't as quick as I thought it was and it cannoned into the corner of the net off my stick.

We had tried to launch a rocket from a canoe and failed. It was Tipperary's biggest championship defeat since the 1800s, a wholly sobering experience. In such a case, each individual must ask himself the question – what did I do in the previous six months to bring me to this moment, to this place where I'm meant to bare my soul? Playing against Kilkenny is the most severe examination an opponent will ever put himself through. Think about the Leaving Cert, multiply that by ten, and you're not even close. The Kilkenny men we face have given up everything in their lives for their cause. I remember Noel Hickey playing against us in a National League game back in 2003. Our forward, Ger O'Grady, went to town on him, scoring 1–6. A few months later, Hickey and O'Grady met again in the League final and this time Hickey ate him without salt. That's the level of commitment you're talking about with Kilkenny, and if you can't match that you'll be hanged, drawn and quartered.

It's why people pay so much money to watch sport, because it guarantees emotion and success or failure at the most extreme levels. Kilkenny showed us absolutely no mercy, crushed us like ants into the ground. Our captain Paul Curran was taken off with ten minutes to go and he didn't deserve that. This man had taken me out of a hole against Kilkenny a year before with that clearance from under his own crossbar, now he was a casualty of war because of the actions of others, 80 or 90 yards up the pitch. And they do say that the first casualties of war are the innocents. I watched Curran trudge off and thought of his family sitting in the stands, proud people. He was cleaned because there was no pressure on the ball coming in. That made me as angry as anything else.

The criticism that came our way was justified, to a point. Larry used his newspaper column to apologize and he'd taken some rough punishment on the pitch too, which should not be forgotten in all of this. The intense levels of scrutiny that followed that game got me thinking. People have to take into consideration the insecurities young players in dressing rooms are carrying with them. The guys inhabiting these intercounty dressing rooms are in the age bracket most susceptible to suicide in this country. They're the ones expected to go out and win All-Ireland titles, be leaders, take the expectations of their families and the hopes of a parish with them into championship battle. Noel McGrath was diagnosed with testicular cancer in 2015. How many people of his age should have to issue a press release about that? That's what our world has evolved into, and I don't like it. Hurlers are now equal to Premier League soccer stars in the eyes of our sports fans. Some can't deal with that and it manifests itself in different ways, through alcohol abuse, depression and the like. Some rebel against the game itself. I've seen more players fall by the wayside than ever make it to the top level.

You have to enjoy it for what it is and understand that people will drop you like yesterday's newspaper, move on and forget about you. What gave me perspective was sitting in a hospital room looking at a dark screen that was supposed to show me images of my unborn child. That's reality. While it is more than a game for the people playing it, and it's more than a game for the people watching it for those seventy minutes, the amount that's invested by people means that the respect shown by players and supporters to each other must be higher. That's where, unfortunately, I believe Larry let us down.

Declan was collateral damage. What disappointed me most about his reign was not hearing that booming voice often enough.

What's seldom is wonderful, and while he never said much as a player, there was one night at training during Nicky English's time in charge when Declan stopped a drill and demanded that we gather in a huddle. He roared at us, making it clear that our work was not acceptable. The passion in his voice that night lives with me now. When he raised his voice, I felt like I was standing near the back of a jet, with the breeze from the engines almost blowing my head off. If that part of Declan had come out more when he was manager, it could very well have unlocked a lot more than what he got.

History will still be kind to Declan Ryan, and rightly so. He was a superb player and with him as our manager we won two Munster titles and contested an All-Ireland final. As players, we must take some responsibility for not building on the platform that had been created for us by Liam Sheedy.

36

Crumlin

Our Lady's Children's Hospital in Crumlin is a special place. It's a place full of inspiration and hope, but sadness and despair lurk there too. Some kids leave there and never look back. Some arrive there and never leave.

I'd visited the hospital on the Monday morning after we won the All-Ireland final in 2010. It's a tradition in the GAA that the All-Ireland champions visit to spread some joy, meet sick children and have photographs taken with them – anything to lift their spirits.

Eoin Kelly and I were asked to wait for a young kid who was on her way back to the recovery ward following surgery. This girl's family told us not to wait too long, that surely there were other things we should be doing. But there weren't. Right then and there, that was the only place in the world I wanted to be. She was no more than ten years old I would imagine, a cancer patient. She was ferried into her room connected to a number of post-operative tubes. We showed her the Liam MacCarthy Cup, happily posed for photographs and were rewarded with a wonderful smile.

In January 2012, I made my way to Castleblaney in County

Monaghan for an AIB GAA skills challenge. Kilkenny's JJ Delaney was there too, along with two footballers, Colm Cooper from Kerry and Dublin's Paul Flynn.

When the skills session was over, a girl ran towards me.

'How's it going, Brendan?' she beamed.

'Well, how are you?'

Her father was with her and he could see by my reaction that I didn't recognize his daughter.

'You don't remember her, do you?' he said, smiling.

'I'm sorry, I probably should know you but I don't.'

It was the little girl who lay in that hospital bed in Crumlin some sixteen months earlier.

'My God! Look at you now!'

She'd made a full recovery. A true heroine. I'd love to know that girl's name now, and hear how she's doing.

That's the power of Crumlin. It's a tough, tough place for sure but there are success stories too. Kids do make it through and go on to live long, healthy and happy lives. On my visit there, I began to understand the true nature of the selfless work the staff undertake on a daily basis.

But I also watched parents struggling to cope, pained expressions etched on their faces. Little did I know that on my next visit to this place, I would be rushing through the entrance doors behind a mobile incubator housing my daughter Sarah.

Sarah was born in Clonmel on 30 October 2012. Our bundle of joy was here and, after the trauma of Pamela's miscarriage, the wheel had truly come full circle. Majella Kennedy works in theatre at South Tipperary General Hospital and was present for the birth. It's an unusual thing, I guess, that a child's godmother is there for the event but this was one of those special days.

Sarah couldn't see me yet, of course, but looking into her eyes was a magnificent feeling. Relief was the overriding emotion, and initial checks suggested that everything was fine. But one of the nurses, a lady named Carmel Byrne, was concerned, as Sarah was panting heavily.

'Give me a minute,' Carmel said.

She arrived back to the room with another nurse.

'We're going to take her down to ICU for monitoring,' Carmel told us. 'Sometimes this can happen with newborn babies as they get used to air.'

Pam and I were worried now. The nurses attempted to assure us that everything was OK, but inside, we suspected differently.

I went down to see Sarah about half an hour later. They had a drip in her arm, a tube in her nose that was feeding her, what looked like a funnel under her mouth supplying oxygen, and she was linked to a heart monitor. I could see that she was still panting heavily. Looking at my daughter, dressed in her little vest dotted with stickers of giraffes and lions, I felt so helpless. Pam was just two doors away, not realizing the full extent of what was happening. I couldn't let her see this.

'It's only a precaution,' I was told. 'We've called the doctor to have a look. There's no problem at all, Brendan. She's fine.'

Beep, beep, beep went the monitor. No problem. OK. Let's not panic.

I had to keep the brave face for Pam but it was difficult to remain composed in the circumstances.

'Where's Sarah?'

'Well, she's below there now and the doctor's coming down to her—'

'What do you mean?'

'Look, I've seen her, she's fine.'

I had asked the nurse to remove the oxygen pump for a moment to take a quick picture.

'Look, there she is, Pam. She's fine. You need to get some rest.'

A specialist examined Sarah the next day. He suspected that she had a hole in her heart but he wasn't quite sure. If Sarah hadn't improved by that evening or the following morning, she would be sent to Crumlin for further tests. He was a lovely man and spoke in gentle tones but being told of Sarah's possible condition was desperate news to process. In my head, I worried if she was going to die. 'Why are we waiting? Can we not go now and check it out?'

Our worst fears were eventually confirmed when we were informed that, yes, Sarah would be on her way to Crumlin. 'I'm sorry,' we were told, 'we have to send her there for tests. We think it might be nothing but we have to be sure. She'll be scanned straight away and if everything is OK, she'll be back here in no time.'

By now, Sarah was in the world two days and Pam had hardly seen her.

I don't know how she managed it, but Pam pulled herself out of bed to make her way down to see Sarah in the incubator. Our daughter was placed gingerly in her mother's arms and the pictures I took of those moments are among the most precious I possess.

Liam Sheedy had been right, like he almost always was. At one of our team meetings, we'd been asked to talk about our biggest fears. Liam's was that anything should ever happen to his family. If you asked me the same question now, I'd answer the same as Liam. That comes from life experience. In 2009 and 2010, nothing else seemed to matter except winning an All-Ireland medal. The fear that something could ever happen to one of your kids was one I could never fully understand until trouble came to my door. Paul was healthy so why would I fear for him? But now a harsh reality had landed on my doorstep. I came to know fear. Real fear.

I sat beside Pam at the side of her bed and cried like the rain. I couldn't talk. I was so bad that Pam might have even forgotten about Sarah for a moment or two. She didn't know what I was going to do next. I placed my head in my hands and cursed God for making this happen.

Crumlin. What did I remember of Crumlin? The faces I saw. Those brave people. I was going to have to find their bravery from somewhere. I was at the lowest point of my life.

A nurse walked in, Mary from Donegal. A guardian angel. I went into the toilet to compose myself as Pam explained how I'd turned into a basket case in front of her eyes. But this lady understood.

The light above Pam's bed cast shadows across the room on this dark, dark evening. It felt like we were waiting for the executioner. My phone rang. It was Eamon O'Shea. I let it ring out and threw it to one side. Not now, Eamon. Not now.

The question had been on the tip of my tongue for hours. Now it was time to blurt it right out.

'What's the story? Is Sarah going to die?' I asked the nurse.

'No, don't panic.'

'What are we facing here?'

And she told us about how she'd been in an ambulance with a child whose heart was the wrong way round when it was born. 'They took out the child's heart,' she explained, 'turned it around and plugged it in the right way.'

'Jesus.'

'The left and right ventricles were mixed up,' she continued. 'When they can do that, surely there's no problem. I've seen this before.'

But I felt that this woman, this angel, was only telling us this to make us feel better.

Friday was D-day. Sarah was transferred to a mobile incubator for the journey to Crumlin. I walked with her to the rear exit of

Clonmel Hospital before running to fetch the car. The ambulance driver was a guy I knew, Stephen Moloney from Cashel. At a time like this, a friendly face provided comfort.

'Don't worry, Brendan,' he said. 'We'll give her a fast spin up.'

Derek O'Mahoney – Sarah's godfather – was with me, and that was huge comfort. Derek is one of those friends who'll tell you that everything is going to be OK, and not to worry. But he was quiet in the car, probably because of the speed we were travelling at. We reached Newlands Cross, on the outskirts of Dublin city, as the ambulance siren wailed and the flashing lights lit up. I stayed no more than ten feet behind all the way to Crumlin. Lights, sirens. But this was no garda escort to Croke Park. It was a serious reality check.

Here I am, driving behind an ambulance to Our Lady's Children's Hospital in Crumlin, following my daughter, who has a hole in her heart. Weaving in and out of traffic, breaking red lights. Through those front doors again. People looking at me sympathetically. 'I hope that poor child is all right. I wonder how sick that child is? Look at that poor man now walking behind that child.'

A new cardiac unit had been built in Crumlin and thankfully we had private health insurance, which meant that Sarah would be seen pretty much straight away. A man informed me that he was performing the scans, but that Sarah would need to be checked in first. The front desk was a fifteen-minute walk away but they were very helpful there. I collected the charts, folders and stickers that were needed before returning to Sarah's room.

Derek was in there, and we watched as Sarah's chest was scanned. Another dark room. Derek stood in the far corner by a radiator, arms folded. Solemn. Respectful. Worried.

I asked the doctor, 'Hey, can you tell me what's going on with this child?'

'I'm not the expert here but it looks like everything will be OK.'

'Thank God.'

'That's not definitive but I've seen enough to know that structurally her heart is fine. The consultant will tell you the rest when he comes in.'

The consultant arrived ten minutes later, studied the charts and explained to us how the foramen ovale – a flap in the foetal heart between the right and left upper chambers – seals naturally in roughly 75 per cent of cases when a child is born. In the other 25 per cent, the opening does not seal. This is a hole in the heart, but thankfully the effects on a human body are minimal.

'Normally I wouldn't need to see Sarah again but the flap is open by four millimetres,' the consultant told us. 'Normally it's two to three millimetres and we'd leave it run. But I want to see her again in twelve months' time.'

I rang Pam, who was waiting anxiously in Clonmel for news. Dr Murchin was there with her. He was brilliant around this time and had called to check on her. It was nice that he was there to hear the good news too. 'Sarah's coming back down the road! She'll be home in a couple of hours!' It felt like we had won the Lotto.

At junction 14 on the motorway back home, we stopped at the Supermac's restaurant where Derek and I devoured the largest burger meal we could find on the menu. I hadn't eaten in two days but we could now sit down and begin to look light-heartedly on what had happened.

'Jesus, what were we worried about? Sure they told us everything would be OK. We should have listened!'

I rang Eamon back later that evening and explained what had happened over the previous few days.

'Look, Eamon. We don't really know what's happening with

Sarah. I don't even know if I'm going back. Hurling's the furthest thing from my mind. I'll ring you when I have a decision made on this thing.'

'Oh, Jesus Christ,' Eamon said. 'I hope everything's OK. I'll talk to you soon. That's no problem at all.'

When Sarah returned to Clonmel, we were told that she wouldn't be allowed home for another couple of days. That was fine because at least we could relax, be parents, and enjoy the moment.

Pam was allowed home on Saturday evening and we monitored Sarah over the weekend. On Monday she was examined again, and the paediatrician, Dr Shana'A, seemed pleased.

'Look, she's fine. Are you happy to take her home? She's good to go if you want to take her.'

On that Monday evening, Sarah was lying in a Moses basket at home in Ardfinnan. Safe.

James Woodlock and Michelle, who's now his wife, called to see us. They thought that Sarah had been home a few days by now and were dropping in to congratulate us, as friends do. They didn't know the full extent of what we'd been through but it was great to have them there. They're really good friends, two people we were more than pleased to share our joy and relief with.

Our baby was home, safe.

You were right, Liam. You were bloody right.

37

Eamon

It was as if people expected that all Eamon O'Shea had to do was flick a switch and, hey presto, we'd be All-Ireland champions again.

Eamon returned to us in September 2012 after Declan Ryan stepped down. I met him in November – the first time we'd been face-to-face since the commemorative squad photo in 2010. I imagined that meeting Eamon again would bring all of the old feelings flooding back. This would be so good, I'd be back on the drug and 2013 would be unreal.

Eamon was catapulted into the role of his own volition. Sure, he was the man that county board officials wanted, but that wasn't the reason why he was coming back. Eamon still felt a huge sense of loyalty to the group, a loyalty that dated back to the time when Liam asked him to be his coach in 2007. I had asked him back then why he decided to join us. 'I was watching you and Eoin Kelly and I couldn't believe that men like ye weren't going to win an All-Ireland,' he said. 'I had to do something about it so I came in, with Liam. I wanted to work with ye, to see what ye were really like. I knew ye from the stands, understood what ye stood for. I wanted to help ye win that All-Ireland.'

History was now repeating itself, but our reacquaintance was as much an eye-opener for Eamon as it was for me. He didn't fully comprehend how badly the camp had unravelled in two years. After severing ties, Eamon had become just a supporter again. I explained to Eamon how the group had lost its way. Discipline, communication and our previously held core values were like pieces of shipwreck floating on the ocean.

I felt that he needed to know how things were because managers are normally the last to hear, and they're the guys who can fix the problems. If Eamon had knowledge of the environment into which he was returning, he could hit the ground running straight away. Eamon himself wanted to know exactly what had happened to the team he left behind. 'Where are the leaders? Where's the system? What's gone on in the meantime that I need to know about?' I answered all of his questions truthfully so that he had the relevant information he would need for the firefight ahead.

I told Eamon that I needed some time to think about my own situation. It had been a tough time with Sarah, and hurling seemed a lot less relevant. In little over a year, we had lost one child and had a major scare with another. I promised Eamon that I would have a definite answer within a fortnight. The main priorities were to make sure that Pam was OK and that Sarah bedded in comfortably after all that she had been through. Ensure normality in the household and take it from there. When you're making decisions with a wife and kids involved, it's impossible to go off on a solo run. I couldn't go home to Pam and say, matter-of-factly, 'Oh yeah, I'm going off hurling with Tipp next year.' That wouldn't have been fair.

We chatted, and Pam was very supportive. 'No bother, off you go. If you want to play, you play.'

I contacted Eamon to let him know that, yes, I was in.

'Good, I'll see you next Saturday morning at 9.30.'

It was a little bit more difficult this time due to the sleepless nights. Sarah was very colicky and we were on half-hour shifts with her. From eight p.m. until 11.30, she was roaring. We tried everything to solve the problem before a guy in Portlaoise told us to change her formula and add infant Gaviscon to the mix. With a wife and two kids, I was slotting coins into the arcade machine for the last time. One more life, one more season. I was fast reaching a point where the walls of my intercounty career were closing in on me.

I could push those walls back to squeeze a second season out of myself but I really didn't want to, and I knew that I couldn't. I could smell the mortar, and intercounty hurling was taking up so much of my time that it wasn't allowing me to be me any more, the person that people see at 3.30 p.m. on a Sunday afternoon, the guy who is cool, calm, collected. This really was it – I decided that 2013 would be my final season.

One night early in the New Year, I was wrecked from running. I cramped up and our physio John Casey ran on to the pitch. We were in the middle of punishing 40-metre shuttle runs after energy-sapping work on the tackle bags.

'John, rub it out.'

'Brendan, you're finished for the night.'

'No, I'm not.'

John texted me later, insisting that I should have called it a night after I'd cramped.

I thumbed a message back to him, which read: 'John, I don't have time to rest. I'm running out of time.'

I had to finish on the high I had started on, to bookend my career. I felt I would be remembered more for how I finished than anything I had achieved. When the door slammed shut, people would remember my last game more than my first. I thought of the great French footballer Zinedine Zidane and the fate that had befallen him in his last big match. On the biggest stage of all, a World Cup final, Zidane was sent off for head-butting an opponent. An extreme example, perhaps, but if you took a straw poll of maybe a hundred people and asked them for their abiding memory of Zidane, I'm sure that head-butt would feature high up on the list of answers.

In mid-February, Eamon announced his captain for the season. I'd also been anxious to prove that I was worthy of consideration for that role. I believed that I was one of the players Eamon had relied on when he was with us as coach. I never actively canvassed for the captaincy during my career but if it had happened I would have been honoured. I thought that if I did get it this time, I could help to develop some of the other players.

The news was broken at a team meeting at the Horse and Jockey. It was an interprovincial weekend and the Tipperary represent-atives were free to leave and link up with Liam Sheedy's Munster squad after the meeting. The rest would train with Tipperary the next day.

We were in the auditorium at the Horse and Jockey, the Derrynaflan Theatre, completing an exercise on what we thought about concepts such as responsibility, trust and attitude, themes we had fallen down on for two years. After a bite to eat, we retired to a separate meeting room and Eamon announced that Shane McGrath would captain the team for the year, with Brendan Maher confirmed as vice-captain.

For a fleeting moment, a selfish part of me argued inside that I should have been told about this in advance. Then again, would I have thought like that five years ago? No, so there was no need to be selfish about it. Shane was captain, more power to him, and though the captaincy had passed me by again, the inner monologue ceased. It takes a unique kind of animal to be a Tipperary captain and, in my career, only two men in my opinion wore the jacket like it fitted – Tommy and Eoin. For sure, I would have liked to wear it to see how it felt, but it was a challenge that was never placed in front of me, and that was fair enough.

I closed the door on my interprovincial career with Munster that same weekend. I was a member of the panel but Cork's Anthony Nash got the nod to play in goal, and rightly so, as he was the All-Star goalkeeper. Liam was manager of the Munster team and after he announced the team on the Saturday evening, I was annoyed that I had sacrificed a weekend at home with Pam and the kids. It was a huge contrast to my first taste of the competition, when I broke on to the Munster panel back in 1996. I was sub goalkeeper behind Clare's Davy Fitzgerald and we won the final that year, hammering Leinster by 2–20 to 0–10 in Ennis. Declan Ryan drove me to the match and back. But seventeen years on, and at this stage in my career, this was another night away from the family. I could have been training with Tipp on the Sunday morning but instead I was stuck up in Armagh and wouldn't arrive home until late on Sunday night. And how was I going to tell Pam that I wasn't playing when I got home?

Paul Curran wasn't picked either, and in our hotel room I bounced my feelings off him. 'Jesus, I wonder what Pam's doing now? She's probably trying to get Sarah to bed.' I had an easy decision to make.

On Monday, I rang Liam to break the news.

'I can't commit to this thing, Liam. We'll have to train twice more before the final and I can't give up another Sunday. I'd rather be away with the family on a Sunday.'

'Can I not talk you around?'

'No. I wish you the best, but I just can't.'

Munster went on to win the interprovincial tournament and Liam rang me a few days later.

'Look, you were as involved in this as anyone else,' he began. 'So I've asked them to get a medal for you. It's only right.'

That was Liam at his finest, yet again. The family was never left behind, the bond never broken.

People often ask me about that bond between players who have won All-Ireland titles. In May 2015, I sat down for an interview with the journalist and sport psychologist Kieran Shannon. He asked me if I'd been speaking to any of my former Tipperary teammates in 2014. I said that I hadn't. 'What's the story, then, with this bond I hear that players have? That ye always keep in touch when you win an All-Ireland together and that it's never forgotten?'

I explained to Kieran that there are normal things people will do for each other every day. A phone call, a helping hand. And then there are the extraordinary things that people do that they know will mean more to you, like that phone call from Liam, like James Woodlock and Michelle calling to the house on the night Pam and Sarah came home. If I pass Philly Maher on the way to work in the morning and he salutes me, that gives me a huge lift.

It's like soldiers going to war. You might not tell everybody the story but when you meet someone that's been there and look him in the eye, you know damn well what he's thinking. That's exactly what it means to win an All-Ireland. We don't have to be on the phone to one another every day still to know what the other person needs at any given point in time, and if we have an opportunity to help him out, we will. Even thinking about Paul Ormond, another guy I soldiered with, is enough to give me goose bumps. Tom Costello the same, when we're chatting on Facebook.

We're not living in each other's pockets, but if I wanted €1,000 in the morning, there's a group of guys from 2001 and another group from nine years later who would say, 'Where will I wire it to?' You don't necessarily need to win All-Irelands for that to happen but, in order to establish that sort of bond for life, the reality is that you need success. Liam Sheedy just knew what delivering that medal would mean to me. It's instinct, and his is rarely, if ever, wrong.

Meanwhile, the settling-in period was difficult for Eamon. When Liam was in charge, players were used to one-on-one meetings with him, but that form of communication wasn't part of Eamon's modus operandi. When he was coach, Eamon was the solution to a challenge that Liam presented us with; now Eamon had to move from a solution-based approach to challenging the players himself. He was now the manager and Paudie O'Neill was the coach, and that was tricky because the players were only mad for Eamon to take the training sessions.

I went back thinking, and hoping, that Eamon would train the team. Paudie was good but he was no Eamon O'Shea. Then again, nobody else is, so Paudie was fighting an uphill battle from the start. Eamon was torn. There were things he would have naturally wanted to do but which he now had to delegate to others, and trust that the job would still be done to his high standards. But if you're as good as Eamon at training a team, and you live and die by results . . . well, he must have been sorely tempted to dip his toe in the water.

When our competitive season got underway, we played Cork in the first round of the National League and took a bad beating. Eamon reacted by taking more of a hands-on approach in training. Much more than a toe, Eamon stuck his leg in the water. For me, the best way for Tipperary hurling to win was with Eamon as coach. If county board officials had their time back, they could have appointed Michael Ryan as manager, and Eamon as coach. Eamon is not an egomaniac whose nose would be out of joint if he wasn't referred to as the manager. He wants Tipperary to win; formal roles or titles are irrelevant to him. Heaven and earth should have been moved for him to train the team. But maybe he was looking at things from a different viewpoint. Did he think that we would go backwards if he returned as coach, or that we'd automatically win just because he was there? Experience might have taught Eamon to keep his distance, but after that Cork loss he couldn't help himself, and we were happy.

Before we played Kilkenny in round two of the National League, a press evening was organized at the Horse and Jockey, a meet-and-greet with members of the media. The Cork game was still fresh in everyone's minds and the vultures were circling. Eamon O'Shea, the great white hope, was back and journalists wanted to know why it hadn't worked out yet – and this was only February. The old reliable was wheeled out to communicate the positive spin and Eamon knew that whatever questions came my way would be dealt with and smashed out of the park. I defended the team to the hilt, but a shock lay in store before the weekend.

At training on Thursday evening, Eamon told Darren to go into goal and hit a few puckouts.

'Sure Darren is playing on Sunday,' Eamon told me.

'What?'

It was a kick in the pants, no doubt. I could live with being dropped. The issue was that I hadn't been told. After all, I'd spoken to the press at the media night, so then to find out that I wasn't playing was frustrating. Not picking me wasn't meant in a hurtful way by Eamon but my paranoia didn't allow me to see that. I needed games to be ready for the championship but it wasn't a subject I felt I could broach with him. Besides, if a player came to me and told me that he wanted to play more, I'd probably reply, 'Yeah, tell me something I don't know. Now show me how much you want to play.' I continued to do that and, as the season progressed, I got better and better.

I played two more games, against Waterford in the group stages and the semi-final with Dublin, which I knew would be my last outing of the League season. In keeping with Eamon's policy of rotating the goalkeepers, I knew he would pick Darren for the final against Kilkenny. My job now was to make his decision as hard as possible. I was flying in training. The prospect of not playing in a national final stung me, especially as it was my last opportunity to play in a League decider.

We played a game against the U21s ten days out and I felt like I was back in Croke Park against Kilkenny in 2003, fighting for my life again. I walked off at half-time and chatted with TJ Connolly and Ken Hogan, who were in charge of the U21s.

'Jesus Christ, you're flying,' TJ said.

'Brendan, I haven't seen you in such good nick for a long time,' Ken remarked.

'I'm not playing in the League final, lads.'

'What? How do you know that?'

'I'm telling ye, I'm not playing.'

38

The Last Supper

'Surely he can see me. I'm looking straight at him, for Christ's sake.'

It's the Thursday night before the National League final and I'm trying to catch Eamon O'Shea's eye. He's not going to break the news to me so I'll have to take matters into my own hands.

'Eamon, do you not have something to tell me?'

'Oh, yeah! I've to talk to you!'

'Look, I know I'm not playing. You haven't talked to me in three weeks, that's how I know.'

'I was tossing and turning this one around in my head. The U21 game nearly turned me but at the start of the year I had it in my head that I'd play Darren in a League final if we got there. He needs the game. I need to test him to see how he'll cope with such a big game.'

Eamon made perfect sense, but he could have told me this earlier. My paranoid head couldn't take not knowing.

To quiet the racing thoughts, I watched a movie on the bus journey to Nowlan Park on matchday. I didn't want to be angry because I'd written the word 'enjoyment' on a Post-it and stuck it to my fridge door at home. That was the key. No matter what happened in 2013, I was going to hurl like I was thirteen or fourteen again, free from worry and doubt. If I found myself on a bench at ninety years of age, I'd want to know that I enjoyed my last year as an intercounty hurler, and squeezed every last drop out of it.

Therein lay the confusion. Kilkenny, League final, Nowlan Park, their back yard. Fuck it, I wanted to play.

Losing the game increased my sense of frustration, but Eamon eased my mind. 'Look, championship's coming now, your time of the year. No more experimenting.' Not playing in that League final hurt but I had a great love for Eamon, and no matter what he did to me, it would make no real difference. I'd come back looking for more, like a dog that's been kicked by its owner. It hurt because it was Eamon leaving me out of the team, but the wound always healed quickly because I wanted to win so badly, for him.

I'd also taken the conscious decision that if a problem arose, I'd take a step back from it. Declan had wondered at a team meeting in 2012 why I hadn't spoken up and offered my view but I felt that the younger players had to learn for themselves. The easy thing for me would have been to stand up and offer a solution but that's no good for a developing player. A short-term fix can work, but it's about the long game. Tipp could win an All-Ireland but not win one again for a long time. That was a major problem, and I wanted to see good characters emerge as much as good hurlers. Liam Sheedy built good people, and Eamon had often spoken about 'men of honour'.

We had a training camp in the build-up to our opening game of the 2013 championship, and though Damian Young had taken time out to compile some really useful footage on Limerick and how they played, the conversation before we watched it centred on where the post-match socializing would take place. I thought of Declan Fanning in that dressing room after the Wexford game in

2010 and how he had urged that there would be no drinking after the game, with three more fences left to jump. We were falling back into old habits.

In the three or four months before you play a championship match, one small thing out of kilter, and with twenty-five heads thinking differently, will take six or seven minds away from the group. Once that happens, the set-up is effectively broken. You find yourself in the middle of the game wondering why you're getting beaten and nobody's fighting back. It's about the little thing inside you that goes the extra yard – that inch that allowed JJ Delaney to catch Seamus Callanan in the 2014 final to execute a goal-saving hook. JJ had given up everything for that one brilliant moment.

A few weeks before the Limerick game, we played a challenge match against Waterford in Carrick-on-Suir. This would be the highlight of my week and I would prepare for the first forty minutes of that game the very same as I would for a championship Sunday. Light up, do my thing, let my game peter out with the game itself. Then I would know that the deposits were in the bank and I could flick the switch on championship day – programme the coordinates and away we go.

We warmed up in Kilsheelan and Eamon called out the team. 'Darren's in the goals . . .' Jesus Christ. Floored again. I was told that I would be coming on for the second half. That was OK but I was empty now; this wasn't the right preparation for me. I wasn't going to just play the second half against Limerick. This was a dress rehearsal, after all. When two people are getting married, they practise the church part of the day, they don't go straight to the reception.

There was a big crowd in Carrick, and on those kind of evenings kids approach players for autographs. Suddenly my mind switched from championship to challenge mode and wondering when the night would be over.

Twenty-three days later, we were sitting like stooges in the Castletroy Park Hotel, beaten by Limerick in the Munster championship. As part of The Gathering celebrations that took place around the country, guests were invited to mingle with the intermediate and senior teams after the games at the Gaelic Grounds. This was a fundraising exercise for the county board and it was obviously hoped that we would have two victories to celebrate. The intermediates did what they had to but we didn't. I felt sorry for Eamon as he had to stand up and say a few words. The intermediate players were pleased, naturally, but we just wanted to get out of there. It was embarrassing.

We now had to wait for our opponents in the All-Ireland qualifiers, and having trained at 6.30 on a Monday morning, a fortnight after the Limerick match, we were drawn against the losers of the Kilkenny–Dublin Leinster championship replay. My immediate reaction was that we would be playing Dublin at Parnell Park, and they would be brittle enough after losing to Kilkenny. But as we watched the Tipperary footballers play Galway while on a weekend away before the qualifier, news filtered through that Dublin were causing quite the stir against Kilkenny. Laura Walsh, a passionate Kilkenny fan and a good friend of mine, was sending me regular text message updates. 'It's not looking good,' she wrote. The football game ended and the result from Portlaoise was announced over the loudspeakers. The ground erupted as this was great news for Galway. It would be Tipperary against Kilkenny, and one of the big guns was gone as far as they were concerned.

We went for a Chinese in Salthill that night, and while it didn't quite have the feeling of being 'the Last Supper', we realized that it might well be. We met on Sunday morning for a stretching session, and when one of our players spoke it felt like a case of trying to wake the dead. It was a false lift because the sense I got from the room was that Eamon was here and everything would be OK. Limerick was only a speed bump and we'd show Kilkenny in Nowlan Park. Talk was cheap. It didn't feel real and we were living in the past. But training went well that week and, walking off the pitch at Semple Stadium on the Thursday evening, it dawned on me that it could be the last time I would ever do this.

39

Finality

This could be it, then, and the familiar feelings are back. It's like the old days against Clare at Páirc Uí Chaoimh, a cauldron of anger, fury dripping from all four corners of the bowl. The key to the rivalry and anger that festered between Tipperary and Clare was the sheer knockout edge to those games, and now we have it against Kilkenny. We're two rats in a barrel. Only one of us will come out of there alive.

I tell Paul Curran that this championship game could make or break us. 'It's the end of us or the end of them. Either they retire, or we do.' If we beat them, I suspect a couple of Kilkenny's elder statesmen will step aside. We missed our chance in 2011, and though you rarely get a second opportunity like this, it has landed squarely on our doorstep.

Our pre-match base was the Lyrath Hotel. Some of the players relaxed on sofas inside but I wanted to experience the sensation of what it might be like on that pitch later. I wanted match temperature for as long as I could. I walked past a fountain and the spray of the water drifted across to cool my face. The droplets dried quickly on my clothes. The sun was high in the sky.

Back inside, it was a surreal time. I looked at the other players and knew that it was almost time to climb into that barrel. We'd go in there and be devoured, or we'd fight our way out. I knew there was something in Larry. This was his type of occasion, and he'd rise to it.

We boarded a bus to take us to a pitch outside Kilkenny city for a warm-up. I wore just a T-shirt and tracksuit bottoms. It was warm, bloody warm, with nobody else around but a guy with keys to the gates and dressing rooms. Pucking over and back, sliotars bounced off the turf as if it was concrete. We stretched under a tree, in the shade, with the sun beating down. I lay down, pulling my leg back to extend a stretch; sunlight filtered through the trees and the flies hummed at ground level. It was perfect championship weather.

Back on the bus, I toss a sliotar in my hand, before extending my arms. Brendan Maher is sitting four seats ahead of me, gazing into vacant space, tuned in. We arrive at Nowlan Park and it seems like there's nobody here. But inside the ground is already full, the air humming with anticipation. 'Next year, I'll be outside the bus looking in,' I think to myself. 'This is mad but I'm enjoying it.'

In our dressing room, I sit in the far right-hand corner, my usual spot. Bonner Maher is on my right, Tom Stapleton on my left. I walk out on to the pitch for a look, to see if the goal-mouths have been re-sodded. Normally that's a problem because the more tufty grass in around the goalmouth doesn't usually knit with the rest, but it's perfect, like a carpet.

Murmurs in the crowd as we wander around in twos and threes. Tipperary are here.

There has been no curtain-raiser before the big one and everybody's sitting there, stewing in emotion. I'm sweating standing up. I stand in the goalmouth and check for the sun. 'If this is it, this is it, but I'm going out with one hell of a bang here.' Kids are hanging over the walls on either side of the tunnel but I pay no heed. That's not being rude – I'm in the zone.

I get ready and head for the shower area to warm up, thumping the ball off the wall and feeling it return safely to my hand. The pre-match team talk and huddle brings a sense of growing belief. I chat to Paddy Stapleton before the off. Paddy will start at full-back because Paul Curran is injured and I'm expecting Kilkenny to deploy their towering forward, Walter Walsh, on the edge of the square. Walsh was man of the match in the 2012 All-Ireland final replay against Galway, parachuted in from nowhere to make a big impact. He's tall, very tall, and Paddy's not. It's an area Kilkenny feel they can exploit. The plan is that Paddy should tackle Walter and I'll come for any ball within a 10-yard radius of the goal. We'll do that for however long it takes Kilkenny manager Brian Cody to change his mind and switch tactics.

The public address announcer has whipped the crowd into a frenzy before throw-in, calling out the Kilkenny team and subs before pausing momentarily to announce that Henry Shefflin is back from injury, and is in the squad. The ground shakes twice when the teams run out on to the pitch. Some of the people have been waiting two hours for this moment, sitting there in the sweltering sun, and the roar is one of utter release.

When the game begins, there's a problem. With ball in hand, I can't see too many options for puckouts, short or long. It's a stark contrast to 2010, when there were so many potential recipients. I sell John O'Brien short with one. He told me that he would drift towards the touchline before drifting back in to collect. John has one hell of a paw on him and is an obvious outlet for a fifty-fifty delivery, but after John cuts back in, I hit the ball to where he was standing originally and Tommy Walsh claims a simple catch, in splendid isolation.

'Shit, sorry, Johnno.'

Larry is flying and scores a goal before his hamstring gives way. He trudges to the touchline with a cacophony of boos and cat-calls ringing in his ears. I don't like this. OK, he was sent off in the League final against Kilkenny, but in 2010 Tipperary fans stood up to applaud Henry Shefflin when he limped off the pitch.

At half-time we're level, and everything is calm. Eamon urges me to mix things up a bit, to take chances. I chat with the backs and forwards and we agree to spread the game out a bit more, but everywhere I look there are Kilkenny players in the way. Nowlan Park is tight and there's precious little chance to place the ball into a gaping patch of grass as a default option. It's like trying to play seven-a-side soccer on a five-a-side pitch. The argument that can be levelled at any goalkeeper here is that it's his job to find space. Maybe I could have, I'm not quite sure, but on that night I played the hand I was dealt. I take a chance, but Walter Walsh picks one off in the second half and sticks it straight back over my head.

Even so, my mind is crystal clear, as good as it was in the 2010 final. I'm immersed in the game and I've rarely felt as happy or content. I know that Kilkenny aren't going to score a goal, I'm gorging on excitement, and it's just a brilliant night.

A key moment turns the game when Eoin looks like he's going to score our second goal but that man JJ Delaney comes from nowhere to make a goal-saving challenge. The resultant 65 drifts wide and Kilkenny fans rejoice. They're relieved because their team is every bit as brittle as ours. Kilkenny are like a boxer who's taken an early punch and knows how much he's got in the tank, rubbing against his opponent but not quite sure how to put him away. The knockout punch isn't in Kilkenny and we're still in with a chance. I make a good save from Matthew Ruth and think that this might light us up. 'It will turn, this isn't the end, and someone will do something!'

But it doesn't happen . . .

Referee Brian Gavin blows for full–time and I fall to my knees. 'No, no.' I pull at the grass, tears flow, and I'm angry, frustrated. Our championship season is over and so too is my career. Game over. No insert coin to continue. Anna Duggan, a Kilkenny supporter I worked with in Portlaoise, will tell me later that she didn't want to come near me as she could see the state I was in. I grab that yellow towel and drape it over my shoulder for the last time. I pick the hurls out of the corner of my net and trudge towards the middle of the pitch, wishing my Kilkenny opponents well for the remainder of their season.

It really begins to hit home the closer I get to the other end of the pitch. I walk slowly, head bowed, gazing at the grass. A Kilkenny woman sees me and asks if I'm OK. 'I'll be fine, it's just the match,' I mumble. She asks me to sign her son's jersey, and I do, before moving on again.

I reach the Kilkenny 45-metre line and their goalkeeper, Eoin Murphy, is there.

'I've always admired you and it was a privilege to share the same pitch as you tonight,' he says.

'Good luck to you, Eoin, and thanks very much. I'm at the end of my career but you're only starting the journey. Best of luck with it.'

I reach the endline and prepare to step into mortality. My right foot crosses before I drag my left foot over, to enter another world. Three girls in the tunnel, teenagers, are full of the joys of life, laughing and joking. They fall silent as I walk past. I let it go now. The tears become sobs and the yellow towel is covering my eyes as I return to the dressing room.

I sit down and Bonner pats me gently on the back – a lovely touch. Here's Bonner, with another ten years left in his career, sitting beside this old stager who's struggling to let go. He's never seen me like this before.

'Sorry, Brendan. It will be all right.'

I hug Hotpoint, John Casey, Mick Clohessy and Dr Kevin Delargy, who works in tandem with Dr Murchin.

It's over.

40

Worm Hunt

'Lads, come on, into your lines there.' I'm at the local pitch in Ballybacon three nights after Kilkenny and a new door is opening. Here I am with the club's U6s, laying out cones for drills. 'OK, we're going to run out here, jab-lift, drop the ball and run on.'

Some of the kids are on their hands and knees, rummaging in the grass.

'Lads, come on! We're doing a drill here!'

One of the kids has found a worm in the grass and the others are now using the noses of their hurleys as shovels to find more. This is one battle I'm not going to win so I give in and join them, scrambling on the ground in the search for worms. I'm home again.

I had now stepped into a world that was still my club, but alien to me in so many ways. There must have been sixty or seventy kids at the field that night, boys and girls, hurling. I walked through the gate knowing everybody but knowing nobody. I wasn't part of this. I was away with Tipperary every Tuesday night for the last nineteen years so how was I supposed to know what happened here? I didn't want to be the county man sauntering in and taking over the show, so I asked if there was anything I could do to help.

That first night back was a real eye-opener, providing me with on-the-spot evidence that hurling had faded big time around the parish. The intermediate team normally trained after the juveniles but just a handful of players turned up. Coach Donal McCarthy had the cones in place for the session before he pulled the plug. I couldn't believe the apathy around the place. Declan Fanning had told me that he found a huge difference when he returned to his club, Killenaule, after finishing with Tipp. Club training would be called for 7.30 and Declan would clock in for 7.10, sometimes left by himself until 7.45 until the other lads arrived.

I was now preparing for a new life outside intercounty hurling but there was still some unfinished business to attend to before I could close the door on Tipperary.

Eamon O'Shea rang me in October. I was working in AIB Portlaoise and he wanted to meet about the following year. I had my mind made up but I suspected that he might try to persuade me. Part of my brain was hoping he would.

'Right, what nights are ye training?' I asked.

'Tuesdays and Thursdays.'

'I suppose there's gym work.'

'Yep, Mondays and Wednesdays.'

'Sure I have a gym set up at home, I could use that.'

'No, there will be collective gym sessions.'

'Right. Are we training on Saturdays and Sundays?'

'Actually, yeah. We'll probably be gone for three weekends out of the first six.'

Any small hope that this might have worked out was extinguished. I'd have Friday night off, and Saturday morning, but we'd be gone from Saturday afternoon until Sunday night. I remembered the night when I was away with the Munster team on interprovincial duty, stewing in the Carrickdale Hotel and wishing I was home. If I said yes to Tipperary again, I'd regret it. Eamon offered me some leeway, suggesting that I didn't have to be there every weekend, but I couldn't enlist and not drill. What we did at that meeting was tease out the prospect of me coming back, with both of us knowing at the same time that it was a non-runner. 'If you do leave, you'll leave as Tipperary's number one, the way you started,' Eamon told me.

Two nights before I confirmed my decision, I was chatting to my friend Derek at home. I told him that I was retiring. 'Thank God,' he said. 'You might leave in a couple of goals in a League match and you're not playing then. I'm not saying that will happen but as your friend, coldly looking at the situation, you couldn't have played much better this year. The time has come now.' It's always your friends that will tell you the truth.

I had been in touch with Marty Morrissey from RTÉ, asking his advice on how this would play out. I placed the job in his hands because he was always very good to me during my career and I trusted him. He met me in Ballybacon to film some footage and put together a package that would air on the Six-One news on Thursday, 17 October. I tried to phone Eamon at six o'clock to tell him, before anybody else knew, but his phone rang out. I tried again at 6.10, and again, no answer. When Eamon rang back at 6.30, the cat was out of the bag.

'It's the last time I go for a run,' he laughed. 'When I came back I found out that my goalie had retired!'

Of course, Eamon knew my mind had been made up, but there were still some loose ends to tidy up. I had given an interview to the journalist Jackie Cahill, which would run in the morning newspapers, and I also spoke with another Tipperary man, Paul Collins from Today FM, who put me in touch with their sports editor John Duggan. Everything was boxed off nicely, the way I wanted it. At thirty-eight years of age, my intercounty career was officially over.

I couldn't believe the reaction that followed. People sent cards, Facebook messages, and stopped me on the street just to say thanks. I was overwhelmed by the goodwill I encountered. In some quiet time, I switched on the TV to watch a programme that had been recorded before the All-Ireland final between Cork and Clare in September. A TV producer, Fintan Walsh, had asked me if I would like to work on a project devoted to the significance of All-Ireland final day and what it's like for players. They liked my suggested script and I was brought to Croke Park with a camera crew to bring it to life.

It went like this:

So, it's finally here. The day these Cork and Clare lads have dreamed about all their lives.

For most of them, it's their first time in this place. But what is the reality of All-Ireland hurling final day for these players?

Are they ready for the emotional roller coaster that lies ahead, even before the sliotar is thrown in?

In the weeks leading up to the game, the outside world is saying, enjoy this special occasion, but within the walls of the dressing room, the message is very clear: finals are for winning.

You're on the bus and the driver points it towards Croker. The closer you get to the ground, the more supporters you see.

Kids draped in the colours, their eyes full of excitement.

From here on, All-Ireland final day becomes real.

For a second your mind wanders and you start to dream with them.

But hang on, you're a player. You've got a job to do.

The blue lights of the outriders light up the inside of the bus, as they whizz by to clear the traffic. The heart beats a little faster.

At last, Croke Park fills the skyline. You take a deep breath, you mosey on up outside the stadium and the masses surround you to get a look.

Your own people roaring words of encouragement, rival fans roaring . . . lots of other things.

Then you disappear under the stand and out of public view. Game face is on, everything dark.

You climb off the bus. There's an RTÉ camera watching your every move.

And you fumble and fooster to get your gear bag and hurls safely into your hands.

You catch a flash of the minor game through a gap in the stand.

Back inside the dressing room, all is quiet, nothing but the hum of air-conditioning overhead.

You strip off, tog out, listen to the battle cry. Last messages are delivered. It's the little things.

Words of inspiration are spoken and bonds are strengthened one last time.

You take a look around . . . you may never be in a room with all these guys again. That plays on your mind.

The main door swings open, it's time to get out beyond the darkened tunnel and run out into the light.

Two sets of gladiators running out to do battle, the roars of the eighty thousand outside filling the arena.

As you run out on to the field, it's more like a circus than an All-Ireland final, guys on stilts and giant hurling balls. Crowd entertainment.

Photo over, it's time to start the warm-up, while the big screen blasts out adverts and shows clips of past games.

It's hard to concentrate if you're not fully focused on the job in hand.

Once the President is met, and the hand is shaken, you get the parade out of the way and it's time to do what you've trained for . . . a game of hurling that could change your life, for ever.

For the Clare players who won All-Ireland medals, their lives did change for the better. When I did it in 2001 and 2010, mine certainly did. Now it's time for a new generation to emerge as I look on, a spectator once again. I'm happy with my lot, although it has taken some time to adjust. A huge void was created in my life but the opportunity to get more involved in coaching and ongoing media work around the game has helped me to bridge the transition. You might leave the game when you retire – but the game will never leave you.

Epilogue

It was the little things that caught me at first, like the day I walked into the Spar shop looking for tickets for Tipperary's first National League match in 2014. The girl behind the counter looked at me as if I'd two heads when I asked for them. 'We don't do the tickets here, that's SuperValu.'

Homer Simpson appeared in my head: 'Doh!'

Down to SuperValu then, wondering where to go to buy these tickets. Are they on sale at the checkout, or the customer service desk? The girl behind the counter there wondered why on earth I was buying tickets because I'd played for so long, but I was just an ordinary punter now, forking out my few quid for the privilege of watching Tipperary play hurling.

Paul came with Pam and myself to that first game, played under lights on a chilly February night against Waterford. It was the first time I'd been able to be with Paul at the game and, walking to the stand, I clutched his hand tightly. I'm not sure whether that was to protect him from the traffic or because I wanted his support, but I needed the connection with him that evening, to reinforce the decision I'd made to walk away. That little squeeze from his hand and the look into his eyes told me all I needed to know – I'd made the right call. Paul had until now been deprived of a simple pleasure: going to the match with his daddy.

Inside, I thumbed a tweet into my mobile phone, summing up how I was feeling. 'Best of luck to Tipperary hurlers tonight in Semple v Waterford. My new view still a little weird. #uptipp.' Paul had enough Coca-Cola and Tayto crisps, I was at peace, and that's all we needed to worry about. I'd wondered how I'd feel sitting there. It was better than I'd expected.

Tipp's first championship game of the year moved things on a little. I parked a long way from Semple Stadium, on the side of a country road, and walked to the ground. We sat in the Old Stand on the 65-metre line, about twenty rows from the back – good seats. Word came down from the radio gantry that Marty Morrissey was there, and would like a word before the off.

Looking down on Limerick and Tipperary going through their warm-ups was surreal. I felt a real disconnect. While I'd have chatted with James Woodlock now and then, I'd never pry too much. James was in the thick of it, I wasn't, and it was more about keeping in touch than anything else. I did text the majority of the lads before the game, to wish them luck, but there was never a sense that I should have been out there with them.

Paul was my touchstone to reality, and it was something that he had said to me earlier in the year that really rammed it home. After I got involved with the Kerry backroom team, as goal-keeping coach, we stayed in Banna Strand one weekend. Seamus O'Regan, known as 'Big Jim', is Kerry's version of Hotpoint and he arranged the accommodation. While pucking the ball to each other out the back, Paul imagined that he was Darren Gleeson, Eoin Murphy, Eoin Kelly or Henry Shefflin, like any kid does.

'Would you like me to go back playing with Tipperary?' I asked him.

'Yeah,' he replied. 'But I wouldn't want you to go to Spain for a week on a training camp.'

Another little moment that told me, yes, I'd made one of the best decisions of my entire life.

As that Limerick game developed, I could see it slipping and I could see changes that could be made to potentially turn the tide. I had the pundit's hat on now. I felt emotionally attached to the game but was also trying to distance myself from it.

Paul wondered where I'd disappeared to for a while and when I told him that I was talking to Marty, he asked me why I hadn't brought him with me. Shit, I'd never even thought of that, so when the game was over I took him up to the media centre to meet Marty. Talk about a child waking up on Christmas morning, because Marty was so good, posing for a photograph with Paul wearing the radio headphones. And do you know what? Paul still talks about the day he met Marty.

Paul was also in the dressing room in 2015 when Kerry got promoted to Division 1B of the Allianz Hurling League – an incredibly big deal for an emerging county. I will say that I'm not a huge fan of having kids around dressing rooms at times, I just don't think it's the right thing to do, but I could hear the players whooping with delight next door and I beckoned him over. 'Come in here to see what success looks like.' I wanted him to witness what happens to a group of players when they win something, and that dressing room was alive with excitement, fun and craic. Players walked around drunk on euphoria, carefree, and Paul was wide-eyed. This is what sport is all about, why we were out the back of the house every night of the week as kids, practising for moments like these. And now when Paul pucks his ball, he's Shane Nolan or Pádraig Boyle from Kerry.

Working with Kerry and Laois as a goalkeeping coach has opened my eyes to new horizons. I had only ever known Tipperary but I don't think anybody with serious managerial or coaching aspirations – very few anyway – can leave a playing career and go straight into a backroom team without some education.

I'm sure the Tipperary job is one I'll be linked to at some point in the future. If the time is right, I will have a serious look at it. Right now I'm happy with what I'm doing, and I couldn't fulfil a role of that magnitude without cutting my teeth elsewhere and learning key skills and experiences that would enable me to do it to the best of my ability.

I've enjoyed media work too since retiring. I love my role as a pundit with RTÉ and there have been columns to write for various print and social media platforms. Many players – and this is unfortunate – finish their careers and sit at home waiting for the phone to ring. I met one of them not long after he retired. This guy was a former Munster senior medallist and one of the finest players of his generation. I asked him how he was doing. 'I suppose your phone is hopping,' I ventured.

'The phone didn't ring at all, boy.'

There was one day when I wished I was back out there, 7 September 2014. All-Ireland final Sunday. At 3.15 p.m., Tipperary were warming up out on the Croke Park pitch and I could picture myself down on that pitch, looking up to where I was sitting in the stand. Kilkenny were up the other end and my heart was thumping because this was the team that had retired me and I'd have done anything to be down there to deliver some sort of payback. As the pre-match parade turned the corner of the Hogan and Davin Stands, I was back down there again, looking up. My eyes welled up and I had such a tight hold of Paul that he must have wondered what on earth was wrong with me. Pam was seated at the other side of Paul, knowing what I was going through, tears in her eyes too. I wanted to run down the steps, stop one of the stewards and tell them that I was playing, but I had to fight it.

The national anthem struck up and I was living All–Ireland final day as a player all over again, looking up at the big screen highlighting the words of Amhran na bhFiann as eighty-two thousand people sang. 'I'll look around any second and it'll be all systems go – but I'm here in the wrong gear, wearing jeans, a jumper and shoes.' My teammates were beneath me, and I reconnected with them emotionally for the first time all year. These were my friends and I wanted them to win so, so bad.

But what if they did win? Would I have thrown away an All–Ireland medal?

At half-time I was pitchside for an interview about the Poc Fada. Players marched off and I ran down, a steward kindly allowing me through. Hector Ó hEochagáin interviewed me as three kids displayed their skills in front of the watching thousands. I was so close to that grass again I could smell it. There is a unique odour that emanates from that Croke Park sod after it's been freshly mowed, an aroma that fills up the senses and tells you that, yes, you're here.

I ran back down the touchline, head down, half embarrassed, and before I'd returned to my seat the Kilkenny fans were on their feet as TJ Reid banged home a goal. With just minutes remaining Tipp were behind and I prayed to God that they would come back, while at the same time wondering if they could. It was such an open game that I felt we had a chance. With the excitement of it all, I thought my heart was about to burst out through my chest. It was a terrible experience. How do supporters sit through something like this? They must feel so helpless, like gamblers with absolutely no control over what is happening but hoping that the horse they've backed has enough to get over the line. The toilets weren't too far away and I felt like going in there, locking myself into a cubicle and closing the door.

Paul sat with his head between his legs and his hands over his ears. I'm not too sure that he knew exactly what was going on but he could sense that this was serious. He escaped, shut down, and when you're six years of age you can do that. At thirty-nine there's no choice but to be an adult and suck it up. Except I couldn't. I held back the tears once again as John 'Bubbles' O'Dwyer stood over a late free that would win the game for Tipp if it went over the bar. Tipperary fans jumped and hugged each other as the ball headed towards goal and Kilkenny supporters remained seated. This was good – but, no, more confusion as HawkEye is called in to adjudicate. It seemed like an hour passed before the video technology revealed its verdict: John's shot had gone narrowly wide and the game finished in a draw.

On the way home I thought of the lads and how they might be feeling. The Burlington wouldn't be too bad because we didn't lose. I texted a few of the lads, with a message along the lines of 'well done on the performance but the job's not finished'. I didn't send them to the lads I wouldn't have been in touch with all year. The last thing you want coming up to an All-Ireland final is texts from people you never hear from ordinarily. You're like a Premier League footballer in the couple of weeks leading up to the game and everybody wants a piece, but when the game's over and the circus moves out of town for another year you're forgotten about, unless you've won.

Pam smiled and asked if we were going the next day. I nodded and told her that we would be.

One of my replay highlights was meeting the comedian Dara Ó Briain, and chatting to him about hurling. Premium level this time, thanks to Liberty Insurance, sitting with Matt Cooper from Today FM and RTÉ's Evanne Ní Chuilinn on either side. As the game progressed, there was never a feeling that Tipp were going to win it, and that brought a feeling of sadness. Seamus Callanan scored a late goal and my heart raced a little. We continued to attack the Kilkenny D, hoping that it would be like the first day and that we'd break through for goals. Kilkenny sat players behind the ball, we fell into the trap, and in a game like that, if it starts out that way, it's difficult to change it mid-stream. Michael Cahill wasn't fit to play, I know that now, and while Eamon shipped some criticism afterwards for not making switches, he didn't have too many options – something he moved to address in 2015. The dream had died again, and once more Tipp looked to regroup.

I walked out of Croke Park carrying a feeling of massive disappointment but also with a sense of a new relationship with Tipperary hurling. It was a far cry from the days when I left my wife and kids at home and morphed into somebody else on the training pitch. I was a man who cried on the team bus listening to his music, focusing on the reasons why he did what he did and who he did it for. I was a man whose regular Sunday night companion was a thumping migraine as he sat alone in the dark attempting to process what had happened just hours before. I was a man who looked at himself in the mirror of a dressing room toilet and pleaded with himself to deliver again. 'One more today, it's in you. Please. I know it's there. Can we have it today?' Now I was just another man leaving Croke Park after an All-Ireland final with his wife and son, happy with his lot. A man who had stood his ground.

Acknowledgements

I was extremely fortunate to wear the famous Blue and Gold of Tipperary over the course of three decades. It was a responsibility I never once took for granted and I realized from an early age that it was important to uphold the values, morals and principles of those who wore the shirt before me.

I met the late, great Tony Reddin a few days before he sadly passed away on 1 March 2015. I wondered what kind of training he did when he was at the peak of his powers, starring on great Tipperary teams in the 1940s and 1950s. A goalkeeper, like me, he told me that he used to run the roads on dark winter nights, steeling body and mind for what would come in the months that followed.

He might not have known it at the time but hearing Tony talk about his preparation provided me with a sense of reassurance that I had walked the right path throughout my career. If a man of his incredible stature put in the hard slog far from the public eye, surely I did something right whenever I ran a six-mile stretch of the Knockmealdown Mountains. There's something quite humbling about knowing that, in some small way, I followed in Tony's footsteps on and off the pitch.

In order to give my all in my intercounty hurling career, I needed a top-class support system around me. I have dedicated this book to Pam, Paul and Sarah. When things didn't work out on the pitch, I always had the lift of a smile or a knowing nod when I came home. They helped to keep me grounded and I simply could not have achieved what I did without their support and love along this great journey.

My parents, John and Anne, were always hugely supportive of me during the early years of my development as an aspiring young footballer and hurler. I thank them most sincerely for that. It's vital to get a head start in life and that's exactly what they provided me with in Gortnalour. My aunt Marie, and her husband Billy, have supported me loyally through the years. Marie sat in stadiums without ever really seeing me play. She couldn't watch – but she still had to be there. The odd glance out of the corner of her eye would suffice.

After our daughter Sarah was born, a brown Nissan Micra wore a path from Ardmayle to Goatenbridge. Pam's mother Margaret was the driver. Margaret and her husband, Jim, are special people whose sacrifices allowed me to play the game I loved for so long. Pam's sister Suzanne, her husband John, Colin and my godchild Clara are other great supporters.

As a player, it starts and finishes with the club. The loyal people of Ballybacon-Grange and Ardfinnan stood by me through thick and thin – and continue to do so. Memories of bringing the Liam MacCarthy Cup over the bridge and seeing those smiling faces will live with me forever. They fuelled me with the desire to try and do it all over again.

Throughout my career with Tipperary's footballers and hurlers, I was privileged to play alongside some great men in both codes. Some of us may have been rivals at club level but when we came together with the county in pursuit of common goals, what always struck me was our unity. We didn't always get the returns our investments deserved. Two All-Ireland senior hurling titles wasn't a bad haul. I just wish it could have been more. Still, I have no regrets.

Behind the scenes, every county needs its administrators. The good ones know when to let players get on with doing what they do best, while removing any obstacles along the road to potential glory. We also had an army of men ensuring that we were patched up and ready to go. Mick Clohessy, John Casey, Dr Kevin Delargy and Ger Ryan, our former logistics man, are top-class operators. Dr Peter Murchin is the man who stitched my left leg, and my career, back together in 1999.

Another army braces itself for battle on an annual basis – the Tipperary Supporters Club. Without their tireless work, it would be almost impossible to keep the show on the road. They strive desperately hard to provide a chunk of the finance that keeps the set-up as professional as possible but it's the ordinary supporters who ultimately dig deep into their pockets to watch Tipp play. In times of worry or doubt, I often close my eyes and hear the strains of 'Slievenamon' all over again. Since retiring in 2013, I often revisit that special place in my mind and relive some great memories. The Tipperary Association in Dublin, another fantastic group, honoured me with Tipperary Person of the Year in 2013. I thank them for that.

Then there was our kit-man, John Hayes. Good old Hotpoint. My God, talk about brothers in arms. He saw me at my highest and at my lowest, picked me up, brought me down. He was the one constant in my career as a Tipperary senior hurler, a true friend and wonderful servant to Tipperary GAA. Hotpoint stood with me on fields of battle. Three fine men also stood beside me on the biggest day of my life, my groomsmen Liam Barrett, Derek O'Mahoney and Mike English. Martin Donnelly, who does so much great work promoting the annual Poc Fada event, has turned what was once an unfashionable event into a real success story. We had the biggest crowd ever on the mountain this year and Martin's hard work and dedication helped to ensure that this was the case.

To my friends and colleagues at Allied Irish Bank, a sincere word of thanks. Working in Kilkenny from 2008 to 2012, I often found myself on the receiving end of some good-natured banter! In my various postings with AIB, I've never been met with anything but respect.

I have met many great leaders in my life. I was honoured when one of them, Liam Sheedy, kindly agreed to write the foreword for this book. He was the man who showed enormous faith in me when he took over as Tipperary senior hurling manager in 2007. Thanks, boss.

Thanks to Eoin McHugh and everybody at Transworld Ireland for their time and attention to detail. As a goalkeeper, I needed a safe pair of hands throughout my career. Similarly, safe hands were needed to put my life in print. In Jackie Cahill, I knew I had the right man. We've known each other for a long number of years. Jackie knew what made me tick before we even started. In 2014, we completed the Dublin City Marathon together. That was one hell of an adventure and this was another. Those long nights of chat, laughter and tears were worthwhile and, more than anything, enjoyable. Behind every good man is a great woman. Jackie's wife, Lisa, probably thought she'd see more of him in their first year of marriage – before *Standing My Ground* became a reality!

We also had some fine early readers who provided us with some essential feedback and assistance. Thanks to Damian Lawlor (another good Tipperary man!), Pat Nolan, Colm Keys and Fintan O'Toole. Thanks to Inpho and Sportsfile for the images in the book. Two local photographers played big roles also. Denis Vahey's work is what you see on the front cover of the book and John Kelly's artistry adorns the picture sections.

Documenting my story was a formidable challenge. It was a project I thought long and hard about before finally putting pen to paper. If I have learned anything along the way, it's that the most important battle to win is the battle against yourself, in that never-ending search for perfection. It's a goal we will never reach, but one we must always strive for.

As my friend, Declan Coyle, always says – live your life on the Green Platform.

Tiobraid Árann Abú.

Brendan Cummins

Picture Acknowledgements

Every effort has been made to contact copyright holders where known. Those who have not been acknowledged are invited to get in touch with the publishers. Photos not credited have been kindly supplied by Brendan Cummins.

First Section

Pages 4/5: Maurice Fitzgerald is tackled by BC 19/05/1996: INPHO 00012700; Tipperary v Waterford SH Challenge, Ballybacon 1997: courtesy of John D. Kelly Photography; BC, Tipperary 2001: courtesy of John D. Kelly.

Pages 6/7: Nicky English celebrates with BC, All-Ireland Senior Hurling Final 2001: Brendan Moran/Sportsfile 072931; Declan Ryan and BC, 9 September, 2001: courtesy of John D. Kelly; Dr Gerry O'Sullivan and BC, 9 September, 2001: courtesy of John D. Kelly; Tipperary players celebrate at Thurles homecoming, 10 September, 2001: Damien Eagers/ Sportsfile 073108; Young supporters celebrate Tipperary success with BC and the Liam McCarthy Cup at the Glenview Lounge, Goatenbridge, 2001: courtesy of John D. Kelly.

Second Section

Page 1: BC facing Rory Hanniffy's strike for goal, Tipperary v Offaly SHC 2003: courtesy of John D. Kelly; Philip Maher, Paul Curran and BC on the line for Tipperary, 2005: courtesy of John D. Kelly;

Pages 2/3: MHC 16/06/2007: Morgan Treacy/INPHO 231372; BC congratulates Damien Fitzhenry, SHC QF, 28 July, 2007: Ray McManus/ Sportsfile 260383; BC makes a save surrounded by Cork fans, MHC 2008, Páirc Uí Chaoimh: courtesy of John D. Kelly; BC appeals to referee Diarmuid Kirwan, All-Ireland SHC Final, 6/09/2009: Lorraine O'Sullivan/INPHO 367381; BC rises high, Tipp v Clare, 2009: courtesy of John D. Kelly; BC with Eamon O'Shea, 14/03/2010: James Crombie/ INPHO 419668.

Pages 4/5: BC celebrates All-Ireland SHC Final, 2010: David Maher/ Sportsfile 457152; Michael Ryan, Liam Sheedy and Eamon O'Shea lift the Liam McCarthy Cup, 5/09/2010: Donall Farmer/INPHO 455728; BC and son Paul at Tipperary homecoming, 2010: courtesy of John D. Kelly; Tipperary team visit Crumlin Children's Hospital, 6/09/2010: Morgan Treacy/INPHO 455956.

Pages 6/7: BC celebrates victory in All-Ireland SHC SF, 14/08/2011: Peter O'Leary/Sportsfile 547629; Slievenamon Hill/Ardfinnan banner, Croke Park, 2012: courtesy of John D. Kelly; BC catches a high ball, Tipp v Cork, 1/04/2012: Cathal Noonan/INPHO 586689; BC leaves the pitch at Nowlan Park, Kilkenny, 6/07/2013: Donall Farmer/INPHO 715508; Jackie Cahill and BC at Dublin Marathon 2014: Ray McManus/Sportsfile 927536.

Page 8: BC with Fr Tom Fogarty at a civic reception held in his honour by South Tipperary County Council in January, 2014: courtesy of John D. Kelly; Pamela, Sarah, Brendan and Paul Cummins at the same civic reception in 2014: courtesy of John D. Kelly.

Index

ABOUT THE AUTHORS

Brendan Cummins was born in Ardfinnan, County Tipperary, in 1975 and made his senior hurling debut for Tipperary in the 1993–4 National Hurling League. His first senior championship game came in 1995 in Páirc Uí Chaoimh against Waterford and, over the next two decades, he went on to make more championship appearances (73) than any other player in the history of hurling. He won two All-Ireland senior medals, five Munster medals and four National League medals, as well as five All-Star awards. At club level he hurled with Ballybacon-Grange and played football with Ardfinnan. He has won the individual Poc Fada competition nine times. Brendan is a GAA pundit and co-commentator for RTÉ and is a regular analyst on the *Sunday Game*. He is married to Pamela and works as a bank official with AIB.

Jackie Cahill is a well-known Gaelic Games reporter who has written for a host of Irish newspapers and magazines. Cahill is a native of Golden in County Tipperary. A journalism degree graduate from Dublin City University, Cahill is also the holder of a Master of Arts in Sport and Exercise Psychology. This is his fourth book.